Brian Pat

My

Lead Dog

Was a Lesbian

A native of Washington, D.C., Brian Patrick O'Donoghue has worked as a cab
driver in New York City, a cargo ship
wiper, an elevator mechanic's helper, a
pipefitter's apprentice, a science museum technician, a press photographer,
and a TV and print journalist. These
days he reports on the oil industry, poli-
tics, and sled-dog racing for the *Fairbanks Daily News-Miner*. O'Donoghue,
40, and his wife, Kate Ripley, live in Two
Rivers, Alaska, with a howling kennel of
retired Iditarod dogs.

My

Lead Dog

Was a Lesbian

My
Lead Dog
Was a Lesbian

MUSHING ACROSS ALASKA IN THE IDITAROD —
THE WORLD'S MOST GRUELING RACE

BY Brian Patrick O'Donoghue

Vintage Departures

VINTAGE BOOKS

A DIVISION OF RANDOM HOUSE, INC.

NEW YORK

A VINTAGE DEPARTURES ORIGINAL, MARCH 1996
FIRST EDITION

Copyright © 1996 by Brian Patrick O'Donoghue
Map copyright © 1996 by John A. Field

Library of Congress Cataloging-in-Publication Data
O'Donoghue, Brian.
    My lead dog was a lesbian : mushing across Alaska in the
Iditarod—the world's most grueling race
    Patrick O'Donoghue.—1st ed.
        p.   cm.—(Vintage departures)
    ISBN 0-679-76411-9
    "A Vintage departures original"—T.p. verso.
    1. O'Donoghue, Brian.   2. Iditarod Trail Sled Dog Race,
    Alaska.   3. Mushers—Alaska—Biography.   4. Sled dog
    racing—Alaska.   I. Title.
    SF440.15.042   1996
    798'.8—dc20
    [B]   95-44516
        CIP

Book design by Cathryn S. Aison

Random House Web address: http://randomhouse.com

Printed in the United States of America
10 9 8 7 6 5 4 3 2 1

This book is dedicated to Doc,
who showed us the way,
and B.L.,
who had the spirit
but none of the luck

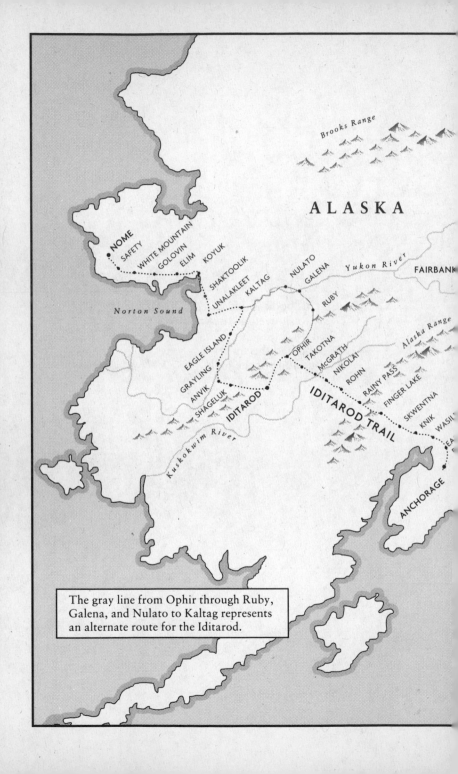

The gray line from Ophir through Ruby, Galena, and Nulato to Kaltag represents an alternate route for the Iditarod.

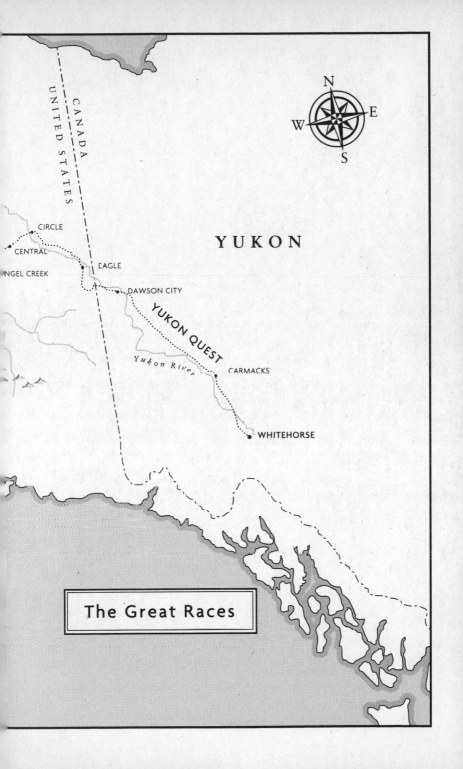

N
W · E
S

CANADA
UNITED STATES

CIRCLE
CENTRAL
NGEL CREEK
EAGLE
DAWSON CITY

YUKON

YUKON QUEST

Yukon River

CARMACKS

WHITEHORSE

The Great Races

Contents

My
Lead Dog
Was a Lesbian

CHAPTER 1

Klondike Lesson

The jitters were gone. I hadn't lost the trail or my dog team. Nobody was limping from injuries or fights. My dogs looked absolutely great, and little Raven was playing cheerleader as usual.

I knew better, but I couldn't resist. With one hundred miles left to go in the Klondike 200 I began imagining how amazed people would be at the finish line. Entering the Klondike, my sights had been set on merely finishing. My farthest trip on a dogsled had been 50 miles. This race stretched 200 and I had to go the distance to qualify for the Iditarod, Alaska's Great Race to Nome. The dogs and I were already signed up for the main event, just six weeks away, but I still had to earn the right to compete. More than six months of preparation and thousands of dollars were riding on our performance here. I had to succeed.

But such concerns were behind me now. As I packed to leave Skwentna Roadhouse, the Klondike's halfway point, a top ten finish looked to be in the bag. This wasn't the way the Coach, Tim Mowry, and I had planned it. Our strategy, developed over a few beers back home at Deadline Dog Farm, called for me to tag along behind other, more experienced mushers. But the dogs were proving more ambitious.

The Mowth was stuck in Fairbanks, pulling the weekend shift at the *News-Miner*'s sports desk. I'd recruited two friends from the Matanuska Valley, Vicki and Cyndi, as my Klondike handlers. None of us knew what we were doing as I steered Mowry's old Ford, loaded down with howling dogs and gear, onto the ice at Big Lake. But then ignorance had become a defining characteristic of this reporter-turned-dog-musher's brief racing career.

I'd drawn the last position, number 18. My parking spot was located at the far end of the staging area. Driving to it, across the frozen lake, we nervously scanned the other racers readying their teams for departure.

I directed my unschooled pit crew sorting through the mess of harnesses and lines. Finally we began hooking up, connecting a pair of dogs at a time, in eight-foot intervals along the gang line. I was taking 12 out today, two more than I'd ever harnessed before. By the time we were done, the gang line, a plastic-coated steel cable channeling the team's power back down the center, stretched over 50 feet ahead of me. Standing rigidly at the far end—"Good dogs!"—Rainy and Casey looked impossibly distant. They looked back at me, impatient to go.

Another friend, Sandy, turned up at the last moment. The big schoolteacher's arrival was perfectly timed, and I drafted her for brake duty, sharing the runners with me on the back of the sled. Cyndi and Vic were positioned along the gang line, ready to lead the dogs to the starting line, which was painted out on the lake ice, some 200 yards away.

Sled dogs begin each run like champions, or demons, depending on their musher's readiness. The trick is to hang on tight until they settle down. But that's easier said than done. It's bad enough setting forth on familiar trails. In the riotous atmosphere of a race, stirred by comradery and fresh smells, a sled dog's inborn enthusiasm reaches a frenzy. Excitement had been building in my team since we began loading the dog truck that morning. They all recognized the signs. We were going some-place new.

I slipped off the knot anchoring my sled to the truck's front bumper. The team bolted toward the starting line. My over-matched crew began slipping. Big Sandy and I jammed our heels on the brake claw, with little effect—besides etching a pair of fresh streaks on the ice. Cyndi wisely let go. Vicki fell but main-tained her grip on the gang line, as she scooted down the lake on her ass.

"Just get out of the way, Vic. We've got it."

She shrugged and let go. Two of my younger males stumbled over her. My eyes remained focused on the trail ahead. A hairpin turn waited at the end of the staging area. What would I do if they headed for the parking lot? I needn't have worried. Out on the lake, over a dozen rippling chains of dogs were visible. Mine rounded the corner in full loping stride, whipping the sled side-ways. They were determined to catch the other teams.

Race marshal Kevin Saiki waved me straight through. Sandy was no longer sharing the runners. I assumed she had bailed out, stepping off the runners as soon as she saw that the team was on track. But I didn't see her in the crowd, which was reced-ing fast. Actually, Sandy had been flung clear at the turn. Cyndi watched her skidding away and was reminded of a bowling pin.

The Klondike's opening miles passed through a network of frozen lakes. Through most of it, the dogs had me at their mercy. I just rode the brake, watching others taste disaster. One dog team went careening down a driveway and over a snow-machine, ripping off its windshield. I saw local kids chasing through the woods after another team that was missing its driver.

I had passed the man, a veteran Iditarod musher, seated in the snow. He smiled and waved at me like a casual spectator. His manner struck me as odd, but I had no time to wonder why. My lead dogs leaped over a fallen log, and the others swiftly followed. My sled smacked the thick trunk, went airborne, and I steered it through the air.

Later I learned the cause for the musher's strange expression. As his dogs jumped that same fallen tree, the unlucky racer had caught a leg under it. Something had to give against the pressure exerted by his 12-dog team. He let go as his leg splintered in a compound fracture. Another racer paused long enough to prop the injured musher in the snowbank, where I saw him, while local kids fetched help. Shock was apparently setting in by the time I passed by.

Leaving the lakes behind, we climbed a few hills then entered a broad lane through thick trees. The trail here was well-packed, a sign of heavy traffic. Not far ahead, I knew, a sharp turn was coming, one I'd been warned not to miss. From that point onward, Klondike racers followed some 70 miles of the Iditarod Trail, a historic gold-rush route to the Interior mines.

I was still looking for that turn when Casey showed signs of lagging. No surprise there. We'd been on the trail more than an hour, and that was Casey's usual limit for leading. I swapped her with Raven, but my little black-haired princess wasn't in the mood to run out front. She kept darting left and right, tripping Rainy, her coleader, and the swing dogs running directly behind. After several pauses to untwist lines wrapped around careless paws, I played a hunch and moved Harley up front.

Harley and Rainy made an odd, but effective pair. Rainy was one of our kennel's smaller dogs, weighing 35 to 40 pounds at most, with brown hair and squirrellike movements. Harley cut a hulking figure, twice her size and splotched black, white, and brown. When he ran, Harley's ears flopped up and down, keeping time with his lumbering stride.

I'd only used Harley in lead once before—on a dark night marked by mutiny and desperation. On that occasion, Harley and Denali, the only dogs still showing any confidence in my miserable sense of direction, led the final miles back to our cabin. Denali was a hindrance. The big young male had no idea what to do. But Harley barreled straight through, dragging his baffled partner along. Listening to me recount the performance, Mowry refused to give Harley any credit. He figured the big dog was probably just hungry and making a beeline for his food dish.

Today Harley's inexperience showed as we entered an icy marsh, where the trail was less obvious. He repeatedly slowed to look back, seeing encouragement. "Go ahead, Harley!" A few firm words aimed at him had a powerful effect on the entire team. As the big leader's attention returned to his work, I felt an immediate burst of speed, as if I'd tugged on a snowmachine's gas throttle.

It was dark as we approached Skwentna, a remote settlement of about a hundred homesteaders, trappers, and lodge operators. I was startled by the sudden appearance of what seemed like dozens of fiery red eyes floating toward me, cloudlike, in the beam of my headlamp. Drawing closer, I sheepishly realized it was merely a musher coming the other way. The unearthly orbs belonged to the front dogs in John Barron's team. The taciturn, grizzly musher from Big Lake had already turned for home. Holding the lead on these familiar trails, he ran with his headlamp switched off to confuse the mushers in pursuit. I'd reported on tactics like that but hadn't yet seen them used.

Several other teams followed hot behind Barron. I gripped the handlebar tightly, braced for calamity, but Rainy and Harley handled the head-on passes without a hitch. Third among the approaching teams came Marcie Heckler, the friend who'd talked me into using the Klondike as my own 200-mile qualifier. Marcie wasn't an experienced racer, but she may as well have been. For years she'd worked as a handler for Old Joe—Iditarod's founder, Joe Redington, Sr.—and her boyfriend, Kevin, was enforcing the rules in the Klondike.

"Almost there, Bri," Marcie grunted as she flashed past.

Leaving the river behind, I followed a line of markers to a circular driveway fronting an old cabin. The Skwentna checker inspected my gear, then handed me the clipboard to sign in.

"Looking pretty good, Brian."

"Beginner's luck," I said, though I didn't really believe that.

Bedding my team in a stand of tall birch, I began preparing the dogs a well-deserved bite to eat. Without even trying, my team had leaped ahead of ten others. Not too shabby. I wasn't going to win this race. But some of those teams ahead of mine were bound to falter.

I studied the dogs. Raven sprawled luxuriously, her tummy thrust outward inviting a quick scratch. Who'd have guessed that the frail, fine-boned little girl possessed the stamina to run all the way to the Bering Sea coast, as she had done for Mowry his first time out? But the princess was a proven Iditarod dog.

We didn't know as much about the racing history of Raven's companions, however. Few seemed tired tonight. Most were still keyed up, licking their paws. Harley and Pig were watching my every move, drooling in anticipation of the feast on its way.

Harley's appetite was the only quality Mowry found impressive.

"He's too big," the Coach had said the day I brought him home. "His build is all wrong. A dog like that will never make it to the finish line."

I put more faith in the assessment of LeRoy Shank. He'd seen Harley racing for Andy Jimmy, an Athabaskan villager from Minto. Jimmy had done well that day, very well. Shank, a former trapper and founder of the 1,000-mile Yukon Quest, knew that sled dogs weren't kept through the winter in Minto unless they were well worth feeding. After the race, he had bought the beefy village husky on the spot.

Shank worked as a pressman at our newspaper. The two-time Iditarod veteran had no plans to race this year, so he took vicarious pleasure in my preparations, stopping me in the hallways for progress reports, badgering me to give the Minto dog a tryout. "Oh, he's a big one," Shank said, after offering to loan me the dog for the season. "Harley could drag you to Nome all by himself."

Handling Harley was a chore. He had playfully knocked me on my ass more than once. Wrist injuries were a definite risk for anyone holding this twisting, excitable husky by his collar. He attacked food like a starving convict, slurping his bowl clean as fast as I filled it. He'd whimper pitifully as he watched me feed his kennel mates. I was a sucker for it. I always gave him seconds, often thirds, and sometimes even fourths. But Harley was never satisfied. Given the chance, he'd eat until he burst.

I poured a bucket of hot water into the sixteen-gallon cooler to soak the mash of dry dog food and frozen beef chunks. We'd come 100 miles in about 14 hours, yet none of my dogs looked tired. All 12 had their eyes fixed on the steam rising from that cooler. If I could hold the team together, we just might do very well indeed.

Gunnar Johnson hoped to squeeze in a trip to Nome before surrendering his life to medical school. He mushed into Skwentna in a horrified state. A dead dog was stowed in his sled basket. The dog had collapsed with absolutely no warning. No warning at all. Gunnar tenderly laid the dog's body in the snow alongside the camp. Moving in a daze, he fixed the other dogs a meal. He was chopping meat when a movement caught his attention. Glancing up, Gunnar saw the dead dog panting for a snack.

Tom Daily also arrived at the halfway point carrying a dog. He'd spent $1,500 flying Zowie, his favorite leader, from his remote training camp to a clinic a few months before, after the dog ate a bum salmon. Zowie had pulled through, but still hadn't regained his stamina. That much was obvious. Daily hated to admit it, but his entire team's performance left a lot to be desired. Short training runs weren't adequate to prepare dogs for a trip of this distance. The former hippie knew that from making his living giving sled-dog rides in Colorado. A once-in-a-lifetime sponsorship offer had landed him here, but the disruption of relocating North had interfered with training. With or without Zowie, these dogs were hurting.

Lynda Plettner wasn't an official Klondike participant. Why pay an entry fee when she wasn't here to race? Plettner was just tagging along. Someone had to keep an eye on Urtha Lenthar, the schoolteacher leasing dogs from Plettner's kennel.

By Skwentna, Plettner had abandoned any attempt at maintaining a casual distance. Barking orders in a voice improbably loud, the Iditarod veteran was directing Lenthar's every move. Her dogs were ready, Plettner decided, but the big goof riding the sled needed a lot of work.

Barry Lee's borrowed dogs were short on conditioning. With that in mind, Lee took it easy the first 100 miles of the Klondike. Driving two hours, then resting two or three.

"This race will more than double some of their mileage," Barry told me, watching his dogs settling down as I prepared to break camp.

I knew Lee from covering past races. He was one of those guys who was always turning up as a checkpoint volunteer. His confession about his dogs' training distances was startling. All of my dogs had at least double, if not triple, that many miles of conditioning, and here Barry was playing catch-up. The dogs weren't the only ones in need of conditioning. The musher's gut was as wide as his habitual smile. Stepping inside the roadhouse, Barry staggered under the weight of the past 100 miles.

In the warmth of the kitchen, Lee munched on a wonderful cheeseburger, washing it down with pitcher after pitcher of iced tea. Then he went into the common room and stretched out on the floor for a quick nap. The musher awoke six hours later, racked by pain. His jaw was cramped. His arms were cramped.

His abdomen and upper and lower legs were cramped. Struggling to a table, Lee grabbed a full pitcher of water and drained it. All that tea had dehydrated his system, causing his muscles to cramp during his long unplanned snooze. Barry suddenly had to pee so badly he wasn't sure he could make it to a bathroom. Fortunately, his bladder was also cramped.

A debate was underway in the Senate chamber of the Alaska state capitol. The governor had hauled lawmakers back to Juneau for a special session to resolve a longstanding conflict over hunting and fishing rights. My newspaper, the *Fairbanks Daily News-Miner*, had sent me down to cover the bickering between unyielding Bush and urban factions, a boring assignment that threatened to waste my fleeting Alaska summer. At the press table, I turned my attention to an application that could change my life.

Mushing experience? All I could list was the Montana Creek Cheechako Race, a 2.3-mile run for novice mushers I had chanced into several years before. At the time, I was working for the *Frontiersman* in Wasilla, a booming highway town of about four thousand located an hour's drive north of Anchorage. Mowry, our stocky sportswriter, was writing a first-person story. I was on hand to shoot photos of his debut as a sled-dog racer.

It was a crisp, brilliant December morning. The temperature was holding in the high 20s. One by one, dog trucks claimed spots near the mushers' clubhouse. The snouts of curious dogs poked through holes in the boxes mounted on the rear of the trucks. Some barked frantically; others harmonized in a howling chorus.

Iditarod veterans Ray and Diana Dronenburg had brought over a dozen dogs to the track that morning, planning to let one of their kennel sponsors compete. Afterward they would take larger teams out on a serious training run. The sponsor was late.

The Dronenburgs went ahead and drew for him, pulling the third position. With time running out, he remained a no-show. Diana asked if I wanted to fill in.

No one could challenge my credentials as a "cheechako," a gold-rush term for newcomers to the North. Originally from the East Coast, I was just starting my second winter in Alaska. I'd never touched a dogsled. My professional driving experience consisted of two and a half years of driving a cab in New York City.

Within moments, I was wearing the number 3 bib and testing my balance on the thin sled runners. Diana coached me on the dogs' names. Ray held them back.

"Three! Two! One!" The sled jerked forward, and we were off.

I wobbled around the opening turn, precariously maintaining my balance. Then I nearly fell off trying to imitate a real sled-dog racer, kicking my heel backward to spur on the dogs. I didn't dare shout "Gee" or "Haw," uncertain which of those fundamental commands meant right and which meant left. Instead I yelled "Hike, hike, hike," a mushing term for "go."

Tongues flapped. Paws flew. Aside from my idiotic cries, the only sound was the panting of the dogs and the whisper of sled runners slicing through the snow.

"Now this is Alaska!" I cried, feeling exultant.

I covered the looping 3-mile trail in 12 minutes, 7 seconds. Good enough for thirteenth place. Better yet, it was 2 minutes faster than Mowry. In the story that resulted, Tim compared his defeat at the hands of this "tall, skinny political reporter" to "a cowboy losing a bull-riding contest to an accountant."

"A dark day for the sportswriters around this country indeed," he wrote.

That had been four years ago. Driving dogs leased from Joe Redington, Sr., the founder of the Iditarod, the Mowth had gone on to race in the 1,000-mile Yukon Quest and two Iditarods, winning the "Most Improved Musher" award for a twenty-seventh-place showing in his second trip to Nome. I'd reported on more big races than Mowry had, but I hadn't mushed dogs more than a handful of times. It was madness to even consider running the Iditarod. But if I didn't try, the missed opportunity would torment me forever. Aware that I was taking action more significant than anything likely to occur on the Senate floor, I signed the application, listing myself as "driver" for a dog team I didn't yet possess.

Those who live in dog country dissect the Iditarod's entry list like the Yankees' batting order on opening day. So I wasn't surprised by the question that greeted me as I entered Blackie's Goose Bay Bar in Knik on the return trip from Juneau. "Brian, whose dogs are you using?" yelled Marcie, who was working the bar.

Drawing a brew, she quizzed me about my plans. We talked about budgets, places to train, and who might have extra dogs to sell or lease. Messages were waiting when I got back to Fairbanks late that night. Marcie had a deal. A whole team was for sale. Twenty-eight dogs. Excellent bloodlines. Many were related, she said, to a dog named Elvis from Swenson's kennel, a claim that later proved untrue. Bottom line: $4,000 cash.

The dogs belonged to a young Knik musher named Spencer Mayer. He was what Marcie called a "dream musher"—a guy who put together a good team, trained the dogs to perfection—but never quite got it together to enter races.

Spencer was married, with a young child. He'd landed a construction job in Dutch Harbor, a booming port in the distant Aleutians. It fell on his father, Herman Mayer, to tend the dogs. Spencer's father had a four-wheel-drive all-terrain vehicle he wasn't using. Marcie and Kevin needed one for training their dogs in the off season. Just watching that fine machine sitting there rusting was more than Marcie could stand.

"Herman," she said. "sell me the four-wheeler."

"I'm not selling my damn four-wheeler," he said.

"Herman, you're not riding it! Give it to me!"

"Well," Mayer said, "I tell you what. You sell my son's dog team, and I'll give it to you."

Marcie always got her way.

Mowry wanted to close the deal without delay. Old Joe Redington had repossessed his dogs, and Tim didn't want us to miss out on these affordable replacements. I wasn't so eager to buy an entire yard of sled dogs. I had planned to ease into mushing, lining up lease deals for training in, say, October. But Mowry had it worked out: He would buy the kennel and rent me a team for $4,000. He had already talked to his father about a loan. The Old Man was agreeable. It was the sort of livestock investment that made sense to his folks back at Mowacres Dairy in New York.

The deal landed me a team for the race at a price within my budget, and it provided me with a coach and kennel partner. The Mowth wouldn't be racing this year, but he owned his own sled dogs at last.

When she felt like it, Raven was our kennel's speed queen. Refreshed by a full belly and a four-hour nap, she was having fun on the return trip from Skwentna as we made tracks toward the Klondike finish line. Bounding gaily, the princess and Rainy set a blistering pace down the hard-packed river trail. It was a windless, balmy night. Sipping chicken-noodle soup, I danced aboard the sled runners, keeping time to a Stevie Ray Vaughan tape wailing through my Walkman. The river here was about 100 yards across. The ice was concealed under a rolling white avenue. Steep banks rose on either side. Old trees leaned inward at the high-water mark, dark silhouettes against the deep blue sky.

The party ended 10 miles from Yentna Roadhouse. Beast was stumbling. The young female kept tripping on the lines and falling with a glazed look in her eyes. The fun gone, Raven began balking, drawing back against the neckline connecting her to Rainy and searching for any escape.

"It's OK, princess," I whispered, stroking the trembling girl between the ears. "You did just fine tonight."

I switched Raven back and placed White Rat in lead. An extremely intelligent female, she remained my personal favorite despite a tendency to slack off at every opportunity. Rat was on her best behavior tonight, but Gnat, a meek unseasoned male, seized every pause, dip, or tangle to sit down.

We'd covered 120 miles in less than 24 hours, and both Gnat and Beast verged on surrender. Mowry had warned me about this: "The thing with young dogs is they have to get past that point where they think they're going to die."

I took a long break and gave the team a snack. The breather refreshed everybody. Afterward Gnat and the Beast shared the work, holding their lines tight as the team hauled my sled up the steep bank fronting Yentna Station, Dawn was breaking through a mist of sprinkling rain.

Other racers were discussing the wisdom of laying over at the checkpoint, delaying their final push until the cool evening hours. It was unseasonably hot—30 degrees. Too hot for sled dogs. But I wasn't listening. Rummy with lack of sleep, I had a raging case of finish-line fever. We were running in the top ten. Who knows how high we could go?

I made arrangements to drop Gnat and Beast at the checkpoint. Had I stayed and rested through the day, I could have taken them with me. But I was no longer treating the Klondike as a mere qualifier, with added benefits as a training run: I had shifted into racing mentality. While the other dogs rested, I went over my sled, dumping every ounce of unnecessary weight. In the process, I set aside the sac holding the team's snacks. I planned to put it back absolutely last so that it would remain within easy reach.

Five hours after our arrival at Yentna Station, I pulled the hook, sending my dogs charging over the bank. Sunshine had burned away the clouds. Over the next hours, it baked us. My Fairbanks-conditioned dogs were reduced to plodding.

It was sundown by the time we finally reached the junction of the Yentna and the Big Su. This kind of passage always scared me. The broad river's uneven surface hinted at unseen forces that might suddenly break loose, leaving unlucky travelers swimming or clinging to teetering chunks of ice. But soon I was treated to a view that brushed fears aside. The sinking sun was firing a rosy salute along Mount Susitna's curves. From the west, a headlike ridge rose to a mountainous shoulder, dipped, then expanded to a hip, which descended in a leggy sprawl. Or maybe Susitna was resting on her back, showing off her bosomlike ridge. From either perspective, it was easy to see why locals called the formation Sleeping Lady.

The wind rose as we passed through Susitna Station, a largely abandoned turn-of-the-century settlement and one-time Dena'ina Indian community. My dogs were due for a break, but I pushed them onward into the forest. I wanted to reach the entrance of the frozen marsh before stopping, so as to position the team for a strong march to the finish line.

I was fooled by the trees and didn't see the marsh coming. We were 20 yards out on the icy flats before I managed to stop. The wind here was fierce, gusting maybe 40 miles per hour across the exposed, barren ice. It was a terrible place to stop, but I wasn't thinking clearly. I dug into the sled bag for my beef treats. The snack sac was missing. Appalled, I remembered placing it in the snow outside the roadhouse.

Belatedly, I tried to get the team moving. But the dogs, seeing no snacks forthcoming, were too tired to pay any more attention to me. Their survival instincts had taken over. Curled in tight balls, backs to the wind, they slept on the ice. The dogs had crashed on me.

My snowmachine suit was soaked from rain and exertion. On a colder day, the situation might have been grave. Today the weather was too balmy to pose any danger. I gave the dogs half an hour, then dished out globs of a pre-prepared meal from the cooler. A fellow racer caught up while I was feeding.

"Everything all right?" he shouted over the wind, no doubt puzzled to see me stopped in this miserable spot.

I pretended everything was under control.

After the meal, the dogs shook themselves and stretched. My athletes looked ready to go. I gave the word. Root, one of my most dependable dogs, was having trouble with her hind legs. She tried to run but couldn't keep up. Jamming the hook into the ice, I unclipped her, figuring I'd pack her in the sled until we reached a more sheltered spot. I had my right hand on her collar and was reaching for the sled with the other—when the team bolted.

With a flying lunge, I grabbed hold of a rear stanchion. The dogs dragged me a good hundred yards on my knees, along with Root, before they finally stopped. Staggering to my feet, clutching a shoulder that felt half torn from the socket, I stuffed Root in the sled and ordered my mischievous friends onward. Amazing what a little rest could do for them.

Intense wind and sleet met us at Flat Horn Lake. The trail was awful. Raven and Harley kept punching through the thin crust and sinking into the powder underneath. The tracks ahead of us abruptly ended in the middle of the lake. Scanning the horizon, I saw the lights from two other teams inching along the distant rim. It was Plettner and her browbeaten disciple,

Lenthar. Raven, always prone to go where she pleased, had skipped a turn. Thankful to have someone pointing the way, I swung my team around.

In the last 15 miles of the race the dogs slowed to a crawl. The heat was getting to Harley. The big dog kept dragging his buddies off the trail to munch snow. I could sympathize. Hills I had hardly noticed a day ago had mushroomed into mountains. My legs were cramping. I considered stopping to camp, but the alcohol for the cooker had somehow spilled. I couldn't even make broth for the dogs, and further delay might even hurt the team.

The dogs and I emerged from a slough onto Big Lake in a near rout. Loaded in the basket were Root, who seemed shell-shocked, and Denali. The weary young male had been having trouble keeping his feet on the icy homestretch. After his third stumble, I let him ride the rest of the way.

Marcie and a few friends cheered when I crossed the finish line in twelfth place, shortly after midnight. The race had taken 38 hours. Stepping off the sled, I couldn't get my legs to work. My feet were concrete blocks.

The dogs saw the truck and hauled the sled to it like champs. They didn't even look winded as I left them, chained around the truck, and went in search of hot water to soak their food. I'd already given each dog a frozen whitefish. Their gnawing could be heard 50 feet away.

Baron was still celebrating his victory when I climbed the monstrous staircase to the inn. Fidaa Daily smiled nervously. She was waiting for news of her husband. Marcie, who'd slipped to seventh in the final miles, declared that her next outing was a shopping trip to Nordstrom.

"I need to remind myself I'm a woman."

The 200-mile ordeal snuffed any interest Marcie might have had in running the Iditarod. "I'd rather go to an Iraqi torture camp," she declared, loud enough for the entire bar to hear.

Sitting in the warm lodge with fellow Klondike mushers, I felt humbled and apprehensive. I'd earned my right to compete in the big race. For the first time, absolutely nothing stood in the way. That was sobering, because my 35-year-old body was a wreck after just 200 miles on a sled. What was Iditarod, more than five times as long, going to do to me?

Grabbing the food bucket, I headed back down to the dogs.

CHAPTER 2

Ready or Not

Only three weeks were left. Self-doubts and potential threats to the team's well-being dominated my every waking moment. Even the home trails felt sinister. Blizzards had buried my landmarks, and I was driving the dogs longer and longer distances, getting lost for hours at a time.

It was warm out, 3 degrees above zero. I set out for Mike Madden's house with an eleven-dog team, intending to make a quick turnaround. The entire 50-mile trip should have taken about 7 hours, including snack breaks, simulating the travel time between average Iditarod checkpoints.

I was using Chad in single lead. That was the Coach's new strategy for handling our temperamental wonder dog. Chad, a quick blond male, trotted with one hip swung sideways. It was an odd gait and often caused him to bump his coleader. Mowry hoped that Chad might be one of those rare dogs who preferred to lead alone. All through the fall Chad was our unquestioned top dog. He was strong, smart, and fast. Having Chad up front amounted to having power steering. Whisper "Gee," or "Haw," and turns were immediate.

One winter day Chad quit on me leaving the lot. He did a

complete nose plant, causing half the team to tumble over him. I assumed that he was injured, but we never found anything physically wrong. It was Golden Dog's spirit that needed nursing thereafter. And the Coach's new approach appeared to be working.

About 15 miles out, I wasn't paying close attention when Chad lunged onto a side trail. I stopped and turned the team around. Next, emerging from a winding slough, I wasn't sure which direction to take on the Chena River. Which way to Madman's house? Upstream? Downstream? Everything looked so different covered by the recent dumps of snow.

Chad glanced back, impatient. "Haw," I said.

I mushed 10 miles along the river, searching for the familiar trail crossing until it was unmistakably clear that I'd guessed wrong. Sighing, I again turned the team around. The snow was soft and deep. The dogs sank and thrashed about in the powder. I waded to the front of the team, then sank to my armpits pulling Chad back toward the trail. A fight broke out between Bo and the normally unflappable Skidders. Back on the hard-packed trail, I separated the two scrappers. Bo was in a surly mood. So I paired Raven with Chad in lead and ran the big troublemaker alone. After stopping for a snack, we backtracked along the river, chasing the setting sun. By nightfall I was lost again, but tried to hide it from the dogs.

At a loss, I directed Chad and Raven up a side trail. We soon neared a dog lot illuminated by blinding outdoor lights. Normally, I would have retreated; people tend to defend their privacy aggressively in Alaska. But I was ready to beg for directions. Our arrival set the dogs chained outside the cabin barking furiously. The cabin door swung open and, to my utter amazement, out stepped Mike Madden.

"Madman, this is your house?"

"Whose backyard did you think you were in, O'D?"

We'd been on the trail five hours. I should have camped and

given the dogs a real meal, followed by several hours of rest, before returning home. But I was on a schedule. So I snacked the dogs and then started them back.

The river was braided with snowmachine trails. Raven and Chad weren't meshing. When they weren't bumping each other, the leaders were wrestling through their neckline, trying to pull each other along different threads of the interwoven trail.

Even so, we were making decent time when I blundered yet again by ordering the team down a side trail. Within a mile I realized the mistake and halted the team for another turnaround. That was strike three for Chad. His confidence in me was shot. Golden Dog buried his head in the snow and wouldn't budge. I dragged him forward several times, roughly standing him on his feet. He cooperated that far. But when I shouted, "All right," the cue to move out—Chad sat down.

I tried Raven in single lead. No way. Her tail drooped, and the little princess tried to hide underneath the swing dogs, creating an immediate tangle. I tried using Gnat and Cricket together. The litter mates cowered. No one wanted the wheel on this doomed ship—not with me in charge.

In training sled dogs, you want to steer them into doing the right thing, while minimizing confusion and discouragement. Building stamina isn't nearly as crucial as instilling confidence through repetition and positive reinforcement, teaching dogs that they can do whatever you, the musher, ask. By building on each success, gradually asking the team to go farther and faster, the dogs develop faith in their all-knowing driver. That was the theory. From the first August night we took our dogs out on a cart—and Chad dug up a yellow jackets' nest in the staging area—training seldom went smoothly.

My reversals had undermined the confidence of every dog out here, and it was the wrong night for a leadership crisis. Rainy, Rat, Casey, and Harley, any one of whom might have bailed me out, were sitting at home. Hitched to this gang line I had Chad, Raven, Cricket, and Gnat: our resident head case and three happy trotters—good for leading so long as it was fun, which it wasn't tonight.

I placed Chad back in lead, thinking he might cooperate after a reasonable break. He was, after all, still Deadline Dog Farm's main dog.

So we sat.

Twenty minutes later, a headlamp appeared.

"How's training going," said Scott, a local musher preparing for the Quest.

"Fine until tonight," I said, a dark edge to my voice.

Chad loves to chase. He perked up and followed Scott to the Winter Trail, a heavily traveled mushing and snowmachine highway, up to five feet wide in places, cutting through the forest northeast of Fairbanks. With the familiar alley in view, I bid the other musher good-bye. Crying "Haw," I sent Chad into a hard left turn. We were home free.

A few miles later, Chad dove down another side spur for no apparent reason. I didn't dare stop him. Nothing is more frustrating than having a dog team quit on you. We were rolling. I didn't care where. The trail lead to a subdivision road. The sled whipped sideways, careening off berms, as the dogs loped down the icy, hard-packed road. I was hoping we'd come across another trail, but the subdivision road spilled onto Chena Hot Springs, the busiest road in the entire area. We were within a few miles of home, and I considered making a dash for it. But it was icy and dark. The sight of an oncoming dog team might send a car or truck spinning into us. I could lose the entire team in an instant.

Stomping the hook into the snow, I walked up front, gripped Chad by the collar, and turned the team around one more time. Chad shrank at my touch and wouldn't even look at me. The other dogs weren't much happier. On a whim, I tried Skidders in lead. The old stud immediately took advantage of his freedom to circle back and sniff the girls. Nice try. And for our next act.

I bedded the team in a sheltered spot near the main road. Cyrus, an 18-month-old pup we'd just acquired from Rattles, was bewildered. He remained on his feet, eager to continue. Five minutes later, he was still whining anxiously. I knelt down in the snow and stroked his tight belly, settling him down at last.

Turning off my headlamp, I was struck by the brilliant stars painting the sky. It was one of those nights when you see dazzling, ghostly depths, hinting at mysteries no mere human will ever grasp. Mushing forces you to spend time outside. That was one of the sport's unexpectedly rewarding aspects. Whether it's watching a woodpecker digging away on a trunk, or catching the sunset through trees ablaze with clumps of ice, some sort of rare experience is always waiting in Alaska's outdoors.

I was sitting there on the snow berm, marveling at the stars, when I heard Mowry's truck chugging up the hill. The sportswriter was on his way home after a late shift. I flagged him down.

The Coach was disgusted by my incompetence. "You're just like Chad," Mowry said, as we loaded the dogs into the truck.

Revolting bloody soup filled our bathtub.

"Christ," I said, recoiling from the fermenting atrocity. "What the hell is it?"

"I'm making honey balls. It's one of Joe's inventions."

Picture 100 pounds of raw chopped beef, 20 pounds of honey, 2 gallons of corn oil, 2 pounds of bonemeal, and other assorted Redington spices—slopped a foot deep.

"I don't know, Bri," said Mowry, stirring the mess with a broken hockey stick. "It seems sort of gooey."

We'd already spent two days cutting meat and stuffing sacks with provisions for Mowry's first Iditarod. He grabbed a handful and tried handpacking it into a baseball-sized glob. Meat goo oozed through Tim's fingers. We scooped a couple bucketfuls and took them out on the porch. There, we dabbed globs of the bloody muck on the surface of flattened garbage bags, hoping it might freeze into something usable. By morning, the honey balls had changed. The Mowth and I now had a porch full of half-frozen cow pies, run together like cookies baked too close on the sheet.

"I have a lot of bucks tied up in this shit, and I don't think it's supposed to look like this," said Mowry, his eyes bloodshot and his dirty blond hair sticking from his head like loose straw.

"Yeah," I agreed, "and our tub is still full of it."

There is, apparently, more than one kind of honey. Redington's recipe called for thick granular honey, not the syrupy brew my roommate had used. The Mowth's dogs did without honey balls that year. And he cleaned the tub. There's a limit to friendship.

Recalling the chaos of Mowry's first big race, I allotted four full days to assemble my own Iditarod food drop. It wasn't enough.

The first setback occurred when I had to unpack twenty-six checkpoints' worth of fish. I'd forgotten to paint my name on the sacks. It was probably just paranoia, but I had been scared the fish might become contaminated in the labeling process. So, dumping the fish, I spread out the sacks in our driveway, thinking I could knock out the job using spray paint and a stencil. It was 40 below, and the paint nozzle froze, forcing me to shift operations inside our cramped A-frame. Space constraints there limited me to painting two bags at a time. And there was no damn room for anything to dry. The quick task ate up three hours.

Two friends from the paper, Mary Beth and Anna, were in charge of my personal food. They came up with a delicious assortment of precooked meals, breads, brownies, and cookies, but it took precious hours to assemble the packets. Anna's efforts, cooking dozens of steaks and pork chops, fell behind when her propane stove quit.

For heating water out on the trail, I planned to use a fancy cooker borrowed from another local musher. But when I tested it against the Coach's battered old unit, Mowry's cooker boiled water in about 25 minutes, or roughly 30 percent quicker, despite the fact that it used toilet paper for a wick. Of course, I wanted that faster heating unit, and that meant another run to town for 50 more rolls of toilet paper.

The Coach concentrated on the real athletes, leaving me to deal with the food drop—and with Rattles, a strutting peacock of a dog man with a handlebar mustache, who'd become a constant presence as the race drew near.

Mike "Rattles" Kramer had earned his nickname working a jackhammer in a hard rock mine. That was before he took up dogs and became a boisterous fixture in the Two Rivers mushing scene. Now he bounced between washing dishes and seasonal farm or construction work. He, his new wife, and their infant son were among the 20 percent of Fairbanks-area residents who lacked running water at home. He didn't seem to mind hauling around water jugs; it provided a good excuse for visiting the neighbors and, perhaps, peddling a few eggs gathered from his chickens.

I enjoyed Rattles's company as long as he didn't get started talking about the Feds, the gold standard, or the threats to personal liberty posed by Social Security numbers. Rattles knew a lot of tricks about tuning snowmachines or rigging sled lines. In his excitement about the race, however, the old musher was getting on my nerves, following me around, but lifting nary a finger to help as he relived his own doggy deeds.

"Rattles," I cried at last, "if you're not going to help, get the hell out of here."

The old musher chuckled, amused by my jitters.

I hit the panic button with 36 hours remaining until supplies were due at Iditarod's Fairbanks collection drop center. I called Anna, my photographer friend Nora, Sam the editor, Wilda and her husband, Charlie, everyone I knew—begging for help. Sunday, the yard was full of helpers bagging toilet paper, fish, spare underwear, batteries, headlamp bulbs, and runner plastic.

Wilda dragged along her dad, who was visiting from Kentucky. He pitched right in, chopping meat with an axe. Our whole operation fascinated him: the dogs watching from the woods; the sleds leaning on the shed; even the cabin interior, strewn with harnesses, lines, and cold-weather gear. The day spent helping an Iditarod musher became the highlight of his Alaska trip.

By nightfall, the work party had filled 60 sacks, each color-coded for one of the 21 checkpoints where we mushers could expect to find our provisions waiting. The next day friends and I delivered the sacks to a local freight company that was assisting with the race. My contributions were weighed, sorted, and added to the pallets bound for various checkpoints. Freight handlers waited until the pallet loads reached about 6 feet tall, then stepped forward to seal them with giant rolls of plastic wrap. Fairbanks handled only a third of this year's Iditarod field, yet the sheer tonnage was immense. My team's load alone weighed 2,094 pounds and cost me $523 to ship.

Rounding a turn, I saw a moose on the river ahead. It was a tall bull, plunging through deep snow. The dogs quickened their trot as they caught sight of him. I lifted my foot off the brake, letting the dogs break into a free lope. It was unlikely the moose would change direction and bother us, but you never knew. Moose are unpredictable as hell.

I didn't want any surprises to mar this gorgeous day. It was 15 below, just cold enough to envelop the team in a flowing fog of exertion. The sun hung low over the river, creating orange streamers between the blue trees. Seven dogs were pulling my sled. The sunlight set their breath ablaze, wrapping the team in a warm glow.

As we neared the river, the trail rose and fell along a series of man-sized dips. Topping one of the rises, I saw a dark mound ahead. The trail dropped again before I could make it out. Something odd was coming up. I braced as the sled climbed another slight hill. Hair, I could see hair. A moose. Oh God.

Then I realized it was dead.

The dogs slowed to sniff the carcass. "All right! All right!" I cried, forestalling any thoughts of stopping. Where there's one, there are often others.

"A person's crazy to go out without a gun," Rattles had said. "With all this snow, those moose are desperate. They won't give up the trail."

I didn't even own a gun, so I was a real Alaskan oddity. I'd arranged to borrow Cyndi's .357-caliber pistol for the race. The gun was waiting for me 360 miles south. Here in town, Madman had offered me his old rifle—if I ever got around to picking it up. I'd been trusting luck to dodge the sort of encounter that postponed Susan Butcher's first appearance in the Iditarod winner's circle.

1985 was supposed to be Susan's year. No woman had ever won Redington's Great Race, but Butcher had placed second in two of the three previous years, and her 17-dog team led the race crossing the Big Su. Traveling through a spruce thicket soon afterward, Butcher and her dogs came upon a large cow moose blocking their path. The musher threw her sled over and braced for the moose's charge, which, experience told her, would carry the brute through the team. But this angry cow was far more de-

structive. Wading into the middle of the team, the moose reared
on its hind legs and began stomping and kicking.

The carnage lasted for about 20 minutes until fellow racer
Dewey Halverson mushed to the rescue. He emptied his .44-
caliber special into the enraged moose, which continued kicking
dogs until the last bullet brought it down. Susan's dog Johnny
was dead. Another dog named Hyde died after five hours on the
operating table. Two more needed surgery, and thirteen others
were injured. The distraught Butcher scratched, clearing the way
for Libby Riddles' march to glory.

This year Alaska's interior was reeling from an invasion of
the long-legged brutes. Starving, irritable from battling the unusually deep snow, moose were in no mood to mingle peacefully.
Finding it easier going on packed trails, roads, and railroad
tracks, many refused to surrender their right of way to anything,
including trains. The carnage was particularly gruesome along
the northern railroad corridor. It got so bad that the Alaska Railroad provided counseling for engineers freaked by the nightly
gore. At least locomotive drivers knew they would come out on
top. Moose held the advantage over unarmed mushers.

Dave Dalton, a fellow Fairbanks musher, could testify to
that. A few miles after leaving his kennel, his Dalton Gang team
had met an angry moose head-on. The moose's charge didn't do
any damage, but it was likely to get a second shot. The team had
no other route home. Dalton had his pistol ready on the return
trip. Sure enough, the moose was waiting. It flared its nose and
barreled into the team. Taking aim, Dalton squeezed the trigger.

The gun jammed.

The moose crashed into the sled, sending the musher flying.
The Gang made a clean getaway. Dave's situation remained tick-
lish. He was chest-deep in snow, looking upward at a huge bull
that was snorting with anger.

Very, very carefully Dalton backed away from the trail,

watching the moose the whole way. When he was safely out of view, he slowly circled around the trail's new owner and walked home. He found the Dalton Gang waiting for him there.

I'd had my own creepy moments—nights when the dogs' ears had suddenly perked up and the headlamp had revealed fresh tracks ahead. So far, today's carcass was the only moose we'd actually touched. Close enough. I was a fool for putting off getting the gun from Madman.

Leaving the river behind, I relaxed. That dead moose was miles behind us. The trail broke into the open, crossing several fields, then turned down a narrow tree-lined tunnel. Midway down that shaded passage, like apparitions, two menacing brown shapes rose from the snow ahead. It was a large cow and her calf. They blocked our path, only 15 yards ahead. The dogs were wild to chase them. I dug in with the brake, but the soft, deep snow offered almost nothing to grip. It was a struggle holding them back. No way could I secure the sled and turn the team around.

The cow moose was eager to avoid us. She lurched into the woods, but the calf wouldn't follow. It continued stumbling down the center of the trail, breaking through the crust with its spindly legs. The cow took a parallel course, plowing a new path through the deep snow blanketing the woods.

The dogs clawed steadily forward. It was all I could do to maintain a gap. The trail finally emerged onto a plowed road. The moose scrambled to get away. I let off the brake, and we chased them until they ran back into the woods. Another crisis, passed.

Mowry and I dropped by Madman's the next day. We left toting a .306-caliber rifle.

Training an Iditarod team made a mess of my working life. At top speed my dogs covered, maybe, 10–12 miles an hour. Add in the time required to get the team ready, then put them away, and it took as long as four hours to complete a 20-mile training run. Try to take a team 50 miles, and a whole day would be shot.

My bosses at the paper were supportive. Sam, the city editor, had grown up with a dog team. He knew what I was talking about when I'd show up an hour late, explaining that Rainy had got loose again and danced, just out of reach, for 45 minutes. But even Sam failed to grasp my overall predicament. Owning a recreational dog team didn't compare with preparing for the Iditarod.

Take the meat shipment from Montana. For nearly a week, Mowry and I were on call, waiting for word from Rick Armstrong, the organizer of Two Rivers' bulk delivery. The day Tim fled east for the holidays, I found a message waiting on my return from the airport. Naturally, the damn delivery truck was finally here. And I was already late to work.

Rushing over to the pickup site, I found Joe Garnie and half a dozen other mushers waiting by the semi in their empty pickups. Garnie was from Teller, an Inupiat village northeast of Nome. He'd recently moved to the Interior.

Like the knuckle hop, ear pull, and other traditional contests held at the annual World Eskimo-Indian Olympics, sled-dog racing has long been a source of friendly rivalry among Alaska's regional and ethnic communities. Athabaskan mushers from the Interior river villages held the edge during the early 1970s, dominating the established sprint circuit and Redington's new race to Nome. Advances in nutrition and conditioning strategies helped mushers such as Rick Swenson and Susan Butcher eventually outdistance the Athabaskan drivers, but the kennel bloodlines of most champions were still rooted in the Indian villages.

Like other racers from the Seward Peninsula, Garnie's dogs excelled in the coastal wind, as his former partner Libby Riddles proved with a famous charge into a storm. Joe had come within an hour of winning the Iditarod himself, something no Eskimo musher had ever done. This year he hoped the change of scenery and the cheap dog food available in the Interior would enable him to correct that previous affront.

Armstrong was finishing his paperwork with Doug Swingley, our Montana meat supplier. Thirty minutes stretched to an hour. I could imagine the questions starting to circulate in the newsroom. "So, any bets on what time Brian will make it in?" But there was nothing to be done. I had $1,866 of meat in that truck: 3,000 pounds of ground beef, 900 pounds of liver, and 600 pounds of lamb.

Deadline Dog Farm's meat was in the very front of the truck, so I had to help clear out everybody else's load before I could begin collecting mine. Stacks and stacks of frozen 50-pound blocks were passed out, forming new piles in the waiting pickups. Minutes ticked away, and I fought the urge to scream.

I finally rolled into work four hours late and physically destroyed. I was exhausted and close to the breaking point, but luckily nobody said a word, and it was a quiet shift. All I had to do was swing by the cop shops, write up the crime blotter, and slap together a graph on historic weather records. Another day in training.

By January the time demands of my race preparations were out of control. Dan Joling, the managing editor, agreed to let me cut back to contributing a single weekly column for the duration. The column, "Off to the Races," described what it was like to be a rookie preparing for Alaska's Great Race. The Associated Press distributed a condensed version statewide. Of course, my pay dropped accordingly, but time was the currency that mattered at this point.

One day in mid-February, less than three weeks before the race, I found a message waiting at the *News-Miner*. Virginia, the newspaper's business manager, wanted to see me. There had been a mistake, she said. As a part-time employee, I no longer qualified for free health insurance. To maintain my medical coverage, I'd have to come up with several hundred dollars in premiums.

"Cancel it," I said.

I wasn't the only one putting dogs ahead of the job.

A year before, Jon Terhune, an abrasive oil company machinist from Soldotna, had approached his plant manager at Unocal Chemicals. Advising the manager of his wish to enter the next Iditarod, Terhune asked what could be done. A month of unpaid leave was subsequently approved, so long as the machinist took the time off in conjunction with his vacation. In July, on the first day entries were accepted, Terhune signed up, becoming the twenty-fourth musher on the list.

The former army paratrooper was a dour man, with little patience for fools. One day in 1969, Jon, his first wife, Nancy, and their daughter, Heidi, had thrown everything they owned in the family's station wagon and left the East Coast for good. Traveling westbound out of Albany, they saw cars on the other side of the highway backed up three lanes deep. The Terhunes learned from the radio that the traffic was caused by people heading to a big music festival. Nancy wanted to turn around and join the procession to Woodstock.

Her husband refused to even consider it. "That's the reason we're leaving," he said, pointing to the traffic. "It's getting to be a rat race."

After settling in Alaska, Terhune began raising malamutes as a hobby. He got into mushing in the mid-1980s, running castoffs from Harry Sutherland. After Nancy died, Terhune found an outlet in the sport. Dogs offered companionship with none of the hassles people inevitably brought into his life. Breeding a few dogs, buying a few more dogs, Terhune gradually built a racing kennel. In 1990 he ran the Kusko 300, a grueling race through Eskimo villages in the Kobuk Valley. It was hellish. All the other rookies dropped out. Terhune spent ten hours searching for the trail in a whiteout and slipped far behind the veteran racers. But he never considered giving up. Not Terhune.

On the home stretch Jon was so tired he fell asleep on his sled, and his team trotted right past the finish line in Bethel. Startled spectators and race officials scrambled after the snoozing racer, whose team continued on its own to the far side of town.

A year later, Terhune entered the Kusko a second time. He viewed it as a final Iditarod tune-up. Instead, the race almost ended his Iditarod hopes. For starters, it was too warm. The race had to be rerouted around open water, and the opening miles crossed tundra stripped of snow by the sun and the rain. Conditions worsened as the trail dropped down on a river. There, wet, slick ice threw Terhune's dogs into a panic. Even worse, Daisy, a recently purchased young leader, was in front. Dandy, the musher's favorite, most dependable lead dog, was running inside the team. It was a protective move: Terhune wanted to spare her from the pressure. But the strategy backfired tragically when Dandy fell on the slick ice. She dragged in a tangle of lines while Terhune battled to slow his runaway team. But he couldn't plant his hook in the hard river ice. Afterward, he spent 20 minutes trying to revive poor Dandy. To no avail. His lead dog was dead.

Terhune scratched from the Kusko. His girlfriend, Dawn, hoped he had learned his lesson. She hoped he was ready to give up his Iditarod obsession. Dawn figured wrong. Though traumatized by Dandy's loss, Terhune wasn't accepting defeat. He chose to protect his team for the bigger challenge ahead. Three other dogs were hurt. If he didn't quit, he wouldn't have enough left to run the Iditarod. He'd invested far too much, endured too many nights on the trail preparing for the coming trip. And he owed it to Dandy to try. Drop out? Each setback further steeled Jon Terhune's resolve.

In February, as he prepared to take his vacation, the machinist reminded his supervisor of the promised leave. The message was relayed upstairs, where the plant manager had changed his mind. Terhune's leave was officially denied. He appealed through Unocal's grievance committee, but the decision was upheld. Terhune was a ten-year employee. He sent the company a letter reminding them of the prior arrangement and reaffirming his intent to run the race.

Unocal officials responded by offering to extend the machinist's vacation by a couple of days, but the request for unpaid leave was again denied. The machinist was ordered to report back to work the day before the Iditarod started. Terhune had a hunch they were calling his bluff, convinced that no one would walk away from a $50,000 job.

"You want to know where I am?" he told his boss at Unocal. "Look in the fucking newspaper."

On my visits home, I always put on a slide show for friends and family in Washington, D.C. After I moved to Alaska, those shows inevitably featured recent sled-dog races, conveying my growing appreciation for the sport. Over Christmas one year, my brother Coleman relayed a message from his father-in-law.

"If you want to run the Iditarod," he said, "Mr. Brown told me to tell you not to let money stop you."

Occasionally I'd daydreamed about entering the sled-dog races I covered for the newspaper, but I'd never given it serious thought. Certainly not the Iditarod. Did Brown realize that it would take the better part of a year to get ready? That it would cost at least $10,000? That I might not make it to Nome?

Coleman smiled, daring me to do it. "I think you ought to talk to him."

For the hell of it, I worked up a budget and arranged to meet Brown at the Kennedy Center cafeteria for lunch.

A retired foreign service officer, Bazil Brown, 59, was a man of broad experience, sensitive to the fleeting adventure our lives represent, and haunted by a son's death and his own bouts with emphysema. Reminders of mortality had led Brown to reflect on the experiences that had brought him the most satisfaction.

Aside from his family life, he told me over lunch, one of his most gratifying experiences resulted from a spontaneous decision he had made at a party, many years before. That night the young diplomat recklessly agreed to invest in a new play. It was called *Sleuth,* and it turned into a huge hit. The play was followed by a movie with the same name. By getting in on the ground floor, Brown reaped continuing financial rewards. His involvement also gave him a backstage introduction to the theater community, a world he would have otherwise missed.

Brown saw my possible entry in the Iditarod in a similar light. He told me he was prepared to put up $10,000 to make it happen.

I couldn't accept the offer. Not yet. There was a lot to consider. I would be putting together a racing kennel from scratch, something that might easily cost closer to $15,000, possibly even $20,000. My life as a reporter was already hectic, involving weeks, sometimes months on the road. I had to decide if I was ready to commit to the months of training that would be necessary if I were to have even a chance of driving a dog team over mountains, rivers, sea ice, and God-knows-what-else I'd find on the trail to Nome.

I told Brown that I would let him know by July 1, the day Iditarod began accepting entries. If I decided to go forward, the $1,249 entry fee would come out of my own pocket, representing my personal commitment to raise any additional capital needed. Brown and I shook on it.

Riding back down the Kennedy Center escalator, I scanned the faces of people ascending toward the cafeteria. For all they knew about the Iditarod, I was headed for Mars.

I wouldn't say that I'm superstitious. But I firmly believe in lucky streaks. Likewise, I believe that there are times when the odds are against you. Entering the final days of training, the omens took a disturbing turn, starting with my car.

My sporty VW Scirocco had never been much of a cold-weather car. I wasn't surprised the morning the engine failed to turn over. It was 35 below, and I had already noticed that the wire to the oil-pan heat pad was beginning to fray. I had meant to fix it.

Living in interior Alaska, you take vehicular setbacks in stride. They are just one more front in nature's eternal siege. I dug a trench under the engine and placed a small Hibachi charcoal stove in the snow, maybe a foot in front of the bumper. While I was waiting for the flames to give way to steady coals—so I could slide the hibachi under the engine—I draped a green military blanket over the Scirocco's hood to help retain the heat. And I hooked a charger to the battery.

Warming an engine this way generally takes an hour. I was chopping meat, no more than a few yards away, when a breeze hastened the heating process. The flames lit the blanket. Then the fire spread from the Volkswagen's plastic grill to the insides of my oily engine. I didn't even hear a crackle until flames were licking around the edges of the wheel wells and grill.

"Tim, Tim, get up," I yelled, dashing inside for our fire extinguisher. "My car's on fire!"

Mowry slowly rolled over and sleepily glanced out his window. A thick column of black smoke was rising from my car.

"You aren't kidding," he said.

I popped the burning hood and pried it open with a shovel. With the inrush of air, a ball of flame leapt up six feet from the engine compartment. I pulled the pin on the fire extinguisher and squeezed the trigger. It spewed froth for a second, then fizzled.

Mowry came running out of the house in his long underwear and bunny boots. We were staring at the fire, paralyzed by the spectacle, when an unfamiliar truck rushed up the driveway. Two men jumped out, each clutching small fire extinguishers.

"Saw the smoke."

The men took aim at the flames, as I had minutes before, and with the same feeble result: foam dribbled out the end of their nozzles, then gurgled to a stop. Retardant gas doesn't work in extreme cold.

Mowry grabbed the shovel and began heaving snow on the engine. A cloud of steam replaced the smoke. So much for technology. The fire was out, leaving a charred carcass in our driveway.

We took 20 dogs out, splitting them between us. The destination was Angel Creek Lodge, a 75-mile round-trip. Call it the final exam.

The temperature was about 25 below as the Mowth and I set out. Trotting past Rattles's place, the mountains ahead glowed with the setting sun's red flare. We met Kathy Swenson, who was returning from Angel Creek. Swenson's team turned around on her, ready to follow us. She straightened them out with an angry shout.

"Swenson definitely has leader problems," Mowry said.

The Mowth's comment wasn't aimed at Kathy Swenson; he was referring to the rumors about her husband, the master himself, four-time Iditarod champion Rick Swenson. According to Rattles, who seldom did anything but gossip—unless he was ranting about the Feds—Swennie was having a rough year. He and Kathy weren't getting along. His training was being hampered by the snow clogging Two River's trail system, and Rick was said to be feeling pressure from IAMS Company, his main dog food sponsor. If that wasn't enough, Swenson's lead dogs were supposedly lousy, a rumor that I could tell Mowry now took as confirmed.

The Mowth and I had first met Rick Swenson in 1987 in Nome when a TV crew was interviewing him near the Burl Arch marking the Iditarod's finish line. Swenson had recently crossed in second place. It was obvious that we also wanted to talk to him, and when the camera stopped rolling, Swenson turned to us and said, "What the hell are you waiting for? I haven't got all day."

At the post-race banquet that year, people shifted uncomfortably as Swenson went on with his odd rambling remarks. "I've got a long way to get back to the top," he concluded. This from a musher whose second-place finish was worth $30,000. The check was no consolation for Iditarod's former top dog, then swallowing his second straight loss to Susan Butcher.

The Iditarod's new queen was more gracious. "In the end," Susan said, "friendship wins out over competition."

Calling Swenson for interviews, I could count on a rash of abuse. "Why didn't you call me in September? I'm in training now." Posteruption, he could be charming. One time when my car broke down during an assignment, Swenson dropped what he was doing to give me a lift.

"You know, Butcher would never do this," he said, becoming friendlier.

Butcher's ascendancy certainly preoccupied him. Back when she was first getting started, Rick Swenson owned the sport, coming within a second of winning five Iditarod victories before anyone else had even won the race twice. For a while, he held the speed records in most of Alaska's big mid-distance races. But Swenson hadn't won anything since 1982. Andy, Swenson's famous leader in all four victories, was sleeping away his retirement years on a couch in Swenson's workshop.

Swenson wasn't the only musher with a Susan Butcher

complex. Joe Runyan's victory in 1989 had cracked Butcher's aura of invulnerability, but she hadn't exactly crumbled, since she finished a close second. A year later she won again, claiming her fourth Iditarod in five years. Susan remained the musher everyone feared. It was her dogs we chased in our dreams.

The press was billing the upcoming race as a showdown. It made for good copy, but no one I knew gave Swenson any real chance. Not without good leaders.

But there was a reason Kathy's team acted flaky. Nearing the lodge we came across a group of snowmachiners salvaging a dead moose. Kathy had shot and killed the moose, after it had barreled into her team, kicking her dogs.

"It was a small moose, and I didn't want to kill it," she told me later. "But I didn't have any choice." She had gutted the animal, as the law requires, then arranged for some folks at Angel Creek to come out and butcher it.

The dead moose cast an ominous presence over our final miles. Mowry and I were relieved when we made it to Angel Creek, where the lodge owner stomped outside to greet us. "You damn mushers," Steve Verbanac said. "You let your dogs piss on that wood pile, and it stinks up the place when we burn it."

After reparking the teams a safe distance from the firewood, we mixed hot meals for the dogs using hot water from the lodge. Most of the dogs settled down, licking their paws. Cyrus continued to pace, whining and looking bewildered at this unnecessary stop. The pup hadn't learned what it meant to be tired.

Cyrus and the other dogs with us at Angel Creek represented every possible candidate for my Iditarod team. We were watching to see who pulled the whole way, who goofed off, who had fun, and who was faltering.

"When we feed them tomorrow, you want to watch for any sign of injury and see who looks stiff," the Coach said, watching the dogs lapping up their dinner.

Inside the bar, Steve's wife, Annette, was retelling the story of Kathy Swenson's epic battle with the moose. Annette had always liked Kathy.

"She doesn't put on airs like Mr. Champion Rick Swenson."

We stayed at Angel Creek for four hours, eating cheeseburgers and drinking beer. Our gloves, mitts, and face masks dangled from the rafters, drying above the lodge's big barrel stove. The Mowth and I toasted each other as Steve bitched about damn mushers and their smelly gear.

By the time we repacked the sleds, the lodge thermometer read 15 below. Practically tropical. The wind was also rising, causing loose straps on my sled bag to flap.

This time we loaded bullets in the rifle. Packing the gun, the Coach left first, again running Chad in single lead. I followed with Rainy and Casey up front. As it turned out, we didn't need the rifle. We had a clean run home.

The skittish brown and grey female wasn't impressive to look at. She appeared to be too small. What first caught my attention was Rainy's ability as an escape artist. Dealing with a couple dozen sled dogs, it wasn't uncommon for one to get loose now and then. The event always triggered a ruckus. Frenzied barks. Dogs rushing out of their houses to join in the joyful prancing. Our escapee nearly always stayed nearby, darting through the kennel, visiting friends, or sniffing the food buckets.

The cause behind a breakout was usually obvious. Most often, a dog had slipped its collar. Chad was particularly good at that. He'd back up and pop the collar over his ears. The empty collar would be lying there, still hitched to the chain. Broken snaps were another common cause for escapes. Or a snap jammed with ice or dirt.

Not so with Rainy. She didn't shed her collar. There was never anything wrong with her snap. The empty chain would be lying there, discarded in the dirt. Rainy never strayed far. But that didn't mean she was easy to find. She liked crawling into other houses. The only giveaway was the excited reaction of other dogs nearby.

One afternoon I heard crying from the lot. Truly woeful whimpering. It was Rainy's neighbor, Daisy, a shy black dog hardly bigger than a pup. She was immobilized between two chains, both of which were clipped to her collar. Our little escape artist was good at her craft.

Rainy's breeding records hinted at qualities beyond what met the eye. The bloodlines of our little five-year-old female spanned the mushing world. Her lineage included dogs from kennels owned by former Quest winner Bill Cotter, sprint champions Bill Taylor and Gareth Wright, Isaac Okleasik, the Lee family, Earl Norris, and, of course, Old Joe Redington, Sr.

Rainy wasn't affectionate. She often hid in her box or watched us from behind a tree. A transformation occurred in her when she observed preparations for a run. Seeing me carrying harnesses or moving the sled into position, she'd cry out and rise on her hind legs, pawing the air as she strained against her chain.

Placed in lead, Rainy displayed a new, bossy side. It didn't matter how big her partner might be, the little female was always in charge. And she was a hard worker, staying out front, bending her little shoulders to the task.

Her shy tendencies didn't apply to sex. Rainy was attracted to any dog within reach. Large or small. Male or female. Given a chance, she'd hump them all. And she'd knock males out of the way to sniff females in heat. We dubbed her Deadline Dog Farm's resident lesbian.

Without realizing it, we came to rely on Rainy. We spent more time discussing Chad and Raven's behavior, Rat's dishonesty, and arguing about Harley's potential. The little lesbian's importance to our kennel was revealed the night I totaled the training miles logged on our kitchen chart. Rainy was the kennel's mileage leader by a substantial margin. As the race drew near, she had recorded over a thousand miles of conditioning—two thirds of that distance as a lead dog.

The morning after our run to Angel Creek she was limping. She might have caught her wrist in a moose hole. Or she could have stumbled crossing a creek. A single misstep anywhere in that 75-mile route could have caused the injury. There was no way we could know.

Mowry and I solemnly brought the lesbian inside our cabin. We wrapped her sore wrist in a rubberized bandage designed to keep the joint warm and speed the healing process. Rainy lay down on a pile of harnesses under the staircase and slept.

"Rest easy, little Rainy," I whispered, watching her chest slowly rise and fall. "I need you."

A heated debate raged between high-level members of my kitchen cabinet.

Madman was starting the race with a 20-dog team, the maximum allowed. He urged me to do the same. "Go for it, O'D!"

The Coach agreed. He had his own agenda to consider. He wanted me to test as many dogs as I could—laying the groundwork for the Mowth's momentous return to competition next year.

No way was I taking 20 dogs. I didn't want to start with more than 16, four more than I'd ever driven at one time. And I might take as few as 14, a fine-sized dog team, easier to feed and care for.

Swenson once won mushing a small team. That was before huge dog strings became the standard, a trend fueled by the paranoia of big men repeatedly being beaten by tiny women.

Besides, top racers were always telling me that the key to assembling a good team was leaving marginal dogs at home. Hell, at Deadline, we had a whole kennel of question marks.

"I don't know," I said. "I'd like to take a small team and get them all to Nome."

"No, no, no, O'D. This isn't a baby-sitting trip," they said. "This is a race."

Worn down by their arguments, I agreed to take 17 dogs, including Daphne, Gnat, and Denali—three dogs in whom I placed absolutely no faith at all.

Root hadn't fully recovered from the Klondike. I was also leaving out Beast and Casey. Both lacked the stamina for the marathon ahead. Mowry pushed me to take Casey.

"Take her as far as Eagle River. Casey's good for twenty miles."

"I'm not taking her. Forget it." I said, flatly refusing to take so-called disposable dogs. I still wanted to reach Nome without dropping a single dog.

The veterans thought my goal was idiotic. Dropping problem dogs was, to them, a fundamental piece of racing strategy.

Watching us loading for the big trip, Cyrus whined, Spook let loose a guttural wail, even old Skidders grew agitated, pacing from side to side on his chain and snapping his teeth. The chorus became raucous as we leaned the bow of my fully-packed sled on the rear of the truck, then slid it into place on top of the dog box. They knew. They always do.

I rolled into Cyndi's yard about 3:00 A.M. Jack Studer, a savvy former racer whose advice always hit the mark, had warned me to take extra care staking out the dogs in Wasilla. They would be frisky from confinement and keyed up in the strange surroundings, he said—a combination that spelled trouble.

Though I took special pains separating the males and other

known troublemakers, a dog fight exploded minutes after I went inside Cyndi's house. It was over before I even got my shoes on to go back out. I wasn't sure who was involved until I spotted the blood-splattered snow near the Rat. She had puncture wounds on one front paw and foreleg. A quarter-sized flap of skin dangled from Daphne's right front leg. This from two sweet females that had never so much as growled.

I felt sick. Rat was supposed to be leading out of Anchorage. Fortunately, a local nurse was staying at Cyndi's. She cleaned the dogs' wounds, soaking their injured legs in Epsom salts and applying an antiseptic.

"I'm sure they'll be fine," the nurse said.

I didn't believe her.

Monday morning I had Dr. James Leach examine the injured pair as he conducted a required prerace veterinary check on the team. The quick actions of the nurse had saved the day, Leach said. The Rat received another shot, and Daphne needed stitches, which set me back an unexpected $144. But the vet assured me that both dogs ought to be ready on Saturday.

Freezing rain was falling as I reloaded the dogs in the truck. I put the truck in four-wheel drive and crept out onto the Parks Highway. The steering wheel had no effect on the glazed pavement. We slowly drifted across the highway. Another car was approaching. The driver apparently hit his brakes, and the car started spinning.

My entire team was on board, and all I could do was watch. The other car finally stopped about ten feet short of my bumper. We both smiled nervously and fled. The highway was soon closed by a collision involving several vehicles.

Get me to the starting line, please!

A jet carrying my family touched down in Anchorage five days before the race. The visit represented their first family trip since

1985, when my mom had hauled the five of us to a wedding in Minnesota. The group included my brother Coleman, his wife Bonnie, my brother Blaine, my sisters Leigh and Karen, my mom Fanchon, and her sister Margo. Only Karen had visited Alaska before.

I couldn't spare any time to play tour guide. The family checked into an Anchorage hotel and drove to Wasilla in a rental van. It was icy, and my mother and aunt barely made it from the driveway into Cyndi's house without falling.

"They're so small!" my sister Leigh said, seeing sled dogs for the first time.

"This one's more like I would expect," Blaine said, pointing to Harley. "THIS IS A DOG! You sure these other scrawny ones will make it?"

Inside the living room, I felt like a contestant on a game show, answering a dozen questions at once. Cyndi's house was equipped with a woodstove and an oil heater for backup. In my rush to get ready, I'd let the stove cool. The room temperature, probably in the high 50s, felt balmy to me, in my long underwear. Along with all their other questions, my mother, brothers, and sisters kept mentioning the weather. I patiently shared what I knew about Alaska statistics.

"Hey Brian," Coleman said finally, "you realize we're freezing here."

My mother seconded that opinion. "If you look around, we're all still wearing our coats."

I got a late start Thursday. Moonshadow Kennel driver Tom Daily and I bumped into each other at a gas station in Anchorage. Both of us were lost, pleading with strangers for directions to the Clarion Hotel, the site of the Iditarod's mandatory pre-race meeting.

The streets were slippery. A guy in a small car rammed me. I jumped out, fearing a catastrophe. The dog truck was unscratched, but the car's grill was smashed. The guy just stood there, staring at the damage.

"Look," I said, "this was clearly your fault. You agree, don't you?"

He nodded yes.

"Good, because I don't have time to mess with cops."

I roared off, leaving him standing by the ruined car.

Twelve mushers, including Daily and me, missed the first roll call. Jim Kershner, who was again serving as race marshal, fined us $500 apiece. Then I found out that fines wouldn't be collected until and unless I again entered the race in some future year. A reprieve. I put the fine out of my mind. Nothing mattered beyond the starting line on Saturday.

The Egan Center ballroom was packed. Last-minute withdrawals cut the number of teams to 75. No matter. My early entry had paid off. My name was number 35 on the list, meaning that I'd be drawing for position with others in the top half of the field.

The actual drawing was a tedious affair. Kershner held up a boot filled with buttons marked with starting position numbers. One by one, we mushers reached for a number, then stepped up to the podium in front of a huge Iditarod banner and thanked friends and sponsors. Folks at my table checked off the positions as they were announced.

I lined up ahead of Terry Adkins and Nels Anderson. The three of us were drawing for the last starting positions in the first half of the draw. Afterward, Kershner would refill the boot with buttons representing starting positions 38–75 for mushers, like Madman, who had signed up after that first day of registration in July, so many months ago.

As we awaited our turn for position, I bantered with Adkins, a true Iditarod legend.

When the mushers set out for Nome in the inaugural 1973 race, Redington talked the U.S. Air Force into letting Adkins, a Kentucky-born military veterinarian, serve as Iditarod's first chief veterinarian. A year later, Adkins returned to Nome mushing his own team to a nineteenth-place finish. Adkins missed the 1975 race, but that was the last time an Iditarod started without the wise-cracking Montanan manning a sled.

Adkins hadn't finished higher than twentieth since 1986. This year promised to be different. He was coming off a stunning victory over Butcher in the 500-mile John Beargrease, and there was reason to believe it hadn't been a fluke.

Following his retirement from the service a year earlier, Adkins had begun experimenting with a new approach to dog training in San Coulee, Montana. Rejecting conventional theories about the dangers of overtraining, Adkins kept his dogs working through the summer, dragging a heavy car chassis through the mountains near his home. By the start of the race, each dog in Adkins's team had over 4,000 miles of conditioning, nearly twice the mileage most mushers considered optimum. The result of his intensive high-aerobic training had been evident at the Beargrease. The Montanan's team hadn't been the fastest in the race, but no one else had dared march over 200 miles in a single shot.

Kershner didn't have a number 1 button in his boot. That position was traditionally bestowed upon an honorary musher chosen by the Iditarod Trail Committee. That ceremonial spot was reserved this year for the late Dr. Rolland Lombard, a sprint-mushing great. The musher leading the way out of Anchorage—launching the largest field in the nineteen-year history of Redington's Last Great Race to Nome—that job belonged to the driver of team number 2.

As we three approached the stage, the number 2 button was still in Kershner's boot, along with button numbers 13 and 33.

No driver in the field was better suited to put that starting advantage to good use than was Terry Adkins, the man standing behind me. Give his marathoners a lead, and they might just hold to Nome. He badly wanted that first spot.

I reached in the boot and fingered the three buttons, finally settling on one of them. I flashed my choice to Kershner, who rolled his eyes. Then I stepped up to the microphone.

"As most of you know, I'm a reporter. Well, I'm going to be able to write about WHAT IT FEELS LIKE TO LEAD THE IDITAROD!"

A hush fell over the room, then slowly gave way to hoots and giggles. I held up the number 2 button and waved it around for all to see. Deadline Dog Farm's team would lead the charge out of Anchorage.

Each musher would take along a handler as far as Eagle River, loaded in the sled bag or trailing behind on a second sled. It was a safety measure. Countless things could go wrong driving a dog team through the crowds and traffic of Alaska's largest city. Kershner gave mushers the option of taking that extra rider as far as Knik Lake, where the Iditarod Trail left the road system for good. My brother Coleman had agreed to ride along on the first 20 miles, with Eric Troyer from the *News-Miner* filling in afterward.

Listening to me onstage, it dawned on my brother that thousands of people would be watching us. Coleman was not at all thrilled with that idea. He hadn't admitted it to anyone, but his shoulders and knees still ached from our test run earlier in the week. His wife, Bonnie, was also frightened. She pictured her husband being dragged to his death in front of cheering crowds of bloodthirsty Alaskans.

A parade of well-wishers came over to our table. Fellow rookie Laird Barron, still waiting for his chance to draw, slapped me on the shoulder. Marcie and Kevin were giddy with excitement, babbling about sled-packing tips and dog-feeding strategies. Lavon Barve, who had drawn the fourth starting position, brought me down to reality.

"I don't want you to take this the wrong way," said Barve, a perennial contender. "But I'm gonna pass you, probably about four miles out. Here's how I want you to handle your team. . . ."

When I got the chance, I split for the pay phones downstairs. Mowry wasn't in a position to help me with the start. The sportswriter and Nora were off in Canada covering the Quest, which was already underway. Before he left, Tim had talked to his old trail partner, Peter Kelly, about helping me at the start. I called the Iditarod veteran from the banquet hall to confirm that he would be available.

"Peter," I said, "you're not going to believe it. We're going to have to have our shit together—I'm going out first."

"Far out," Kelly said.

Mowry refused to believe the news at first, but then he became excited. Going out first virtually guaranteed our team would beat the mob to Skwentna, the Coach reasoned, providing me with a tremendous advantage.

CHAPTER 3

Leader of the Pack

I'd snatched barely two hours of rest before Peter Kelly and his friends showed up at Cyndi's on race day. Kelly was impressed that I got any sleep at all. It was 4 A.M., but I didn't feel tired. The Day was here.

I took advantage of the hour-long drive to interrogate Kelly about the trail. He listened to me ramble for a while, then passed me a cup of coffee laced with a strong shot of Kahlua.

"You need to settle down, man."

We arrived at Iditarod's staging area about 5:30 A.M. One of the 225 volunteers assisting with the start checked off my name and directed us to the front of the parking lot. After a wait of about 20 minutes, we were waved through a corridor of downtown streets to Fourth Avenue. Parking spots were assigned in reverse starting order, providing handlers with an easy exit route. Our space was located at the far end of the closed avenue, four and a half blocks from the starting line. "A long, long, long way," decided Nancy Marti, as she surveyed the scene. Nancy dreaded the moment when she and my other handlers would begin shepherding the team toward the distant countdown area.

Kelly noticed that the stars were exceptionally bright. It was crisp and cool in the predawn hours, a good morning to be mushing. He removed dogs from the truck, one at a time, and fastened Iditarod's team ID tags on their collars, a ritual that brought back memories of his own grand departures. In his two Iditarod starts, Kelly had relied on cues from the mushers nearby. He watched to see if they thought snow conditions warranted booties. The movements of teams ahead of his signaled it was time to harness the dogs.

Today was different. "Everybody is keying off us," Peter realized with a shudder.

We positioned the sled and uncoiled the team's gang line. The length needed for 17 dogs was staggering. Each pair of dogs extended the line another 8 feet in front of my sled. The leaders, Rainy and Rat, would be almost 80 feet ahead of me. Turns were going to be real interesting.

My family soon turned up, as did Eric Troyer, *News-Miner* managing editor Dan Joling, and a growing swarm of friends and spectators. Rigging chains around the truck, we brought the dogs out for good. I posted the volunteers at strategic places, ready to intervene if fights broke out. "Your basic midmanagement job," Joling said.

At 8 A.M., with 62 minutes to go, the sun was high and bright. Crowds were building along the barricades. A crew of veterinarians examined the dogs, but found nothing amiss. Jim Kershner was next. The race marshal inspected my sled for required gear, including a bundle of U.S. mail to be delivered in Nome, a tribute to the mail carriers who served Alaska by dog team as late as the 1940s. Finding my snowshoes, booties, axe, sleeping bag, and the mail packet were in order, Kershner wished me luck.

With 45 minutes to go, we harnessed the dogs, rechaining them outside the truck. Aunt Margo was stalking me with a videocam and a newspaper map. Where should she stand to get the best pictures?

"I haven't got a clue," I snapped. "I'm just following the damn arrows."

News photographers and video crews shadowed my movements. This rookie's lucky draw couldn't have been scripted better.

"I'll be leading the Last Great Race, and not many people can say that," I said over and over.

Another reporter asked how long I expected to stay out in front of the pack.

"For three or four blocks."

Thirty minutes to go. My handlers began assembling the team. I directed the placement of each dog, working from a chart scrawled on a legal pad. From front to back, the lineup called for Rat and Rainy in lead; followed by Cricket and Raven; Screech and Daphne; Chad and Scar; Denali and Pig; Spook and Digger; Bo, Skidders, and Harley; with Cyrus and Gnat in wheel. Bo, our kennel scrapper, got a solo spot to ensure that the Iditarod's live telecast didn't begin with blood spilled in the snow.

Twenty minutes left. Handlers and several Iditarod volunteers assumed positions along the gang line. Troyer knelt in front, calming the leaders. Digger madly shoveled snow with his front paws. Spook uttered his keening wail. Other dogs whined anxiously or jerked on the gang line.

Joling was assigned to the ballerinas, Raven and Cricket. "Approximately ninety pounds of yelping fury," he called the pair.

I left Cyrus chained to the truck until the very last second, a slight that drove him insane with worry. He whined. He stood on his hind legs pawing the air. Other dogs were going someplace. Why not him? Why not him?

I remembered the day Rattles had brought over the young black-and-white dog for a tryout.

"This is Cyrus. He's a Rum dog, a Rummm dog," said Rattles, chanting the phrase like a mantra.

We had been hearing tales of the late great Rum for months. Rum was merely the leader immortalized, according to Rattles, in the Quest's official sled-dog logo. His bloodline was marked by distinctive barrel-chested dogs with pointy snouts.

Barely two years old, Cyrus was Rum's grandson. Like his proud owner, the pup was painfully loud. The dog whined day and night and whooped for joy when Rattles's pickup entered our driveway. At 50 pounds, the big lunk was prone to knocking food pans out of my hands and chewing anything within reach.

"Jesus, Rattles, has that dog even been harness-broken?" Mowry said after wrestling Cyrus into the team for the first time.

"He's a Rum dog," Rattles replied, as if no other answer was needed.

Mowry tested the dog during the week I was away on the Klondike.

The Coach began cautiously, taking Cyrus on a 15-mile run. The young dog was hardly panting when he returned. So Mowry ventured to try him on 30-milers, several days in a row, then 35, then 50 miles.

"I can't tire that dog out," the Coach said when I got back, for once truly impressed.

Today I had a special slot reserved for Cyrus. He'd be leaving town paired with Gnat in wheel position, which locked them down directly in front of the sled. Rattles's pup was too wild to trust anyplace else, and I wanted Gnat where I could keep him under close watch.

It was time.

Coleman stood ready on the back sled. "Let's go!" I shouted, pulling the rope. Feeling give in the gang line, the dogs plunged ahead. Clawing and straining they dragged the sleds and handlers forward. My handlers skidded and struggled to keep their footing in the mushy snow, which had been trucked in to Anchorage and dumped on the barren street for the occasion.

"Like walking through a big pile of cornmeal," Troyer told himself. He glimpsed Butcher directing a swarm of handlers attired in matching suits. Passing by Redington, Swenson, and other famous drivers preparing for their own approaching departure, Troyer noted similarities to the pits at the Indianapolis 500. He was amused at the thought of his former Yellow Press bowling partner competing against these legends of the sport.

I didn't notice any of that. My eyes were fixed straight ahead where I couldn't see through the crowds blocking the street. But the sea of parkas, cameras, and barking dogs kept parting mere yards ahead of our advance, as ranks of race volunteers screamed for people to clear the way.

Officials halted us a few doors down from the Iditarod starting-line banner, which was fluttering grandly above the avenue. After a brief pause marking the late Doc Lombard's honorary departure, my team was waved into the chute. A crew of burly guys grabbed my sled. An announcer boomed out my name, giving a brief biography. I walked up the length of the team, petting each dog and talking to him or her for a second. Cricket's ears drooped. The commotion had her cowed. But looking at me she shyly wagged her tail.

"Five," the voice boomed. "Four. Three. Two . . ."

The howls ceased. Noses dipped toward the snow. Tug lines snapped taut as my 17-dog team bent to business, effortlessly yanking our two sleds forward. Loosely fastened booties flew from the paws up front. I briefly scowled, conscious that I faced a booty shortage, but the regret was soon overwhelmed by the thunderous cheers greeting my team.

Pumping my right fist at the sky, I mushed the dogs down the center of Fourth Avenue, savoring my moment as front-runner on the Iditarod Trail. Butcher, Swenson, Runyan, Buser, and King—all the name mushers were chasing me out of Anchorage today.

The start was broadcast live across Alaska. Watching at a friend's house in Two Rivers, Rattles leaped to his feet as the camera zoomed in on a manic dog in the rear of my team.

"That's CYRUS! That's CYRUS! CYRUS!" the Rattler shouted. "He's going to Nome!"

Five blocks from the starting line, the trail hung a sharp right turn onto Cordova Street. Rainy and the White Rat guided the team through the curve in a fine tight arc. My sled neatly skidded around the berm piled on the corner. Riding the handler's sled, my brother Coleman wasn't so lucky. Slamming into the hard snow wall, his sled flipped over sideways. Coleman understood that I wasn't going to stop, certainly not as long as we were leading the pack. Fortunately this was the one mushing maneuver my brother had actually practiced.

The week preceding the race had largely been consumed with official meetings and last-minute chores. The dogs, sitting on their chains in Cyndi's yard, had energy to burn. My brother Coleman also needed a sled-riding lesson if he was going to man that second sled. Finding a few hours free, I grabbed the chance to take the dogs on a short run. It would be my family's first chance to see a real dog team in action. Bonnie, who was three months pregnant, asked if she could go along for the ride.

I shook my head. "I'm sorry, but I don't think it would be a good idea, Bon."

She was disappointed and somewhat offended by my protective attitude. I felt guilty. Her father had made this thing possible. But bringing her along would be asking for trouble. I was taking 14 dogs, leaving behind only Skidders and the two casualties. Too many things could go wrong.

We didn't get started until after dark. Coleman was zipped inside heavy Carhartt coveralls, wearing bunny boots and a headlamp for the first time.

"These dogs are stronger than they look," Blaine said appreciatively, unloading them from the truck. Until that moment, when he felt his arm being twisted by my squirming bundles of muscle and fur, my younger brother hadn't been impressed by sled dogs.

As the moment of departure drew near, Screech and Digger began leaping in place, straining to go. The excitement spread, and my sled bounced and wobbled under the team's pressure, but we were firmly tied to a pole. I positioned the second sled about ten feet behind mine, attached by a thick poly towrope. Coleman planted himself on the runners.

Bonnie was feeling apprehensive. The dogs were much wilder than she had imagined. The landscape stretching before her, an icy field giving way to a dark mass of trees, was forbidding. "I would feel a lot safer if we were doing this in daylight," she said.

Coleman's sled trailed slightly at an angle to mine, but I figured it wouldn't matter.

"Ready?"

"You got it," Coleman said.

I yanked the anchor rope. The dogs surged forward, whipping both sleds across the hard-packed crusty snow.

Coleman's sled slammed into the anchor pole, and he lost his footing on the runners. Remembering what I had said about never letting go of a dogsled, he hung on for all he was worth. The dogs dragged him, facedown, into the darkness.

My eyes stayed glued on the dogs, alert for hints of a tangle developing in those first crazed minutes. Coleman's sled remained upright, and I didn't realize he was down until we had traveled about a quarter of a mile. When I finally stopped the team, Coleman staggered to his feet. He was weary and winded, his hair was gray from sprayed snow, but otherwise he was fine. He'd been shielded from harm by the heavy coveralls.

"That was a rush!" he said, chuckling as he dusted himself off. "You dragged my ass a long way."

Coleman strapped the headlamp back on his hat before we continued, but the light slipped free. He was too nervous to let go of the sled and reach for it, so the headlamp dangled, still lit, from the end of its power cord.

As they stood and watched, Bonnie and Blaine couldn't see much beyond the two lights steadily moving across the open field. The lamp in front moved smoothly away, floating several feet above the dark line of dogs. But the trailing headlamp, the one Bonnie knew was strapped to Coleman's forehead, continued bouncing on what had to be the hard, icy ground. Bonnie was horrified by that awful dancing light; she pictured her husband's head being battered to a pulp. Blaine bellowed with laughter.

After the lights were swallowed by a line of trees, Bonnie was nearly overcome with dread and grief. Coleman had only recently gotten over pneumonia. Even if he wouldn't admit it, Bonnie knew that her husband was still weak. What kind of insanity had brought her here, to Alaska, to this dismal edge of known creation, to watch him dragged to his death? Bonnie hugged her stomach, swollen with the pregnancy. To think that she had wanted that dogsled ride. She felt tears coming as she imagined having to explain Coleman's death to Sarah and Devin, the children they left at home. She and Blaine drove back to Cyndi's. The waiting was just too awful to bear.

Coleman and I took the dogs on a ten-mile loop. After the rough start, Coleman remained tense for several miles, expecting the sled to flip again. Nothing bad happened, and he finally relaxed, leaning into the corners and having fun. Riding a sled was like getting your sea legs, he concluded.

Coleman put on a show for the crowds lining Anchorage's Cordova Street. He was dragged, facedown, for about a hundred yards, then righted the sled with a twist and pulled himself aboard the runners. He was riding the brake with one knee when he noticed a pedestrian running alongside.

"I've got your hat! I've got your hat!" cried the sprinter. The man had snatched the hat from the snow and dashed after us. He had chased the team three blocks before Coleman heard his cries. With his sled righted, we were pulling away. The man made a last desperate throw with the hat. It fell short.

Unbeknownst to us, *Daily News* photographer Fran Durner caught the incident with a telephoto lens. Safely ensconced in his hotel bed the morning after the start, Coleman was awakened by Bonnie's shrieks. Somebody had slipped a copy of the paper under the door. The back page was illustrated with a six-inch-square color photo. It showed me shouting at my brother as he belly-surfed through downtown Anchorage.

That first morning I didn't expect my two-minute lead would hold up long. Team number 3 was driven by Brian Stafford, who had dusted us in the Klondike.

"We got company," Coleman shouted, as Stafford's dogs began closing in on us. We held him off for a few more blocks. But he was coming on strong as the trail shifted to a bike path and continued on into the woods.

A short tunnel gave me the edge. Rainy and Rat sailed through it. Stafford's leaders threw on the brakes. I pulled away as he sorted out a tangle. Fifteen minutes past the starting line, the lead in Redington's Last Great Race remained mine. All mine.

Minutes later, Barve's team appeared from behind. I had to hand it to the veteran. We were approaching the exact spot he described at the banquet.

"Stop your team. Now," he cried, pulling alongside.

I braked. The Iditarod had a new leader. But, it had been fun while it lasted.

Beginner's luck had run its course. Seconds later, rounding an easy turn into the woods, Gnat dodged the wrong way around a tree. His thin neckline snapped, as it's designed to, but that didn't arrest the accident in motion. A 17-dog team doesn't stop without major persuasion. "Whooa!" I shouted, braking as hard as I could. The team rolled on, yanking Gnat backward by his tug line. He slammed into the tree and spun back around its trunk, yelping horribly.

Damn wolves with collars, that's what the ranchers in Colorado called Tom Daily's sled dogs. Real dogs wouldn't raise the unholy howls that were heard coming from the hippie's place. The simmering resentment was getting to the easygoing, long-haired musher. Tom and Fidaa, his Saudi Arabian–born bride, were itching to move to Alaska, where Tom dreamed of mushing the Iditarod. But where were they ever going to get the money?

The snow was on the way out. Daily figured his season was over, when a four-member group booked rides. The party included the owners of Track 'N Trail, a sport-shoe company. Daily had his hands full, keeping his dogs in line while answering their usual questions. The Iditarod came up, of course. Daily admitted that competing in the great Alaskan race was his personal goal. He described how he had once spent a few months helping at Redington's huge kennel in Knik. It was nothing he hadn't told tourists a thousand times before. He almost hated talking about it. The dream felt tainted by such small talk. Daily didn't take it seriously when the clients mentioned that they might be interested in sponsoring him.

"It costs a lot of money," he snorted. "Thirty thousand or so. You don't even want to think about it."

Two days later, the shoe-company owners called Tom and offered him full Iditarod sponsorship for two years. It was like winning the lottery, only he hadn't even bought a ticket. It was karma. Fate. The gods were speaking through his dogs. Packing their lives aboard a truck, the Dailys moved to Alaska.

As Iditarod's opening day for registration approached, Tom began to panic. He and his wife were penniless. They were living in a cloud of mosquitos, surrounded by hungry dogs, and they hadn't seen a dime of that promised money. Tom wondered, Have I been faked out? Was this whole thing some kind of rich man's joke? Full of doubts, Tom went into town and called the sponsors collect. He described his preparations for the race and demanded a check to cover the $1,249 entry fee. The check arrived on schedule, followed by others. Daily's sponsorship was real. Moonshadow Kennel's driver was bound for Nome.

Hectic months later, the musher and his wife were entertaining Tom's shoe-company sponsors in Anchorage. It was the last thing they wanted to be doing the night before the race. The couple hadn't slept in two days. The packing wasn't finished. But the sponsors suddenly turned up in Anchorage, eager to see their musher start the race—made possible by Track 'N Trail's money. What choice did Daily and his wife have? The meal dragged on for hours. Fidaa's self-control was strained to the limit. After dinner, she and Tom pulled an all-nighter finishing preparations for the race.

Daily had drawn position number 20. His pit crew was weak beyond his wife and Big Larry, a bouncer from The Bush Company, a local topless joint. The rest were inexperienced helpers from the shoe company.

"Oh no," Fidaa cried, watching one of their volunteers fumbling with a dog harness, "we have to train the handlers."

Kershner's inspection added to the stress: the handle on Daily's axe was shorter than the 22-inch standard specified in the race rules. The race marshal could have forced the team to wait until a legal substitute was found. Instead he ruled that Tom could leave Anchorage on time, but the team wouldn't be allowed to continue past the first checkpoint until Tom's gear met Iditarod standards. The crisis appeared resolved when friends in Eagle River promised to meet the team there with the necessary replacement.

"Still ahead of Butcher and Swenson!" I shouted, playing to the trailside gallery lining the first miles of city streets, parks, and power-line trails. A lot of people knew who I was from the publicity surrounding my going out first. Others relied on the photos and starting positions of each musher that had been published in the *Anchorage Times* that morning. True fans used the photo spread as a program to greet us by name.

I had to change my script after Swenson joined Joe Runyan, John Barron, Garnie, and a half-dozen other top mushers streaking ahead of us. I yelled to Coleman not to worry. "Those guys are contenders." Nome wasn't the only goal for those top drivers. A series of prizes awaited the first musher into half a dozen of the checkpoints ahead, starting with a new pickup parked in Skwentna, 100 miles up the trail. Those guys were out of my class completely.

It was a different story to be passed by driver number 15. Kraft General Foods employee Larry Munoz, who crept by us during a tangle, riding a sled decorated with a huge Oscar Mayer wiener. I wasn't going to take that without a fight. I got my dogs loping, and we caught and passed the damn Hot Dog Man. Alas, my team again balled up and Munoz slipped by.

Big Larry lost his grip on Tom's sled as it moved toward the starting line. The other handlers were flung aside, leaving Daily powerless to slow his surging dogs. Fidaa sprinted after her husband's team on the snowy avenue. Like Tom, she was decked out in new Northern Outfitters gear. The bright parka looked sharp, but it was too warm for the day. By the end of the first block, Fidaa was drenched in sweat. Daily was using a single sled. Fidaa was still running when the announcer called her husband's name. He couldn't start without a handler and she barely made it, jumping into the sled bag as the countdown ended.

The excitement of the city gradually faded. With their sled gliding through the woods, the long hours of preparation caught up with the musher and his wife.

"Tom," Fidaa said, "I'm falling asleep."

"Yeah, I am too."

The Dailys exchanged foolish grins.

Back in the city, Madman and dozens of other mushers were still fussing with their teams, awaiting their turn in the starting chute. Noon was approaching before the last musher, Mowry's old trail companion Malcolm Vance, heard his countdown.

Miles ahead, Tom and Fidaa were sleeping soundly while their 20-dog team trotted on, navigating the forest without any guidance. The Dailys didn't awaken until their sled flipped and went crashing through a trail barrier. Tom sleepily righted the sled, and his frisky dogs resumed their march on a hiking trail that followed Ship Creek up into the mountains. Daily had flickerings of doubt as the trail split from the creek bed and began climbing a high canyon. He had gone a long way without seeing a marker. These curves were dangerously sharp for long strings of dogs. But this had to be right.

The trail dead-ended at a tall fence. Daily's leaders, some 80 feet ahead, turned and ran alongside the fence, halting finally on a cliff overlooking Ship Creek. Tom now found himself in an awful fix. It was a treacherous place to turn any dog team, let alone a full Iditarod string. Fidaa couldn't offer much help. Not from her position inside the sled. Topping it off, Tom's damn suspenders were screwing up, dropping those high-tech pants down around his knees, and this was no place to make adjustments.

Barry Lee had just 13 dogs—one of the smallest teams in the field—but most were proven Iditarod finishers. He had Louie, an old lead dog from Dewey Halverson's third-place 1987 team; Onion, from Bill Hall, whose wife Pat Danly was also running the race; Mutt, from Dave Allen; and a young leader named Chiko from Mitch Brazen. Of course, Barry Lee also had dogs from his older brother's kennel.

Former race marshal Bobby Lee was working in the chute with a microphone, interviewing racers for the live TV broadcast being fed to stations across Alaska. Musher number 46 got the standard questions. Then Bobby switched off the mike.

"You made it. You made it," he said, hugging his younger brother.

Listening to the countdown, Barry Lee reveled in the moment. His eyes were puffy and red from three weeks of sleep deprivation. His smile was huge. Others were chasing prizes in the days ahead. Lee was already savoring the achievement of his lifelong dream.

The musher gave the signal. His dogs bent to work, cutting a slow but steady pace past the crowds still lining Fourth Avenue. Only a few blocks passed before Lee's weariness made concentrating difficult. He was thankful that he didn't have to worry about getting lost. The route followed trails familiar from a childhood spent near the Tudor dog track in Anchorage. He could handle this on automatic pilot.

"Yea Barry! Go Barry!" Lee reveled in the cheers, but how did all the fans lining the route know his first name? Was there a radio announcer on every corner telling them who was coming by? He was chagrinned when he finally noticed the newspapers in people's hands. The musher sporting number 46 on his chest had cheered on others for years using that same information. It unnerved him how long that information took to process. Fatigue was affecting his thinking. Lee knew he ought to keep that in mind.

The Hot Dog Man was faltering. Sensing a chance to catch him, I jumped off the runners and ran, giving it everything I had, pushing my sled up the short hill crowned by the American Legion arch. But it was no use. We coasted into the legion hall parking lot in thirteenth place, 34 minutes behind Barve, the first musher into Eagle River's checkpoint 20 miles from the start, and 2 minutes ahead of fellow rookie Joe Carpenter.

I sent friends for a veterinarian to examine Gnat. Two vets promptly appeared. They knelt over the young dog, flexing his limbs and probing for sensitive areas. A local TV crew raced over to catch the action. Just what I need. "Reporter cripples dog. Footage at six."

Blaine, Jim, and Nancy tossed the other dogs chunks of whitefish and dished out a meaty broth to those willing to drink. Kelly pulled off any remaining booties, which were reduced to shreds, and checked the dogs' feet for cuts.

"Nobody is putting on those booties the right way," I shouted. "From now on, I am the only one putting on booties."

Nancy figured I was freaking out because my mom had sewed them. She didn't know that I faced a booty shortage. If the bundles I mailed out after the food drop weren't waiting at the checkpoints ahead, I'd need every last one we had.

I calmed down after hearing good news from the veterinarians. Gnat's back was bruised, but it didn't appear to be serious.

"See how he acts in Wasilla," a vet said. "If he looks all right, put him back in the team and see how he handles the run to Knik. That's only fourteen miles."

Coleman watched the action from the second sled, chin

planted on his fist. He hadn't budged an inch since arriving in Eagle River. He looked like a crooked old man to our sister Karen.

The day was looking good to me. My team hadn't mutinied in front of the ABC cameras. I hadn't lost the dogs, or Coleman. We hadn't been run over by snowmachines, mail trucks, or damaged by any of the freak hazards awaiting people crazy enough to mush dogs through Alaska's largest city.

We loaded the dogs back into the truck. With Blaine at the wheel, Team number 2 rolled up the highway, bound for Wasilla, where the serious race for Nome would begin.

Coleman stayed behind. A nice smooth ride in the van with the rest of the family sounded appealing to him. "It's nice to have completed my part of the race without a train wreck," he declared, as my aunt zoomed in with her video camera.

Descending the hillside, Tom Daily's leaders decided that the frozen creek below looked more appealing than the narrow trail they had used on the way up. When the chance presented itself, the leaders plunged down the bank. By the time the musher managed to stop the sled, ten dogs were standing on the creek ice below.

This is absolutely nutty, thought Tom, who could see water gushing through open holes in the ice. His sled was precariously balanced. If he let go to haul his leaders back up the slope, he knew he might well lose the entire team. Fidaa spied a sign alerting hikers about the dangerous cliffs. She wondered what advice authorities had for sled dogs.

Bowing to the inevitable, Tom launched his sled over the bank, sending the team on a careening descent along the narrow frozen creek. The ice offered nothing for his brake to grab, so Daily concentrated on steering the sled past massive rocks, stumps, and the holes he couldn't skate over.

For the first time ever, Fidaa saw her husband was terrified. "Tom, just scratch!" she cried.

Tired, sweaty, and scared, Daily considered bailing out. His wife, the love of his life, was in danger. Assuming he could figure a way to save her, he might just let go. But the musher thrust such thoughts aside. Of course, he wasn't going to let go of his dogs. Hanging on to that sled, Tom Daily felt intensely protective of those childlike companions in front. His whole life was tied up in those dogs.

Eighteen teams skipped past Daily during his team's adventurous detour. Yet Tom was only two hours behind Barve checking into Eagle River. That wasn't so bad at all. The bummer arrived in the form of the replacement for his illegal gear. His friend's wife hadn't understood. Instead of meeting the team with a legal axe, she brought Tom Daily a bow saw.

Friends expected great things from Sepp Herrman. The long-haired, blond-bearded German expatriate was a newcomer to the Iditarod, but no one questioned his ability as a dog musher. The reclusive Herrman spent winters trapping out of a remote cabin, 50 miles from the closest road, in the Brooks Range, a mountainous region north of the Yukon River. Sled dogs were his engine of survival in that treacherous, unforgiving wilderness. The trapper's savvy and grit were matched by excellent dogs. He had several on loan from Rick Swenson. The master musher respected Sepp's ability to train good leaders.

Herrman drew position number 71 in the chute, putting his team's starting time nearly three hours behind mine. High noon overtook him as he mushed those tundra-seasoned dogs through unfamiliar city streets. By that time the snow, trucked into the city for the occasion, was getting thin and dirty. The sun felt scorching. It was easily 80 degrees warmer than the conditions the team had so recently left in the Brooks Range. Dogs capable of breaking their own paths through deep snow and fierce winds, dogs upon whom the solitary trapper routinely staked his life—those same dogs faltered on the warm, well-groomed trail to Eagle River. Twenty miles into the 1,150-mile race, Sepp Herrman was third from last in the standings and was packing three dogs in his sled. His entire race was in jeopardy.

Larry Munoz rode his big wiener out of Wasilla at eight minutes past four. I was scheduled to depart a minute later. Ushering my dogs toward the chute, Vicki noticed I wasn't wearing a numbered bib. It was required gear, because the restart was also being televised live.

Vic sprinted back to the truck and fetched it. Friends were tying on the bib as my name again blared through the surrounding speakers.

Bobby Lee, seated overlooking the starting chute, was providing running TV commentary. The former race marshal took note of my rapid fall from first to thirteenth position in the overall standings. Lee added that I was still keeping good company for a rookie.

"I'm sure Brian would be glad if he could keep that position—but he won't."

The safe approach was to leave the White Rat and Rainy in lead. That had been my prerace strategy. On the spur of the moment, I now scrapped that idea. Moving Rat down inside the team, I shifted Cricket into lead with Rainy. Gnat's tiny sister was much faster than Rat.

The player change looked brilliant as my little girls set a swift pace leaving Wasilla. Trouble hit when the trail emerged from trees, and we entered Lake Lucille's glassy, wind-polished ice. Alone, I'm sure Rainy would have made straight for Munoz, who remained visible in the distance, hunched over his sliding wiener. There were scratch marks to follow and a handful of marked tripods. An experienced dog might have noticed such clues. It was all new to young Cricket.

There were scattered clusters of people, some of them seating on folding chairs. There were cars and trucks, haphazardly parked. Groups of children were playing. Snowmachines were zipping in different directions. Confronted by all these strange sights and sounds, my little girl freaked, peeling Rainy and the team away from the trail at a 45-degree angle.

I yelled. I hit the brakes along with Troyer, who'd replaced Coleman on the second sled. But the sheer ice offered nothing to grip. Spooked, little Cricket remained on a tear, propelled by 64 additional flailing paws. Both sleds swung wildly behind the team, which twisted like a mad snake. We slammed into several hard-packed mounds of snow before my hook took hold, finally ending Cricket's charge.

In the distance, I saw other mushers trotting past us in neat formation. I would have changed leaders, but the situation remained precarious. One slip and Troyer might be on his own. All I could do was coax them. "Go ahead, Rainy, go ahead. Good girl Cricket! Good dogs!"

The leaders were finally headed in the right direction, when they spotted a spectator's dog.

"Put that thing in your car!" I yelled.

"My dog has every right to be here," the guy shouted back, ready to debate the point. The man reconsidered as my excited crew barreled down on his lone mutt. Scooping up Fido, he dove into his car.

We continued skidding in the general direction of the trail. Just short of a dangerous cluster of spectators and parked vehicles, I again stopped the team.

"I think we'd be all right if you could just please steer my leaders past these cars," I called to a woman standing near Rainy and Cricket.

The woman crouched down and gave the pair directions,

pointing out relevant land marks. Cricket wagged her tail, sensing an opportunity to be petted. Rainy held the team in place, but she shied away from the woman. My lesbian didn't know what to make of a talkative stranger.

Troyer was too busy laughing to be of any help.

"Lady," I shouted, "just grab the dogs. Please, grab their collars and drag them to the trail."

As the trail joined Knik Road, my old landlord, Tom Renggli, appeared alongside up in his van, waving madly and pacing my team. Rushing ahead, he parked and greeted me at a road crossing.

"Need anything, Brian?"

Several friends were throwing a bonfire party on Knik Lake, the trailhead first used by dog teams hauling gold miners and their supplies to a place called Iditarod. This year Big Sandy had gone all out, renting a portable john for the festivities. As the team trotted past, I urged my landlord to meet us out on the lake. "Look for the john," I said by way of a landmark.

He recoiled at the suggestion.

The van again zoomed by. Minutes later, I saw my old landlord perched on a berm overlooking the trail. Worry creased his brow.

"Bri, you need a porta potty?" he shouted. "I got one at home."

"Thanks," I said, realizing I couldn't begin to explain, "but I'm fine, really I'm fine."

Tom Daily realized his sponsors were disappointed. They wanted to see more fire in their musher, more dedication toward winning the Iditarod his first time out. As if that were as simple as tying on a new pair of sneakers. They might be generous with their money, but these folks had no idea what this sport entailed. None. Tom's current objective was to escape town without any more disasters.

The musher arranged with race officials to drop four dogs from his team at Wasilla. Those he left behind weren't injured. Driving 20 dogs was just too crazy; after careening down that creek, Daily wanted absolute control. But that hope was crushed before Tom even made it past the restart banners. One of his shoe-company volunteers had meticulously fastened each dog's neckline to a thin tag clip, instead of to their sturdy collar rings. The weak clips held so long as handlers were there restraining the dogs. As soon as they let go, necklines began popping loose.

The force exerted by a working sled dog is primarily channeled into the team's gang line through a tug line, which is clipped to the rear of the dog's harness. Those tugs were properly connected, so Daily's dogs were still pulling, and his sled was launched forward. The neck lines served to hold the dogs in neat formation. Without them, the team fanned out like a riotous mob.

Tom wondered what new bad thing would happen next.

The first time his lead dog collapsed Bill Peele was thunderstruck. The kindly musher from North Carolina assumed that poor Charlie was stricken with a heart attack, or something else catastrophic. Peele was relieved to detect a strong pulse.

Charlie's eyes popped open. He sprung to his feet. Ready to go.

Peele, 56, didn't know what to make of it. The lanky, bushy-bearded rookie had no illusions about being a mushing expert. But this didn't fit with anything he'd learned since coming to Alaska in December to lease a dog team from Redington. Proven Iditarod dogs like Charlie, a trained leader, didn't crumble in a heap without good reason.

Knik was less than about ten miles away. Peele would have the dog thoroughly checked out when he arrived. He pulled the hook free and resumed his march. The team had hardly moved before the dog went down again. Peele cursed his foolishness. Charlie was dead for sure. He should have loaded that dog! Yet Charlie's pulse still felt strong. His chest was heaving regularly. Sure enough, the dog quickly regained his feet. Peele was thankful, of course, but the darn dog's behavior was mystifying.

When Charlie dropped for the third time in barely a hundred yards, Peele became suspicious. This time the musher didn't stop right away. Instead he watched as the team dragged its prone member through the soft snow. Funny thing. The musher sensed that ole Charlie was watching him.

Stopping the team, Peele knelt over Charlie until the dog finally looked him in the eye. It was as if Peele could read the thoughts underneath that furry brow: "Well, dummy, you best leave me here, cause I ain't going to Nome again."

Peele loaded Charlie in his sled. He told himself he was imagining things. A sled dog couldn't be this devious.

It was Mardi Gras time in Knik. Inside the bar, Hobo Jim's foot-stomping and slashing guitar work had the crowd in a frenzy. The windows were so steamed from perspiration you couldn't see through them. Outside, the view of the race was blocked by the mobs of spectators, friends, and handlers swarming each incoming team.

Big Sandy tracked down Kelly and Davis and told them about the party out on the lake. She gave them directions and asked them to guide the team over.

"No way," Kelly told the other handler after Sandy had left. "Our job is to GET BRIAN OUT OF HERE."

As my team entered Knik, Rainy bravely trotted through the tunnel of parkas. Digger and Spook flinched at the human tumult, but continued forward, ears low. Somehow I picked Marcie's face out of the crowd. She chased us to the checkpoint and gave me a hug.

"The dogs look good, Brian. Really good."

I had a million things to say. But Knik offered no refuge. The race was ON.

"Can't stop here. Can't stop here," an Iditarod volunteer shouted, determined to keep me from parking next to my truck. Kelly ran the guy off, then stuffed a Burger King cheeseburger in my pocket. He and the pit crew were cranked.

While Kelly and Davis unhitched the second sled, Nancy snacked my dogs. I placed on new booties, by myself this time. Cyndi was standing by with the thermos I had asked her to fill.

"Hot Tang," she said, "just what you ordered."

Kelly pulled Troyer aside. "Look, we can't let him stop for this barbecue thing."

Half a dozen teams had passed mine on Lake Lucille, two more caught us along Knik Road. Countless others were streaming in and out of Knik. I fussed with my sled. Did I need anything else from the dog truck? An important question, since I wouldn't see it again until my return home.

"You're ready. Get out of here!" Kelly said as Dee Dee Jonrowe, a top driver, parked her team adjacent to us.

Stepping on the runners, I reached for the hook. Troyer climbed aboard one side of my sled; Kelly took position on the other. Jim and Nancy ran ahead of the dogs, leading Rainy and Rat through the crowd.

Sandy intercepted the team as we approached the open part of the lake.

"This way," she said, grabbing the leaders to steer the team over toward the bonfire.

"What? What?" I said, having completely forgotten the party, where my family and dozens of friends were waiting. Kelly rushed to the front of the team.

"Forget it. Brian's not stopping. This is a race!"

We left Sandy on the lake, looking disappointed.

My dogs were pulling like an engine in fine tune. I shook hands with Troyer and Kelly, and they jumped off. I was looking backward, waving good-bye to my friends, when the team balled up in a tangle. Both handlers saw it and came running. Another team slipped by as I lined out my dogs. Kelly was waiting on the sled when I trudged back. I slapped him on the shoulder, then turned to the dogs.

"All right," I shouted. The dogs chased the team ahead.

I leaned into the turn rounding the old Knik Museum. When I looked up, there it was, waiting for me: a curving fence rising toward a gap in the trees—the Iditarod Trail.

Dandy should be here. Mushing out of Anchorage, the absence of his trusted leader cast the only shadow touching Jon Terhune's trail. His Kenai-conditioned dogs breezed through the warm passage to Eagle River, climbing a notch to forty-fifth position.

Watching other mushers streaming through Knik and racing off into the darkness, Terhune's girlfriend, Dawn, brooded about the unknown dangers ahead. She couldn't quit thinking about the money, time, and energy being squandered on this mad perversion of a sport. She thought about Terhune's refusal to return to work the day before, as his company had demanded. Ten years with Unocal and her boyfriend had thrown it away— for what? By the time Terhune arrived at Knik Lake, Dawn was seething.

"You're crazy," she told Terhune. "And Joe Redington should be put in jail for starting long-distance mushing."

It was a familiar argument. Terhune didn't need a rerun. Certainly not there in the middle of Knik Lake. But he let her rage. He was going to Nome, regardless. And he really had no adequate response to Dawn's main question: "Why do you do it?" Terhune figured the only answer to that was spiritual. You either saw that or you never would.

"How can you do this for a hobby?"

"It's NOT a hobby," Jon snapped.

The musher kept his cool. This was Dawn's scene, and he let her play it out. Three hours slipped away in a breathy cloud of angry words. Every minute of the delay represented a major sacrifice to Terhune. But he knew she'd never appreciate that.

Barry Lee was disgusted with himself. The little cook pot for his personal food was missing.

While Lee fretted about this screwup, Dr. Nels Anderson faced a painful decision. His admirable, thrilling start was being derailed by illness. The two-time finisher hadn't come back to the Iditarod Trail only to nurse a sick team to Nome. He resolved to scratch.

Lee hated to profit from another man's distress, but he couldn't let this golden opportunity pass. He talked the doctor out of his cooking pot. Anderson also sold him a spare set of runner plastic, dirt cheap. Depending on the hardness grade, a single set of runner plastic sold for $20 to $50. Lee had lacked the cash to buy spares in time to ship them out with his food drop. Lee was particularly pleased with this last acquisition. He didn't have any runner plastic waiting at checkpoints ahead.

Jeff King, of Denali National Park, trailed Barry into Knik. In the decade since he had made his one and only Iditarod bid, placing twenty-eighth, King had emerged as a champion sled-dog racer, winning the Quest, the recent Kusko 300, and numerous other mid-distance events. None of those victories counted against the competition here. They were tune-ups for the intense, jockey-sized musher's return to this trail.

Anxious to test the dogs and himself, Jeff King overtook Lee in a narrow section as the teams were descending a steep slope. It was a lousy place to pass, but the driver from Denali managed it with style, dogs loping, steering his sled past the rookie's team on one runner.

The slick demonstration of dog power and control left Barry Lee truly awed. He felt like pulling over and waiting for the snow to settle.

Daily needed to regroup. He felt lucky to have made it to Knik. That crazy trail out of Wasilla had been lined with badly parked trucks. Already exhausted from the hillside detour after leaving Anchorage, Tom was spent by the time he wrestled his sled past all the obstacles. The dogs dodged through without damage, but his sled had slammed into several of the trucks. Each time Tom feared the blow would finally kill his poor wife, who was still riding in the sled bag. But Fidaa managed to ride it out.

The passage to Knik was further enlivened when Daily lost his snow hook because of an improperly rigged line. Tom was retrieving the crucial hook, entrusting Fidaa with the dogs, when Jeff King mushed past them. Like Lee, Daily and his wife were impressed by the Denali Park musher's smooth, powerful dogs. It gave Tom a thrill just watching them. Give me ten years, he thought, and my dogs MIGHT look that good.

The shoe-company sponsors were gone. They hadn't bothered coming to Knik, and Tom was sure they were ready to dump him. They probably wished they had given money to the asshole shouting at him in Wasilla. So his own team took an extra minute getting out of the chute. Daily couldn't believe the way the other racer had carried on.

Tom rested nearly seven hours in Knik. Midnight wasn't far away when he adjusted his headlamp, hugged Fidaa good-bye, and pulled the hook, sending his team trotting across the quiet lake. The stars above were bright, and the woods ahead looked friendly.

Driving the last-place team—thus making him custodian of the Red Lantern in the largest Iditarod field ever seen—Tom Daily laid fresh tracks toward Nome.

CHAPTER **4**

Early Casualties

Bonfire parties raged through the forest for miles. The festivities were widely spaced among the thick alders and stands of spruce. I'd be traveling alone with the dogs, then enter a clearing ringed by snowmachines and cheering fans.

My fleeting lead in the Last Great Race was gone for good. I knew that I'd probably see Nome before catching Swenson, Runyan, and the rest of the serious racers. But I hadn't completely surrendered my bragging rights.

"Still ahead of Susan Butcher," I shouted to the clusters of merry celebrants, attired in thick parkas and fur hats. It was a claim any Alaskan could appreciate. Thick mitts raised toasts in my honor.

Though well intended, my hurried departure from Knik backfired about ten miles out. Passing through a narrow, tree-lined alley, faster teams kept catching mine, resulting in a series of bruising passes. The trail here resembled an icy gutter. Burt Bomhoff, the old Silver Streak, was one of the few who successfully muscled his sled past us without slamming into my leaders. The blows left Rainy and Rat increasingly skittish, further slowing down my team.

It got so bad that I stopped each time someone approached and ran forward to protect my dogs. That was the situation when Dee Dee Jonrowe tried to pass. Her dogs were sailing ahead when her sled snagged my snow hook. Jonrowe continued on, probably unaware of the problem, and dragged my sled backward through the team, scattering dogs everywhere until the lines finally tightened, halting Jonrowe's progress.

"Sorry," she said, noticing the predicament at last.

Freeing my hook, Dee Dee casually tossed it back.

I was left standing knee-deep in a spaghetti pile of tangled lines. Seventeen dogs were balled up against my reversed sled. More than a few were growling.

Tying a midsection of my gang line to a tree, I began methodically sorting out the dogs.

Bill Cotter, a bona fide contender in this year's race, rolled up behind my roadblock.

"What's the problem?"

"Sorry, I got a big tangle here."

"Well, we're going to have a big pileup in a minute," he said.

"Blame it on Dee Dee Jonrowe!" I shouted, feeling like an abused hit-and-run victim.

Cotter's fears were realized as Roger Roberts, the cocky Loafer from Ophir, barreled into him from behind. Curses flew through the woods as Roberts tried to pass Cotter, creating another tangle.

"Sorry Bill," I said as Cotter finally passed me after a 10-minute delay.

The Loafer cursed as he followed Cotter on by. Couldn't blame him. I was a lousy rookie. He was a three-time veteran with hopes of winning real money. Then he turned and kicked Rainy as he passed her. He deliberately kicked my lead dog!

"You son of a bitch!"

He was lucky Cyndi's .357 was stowed in the sled. In my state of mind, I might have shot him.

Young Daphne couldn't handle the freedom of traveling in a long Iditarod string. Each dip or bump caused a break in the tension of the gang line, the center cable that connected the pairs of dogs from the leaders back to the sled. Daphne kept taking advantage of the slack in the gang line to leap to her partner's side to catch a paw in one of the lines. An experienced sled dog might hop for a few steps, but usually cleared such easy tangles with a swift kick. Not Daphne. The little black-haired dog merely looked back at me, stumbling forward as she begged for another rescue.

On, perhaps, Daphne's hundredth tangle in the first 15 miles out of Knik, Gnat crumbled. He lay whimpering in the snow, squealing horribly as I tried to raise him to his feet. When I backed off, he just stared at me in abject surrender. Why did I ever agree to bring this quitter?

But Gnat had smacked that tree. Something could be seriously wrong. Unhitching him from the team, I loaded Gnat in the sled bag. Seventy miles from Skwentna and over a 1,000 miles shy of Nome—I had my first passenger.

The sun was setting on the first day of Iditarod XIX. I heard a dog team behind me, closing fast. The musher was wearing a bright red parka. As the lead dogs nipped at my heels, I recognized the driver. It was the Butch.

"You want to pass?"

"Not here."

By waiting for the point where the trail branched into several interweaving paths, she eliminated the risk of contact with a rookie's potentially ill-mannered team. Butcher urged her dogs ahead, leaving me to admire her form. Hell, it was thrilling. We shared the trail with the Iditarod's defending champion, if only for an instant.

Coal black darkness filled the thick forest. Cricket and Daphne had taken advantage of my ineptitude to suddenly backtrack, twist, and turn, knotting the team in what my headlamp revealed was another unbelievable tangle. I was shifting bodies to sort out the mess when Gunnar Johnson drove his dogs past us, then abruptly stopped.

"Do you think you could get it?" shouted Gunnar, shining his headlamp at a spot roughly 20 feet behind me. His snow hook, completely unattached, rested in the center of the trail.

It was a tense moment. The hook lay in the direction no musher wants to walk: backward from the sled, where even a lunge can't prevent the team from escaping.

"I'll stop your team if they get loose," he said, pleading.

I gently let go of my sled and tiptoed back. The dogs remained quiet as I picked up the hook and carried it to him.

"You owe me one."

Mike Madden caught me at the bottom of a hill, where I was providing Daphne with yet another assist.

"Hey, Madman, I led the race for twenty-five minutes."

"So what are you still doing here?" Madden had made up some two and a half hours already. "Let's get out of here O'D. Let's go to Skwentna."

Though my dogs exuberantly chased his, Madden's headlamp floated steadily away. Fair enough, I thought. I'll catch you in Skwentna.

The strains of the last few weeks were catching up. I caught myself dozing before the team even reached Flat Horn Lake, a mere 35 miles from Knik. A crackling bonfire cast dancing shadows on the bordering bank. A half-dozen teams were camping, including one of the Russians and Don and Catherine Mormile.

Pulling my team off the trail, I stomped the hook into the crusty snow.

I threw the dogs frozen chunks of liver and beef. Leaving them contentedly chewing, I walked over to the bonfire, hoping to beg a soda. Cyndi had filled my thermos with Tang mixed so strong it was more suitable for peeling paint than drinking.

I had a nice conversation with a young couple curled up near the fire, but they didn't have anything to drink. Chewing snow, I returned to my camp. The team was resting peacefully. I stretched out on top of my sled bag. The dogs can use this, I told myself.

Dawn was not quite breaking. My team trotted past the quiet remains of Susitna Station, bringing the Big Su River into view. Little more than a month had passed since I had last made this crossing to retrieve Beast and Gnat after the Klondike 200. To the southwest, Sleeping Woman reclined across the horizon, luxuriant and majestic as always. The river itself was barely recognizable. New folds in the snow-covered ice gave the landscape the appearance of a huge rumpled comforter. Crossing the river the trail rose and fell as much as ten feet between each wrinkle. The team and I crossed the river like tiny ants.

Entering the Yentna River, I came upon a cluster of tents. Sagging banners proclaimed a rest stop sponsored by a long-distance telephone company. The fire was smoldering. I wasn't planning to stop, but then I spotted a cardboard box with a fruit-juice logo. Thank God! I was desperate for something to quench my thirst.

Rummaging through the supplies left on an outdoor table, I found plenty of juice packets. Each one frozen solid.

One of the hosts stumbled out of his tent. While I babbled about the Death Tang, he found me a couple of semi-thawed juice cans. I chugged them. Stuffing a few juice containers in my pockets, I prepared to depart.

The guy stopped me. "For some reason, teams leaving our camp are having problems with that tree," he said, pointing to the left, toward a low-hanging branch leaning over the river.

"Sure, sure," I said, wondering why anyone would stray so far from the marked trail.

When I pulled the hook the dogs bolted left and dashed under that low branch. The route wasn't the one flagged by trailbreakers; it was the path countless dogs had already picked. And any dog that came later was bound to check it out. Trailing other dog teams in a crowded race field, most leaders are so reliable about following the common path that it's easy for a musher to slip into autopilot. This time I was almost knocked flat.

It was bright, incredibly bright on the river, as it can only be with snow reflecting the sun from its white surface. Hundreds of weaving paths stretched before us, attesting to the heavy traffic accompanying the race. People scooted by on snowmachines. Small planes flocked overhead like migrating birds. Many of the planes looped past two and three times, often tipping their wings in salutation. Some buzzed the team, passing so low that Screech, Cricket, and the other shy dogs dropped their ears.

I saw a team camped in the middle of the river. As I approached, the musher waved his arms for me to stop.

"I'm really in trouble here," Joe Carpenter said. "Bad, bad trouble."

I looked around. A beautiful day was taking shape. There weren't any holes in the ice. His dogs looked peaceful. He was outfitted in a fine blue Northern Outfitters parka. So what's the trouble?

"The team quit on me," Carpenter said. "The dogs won't go. Won't go at all."

I suggested that he rest them, maybe in the shade by the bank.

"No, no," Carpenter said. He explained that he had no food, no supplies and HAD TO GET TO SKWENTNA without delay.

The Coach had warned me to stay clear of mushers who were losing it. Carpenter, wide-eyed and panicked on this peaceful morning, fit the description. Well, I was going his direction. Wouldn't hurt to try.

"I'll pull in front," I said. "See if you can get your dogs to chase mine."

The jump start worked. Carpenter's team chased us. But, alas, his swing dogs began overtaking his leaders.

"Ride your brake," I shouted. He needed to keep his team lined out—moving slower, perhaps, but moving.

Instead Joe screamed holy murder. His leaders faltered under the verbal abuse. I left him there on the frozen river, yelling at his demoralized dogs.

Dozens of resting dogs dotted the snow fronting Yentna Station's big log cabin. The skies were sunny, and the temperature was pushing the 40s. And there was John Suter slipping coats on the dogs responsible for his notoriety as the one and only Poodle Man. Most Iditarod veterans were embarrassed by the presence of Suter and his poodles, whose fur was so ill suited to Arctic conditions that they stuck to the ice when they slept.

As a rookie, Suter had stunned Mowry and five other Iditarod mushers when he passed them in a storm on the final day of the race. The team's complement of Alaska huskies made that possible, but those dogs got little credit in the publicity surrounding the three poodles who had gone the distance, or the four who made it a year later. Poodles were Suter's ticket to network TV appearances and the pages of *Sports Illustrated*. As

John Suter liked to brag: "There's five billion people on the planet, and only one of them mushes poodles."

Mowry dedicated his second Iditarod to beating the Poodle Man, which he did. I wasn't as competitive as the Coach, but I didn't intend to lose to Suter.

Ken Chase saw me throwing my dogs chunks of whitefish. He asked if I had any to spare. The Athabaskan from Anvik was one of the mushers who had defined Iditarod in the early days. He was renowned for racing with a light sled, trusting good dogs and a lifetime of experience to overcome any lack of supplies.

Mushing toward Unalakleet several years before, rookie Mark Merrill had been flagged down by a trapper traveling by snowmachine. "Man, you're crazy," the fellow said. "A bad storm's coming this way."

Merrill, a proud woodsman from Willow, spent several hours building himself a survival shelter.

"What are you doing?" Chase asked, mushing up from behind. He was amazed that someone would stop with a storm moving in.

Merrill told him about the snowmachiner's warning.

"Trappers! They aren't dog mushers," the Indian snapped. "What do they know!" He advised the rookie to quit wasting time and get moving to Nome.

Merrill hadn't ever heard of Ken Chase, and he wasn't impressed by the stranger's ragged outfit. He stayed put in his nifty shelter. Within 48 hours, Chase was mushing into Nome, beating Babe Anderson, an old rival from McGrath, by 10 minutes. The failure to heed the old veteran's advice caused Merrill to spend 2 days pinned down on Topkok Hill, battered by wind so fierce it blew his dogs backward.

"I didn't know who Ken Chase was," Merrill sheepishly told me. But Merrill had come from behind to preserve his honor by beating the damn Poodle Man.

Chase's eleventh Iditarod wasn't going well. His dogs were

bummed after cutting their feet on the icy trail out of Knik. A few whitefish might perk them up, he said. Unfortunately, I was only carrying snacks. By the time Chase asked, my one small bag of whitefish was gone.

The roadhouse radio was crackling with discussions about Carpenter, the screaming idiot "in trouble" down on the river. The musher's wife and handler were desperate for information. Apparently this was Joe's second flameout. Five years earlier, Carpenter had scratched in Skwentna. He had better dogs this time, "a great team," his handler said. What was going wrong? The musher's friends had access to a plane. They wanted to fly out and DO SOMETHING. The handler asked Dan Grabryszak to pass a message to Carpenter that there would be a meal waiting for the dogs in Skwentna.

Dan assured the callers that Carpenter was in no immediate danger. He also gently reminded them that Iditarod has rules limiting outside assistance.

Barry Lee sacked out in the frozen marsh. Back on the trail by 5:30 A.M., he quickly caught and passed Gary Moore. Two hours later, Lee camped a second time near the Yentna, building a fire and serving the dogs a hot meal. It was part of Barry's schedule for working his dogs into shape.

He was napping on the sled when Moore found him.

"Everything all right, Barry?"

Lee smiled and waved Moore by, appreciative of his concern.

He'd hardly closed his eyes before two snowmachiners drove up. It was Craig Medred, a reporter from the *Anchorage Daily News,* and photographer Jim Lavrakas, who snapped a few pictures of the "sleeping musher."

A few minutes later, Lee was disturbed yet again. A bicyclist no less! The guy was training for the Iditabike, an upcoming 200-mile mountain-bike race.

"There's a guy a mile or two up the trail who can't get his dogs to go," the bicyclist told Lee. "Said he's been stuck there for nine hours."

Nap time was over. Lee got his team rolling to see if he could help. He found Moore rigging a tow line for Carpenter's team.

"You know, Gary," said Lee, as he helped Moore fashion a connector that wouldn't drag the trailing leaders by the neck, "he'll be out of the race."

"I know, but he doesn't see any way around it."

Carpenter stood on his sled, out of earshot, awaiting Moore's cue. With the tow line in place, Moore's dogs ambled forward. The Good Samaritan supported the line to Carpenter's leaders in one hand.

The incident was observed by the reporter, the photographer, as well as Carpenter's wife and handler, who had just landed on the river in a ski plane. Lavrakas pulled out his camera and documented the rescue.

"Too bad that Joe has to scratch," Lee remarked to the musher's wife as they watched the two teams depart.

"Why would he have to scratch?" she asked.

"He can't accept help like that," Lee explained. "It's explicit in the rules."

Rule 26 stated that teams could only be tied together in an "emergency situation," which had to be declared at the next checkpoint. Dogs quitting on a mild, sunny day was not likely to constitute an emergency in the eyes of the race marshal.

"I don't think he knows that," Carpenter's wife said.

"I'll tell him," said Lee, whose dogs were anxious to chase anyhow.

The tandem pair were barely creeping along. Moore was trying to cut Carpenter loose. But every time he relaxed the rope, Carpenter's trailing leaders faltered. Lee quickly overtook them.

"Joe, you know you're going to be disqualified," Lee shouted.

Carpenter protested that his situation certainly amounted to an emergency. "I don't have any food. I don't have any fuel," he cried.

"OK," Lee said, shrugging. A reformed alcoholic well versed in self-help litany, Barry recognized denial when he heard it. He'd tried. If Carpenter was too freaked out to accept the inevitable, so be it.

The Coach hadn't wanted me to even stop at Yentna Station, let alone stay six hours. I thought I was being prudent. In covering sled-dog races, I had seen a lot of people blow out their dogs the first day. I was still there when Carpenter finally made it to Yentna—showing no signs of grasping his predicament. He was talking about schedules. Talking about those supplies waiting in Skwentna. Lee and I shared uneasy feelings listening to Joe rant. It was like watching a driver babbling about scratches on a totaled car.

I headed upstairs for a nap as Carpenter and Medred began arguing. The musher couldn't understand what was so newsworthy about his little delay. Why would Medred want to write about this? Carpenter's Iditarod was history, and he just didn't see it. Lavrakas's photo of the illegal tow was destined for page 1 of Alaska's biggest newspaper. Medred was gathering details for the next day's lead story: the first disqualification of this year's race.

Had anyone asked, I would have said I was traveling somewhere in the middle of the 74-team field. Like Carpenter, I was deluding myself. Lee better understood our plight. He knew there was no one left behind us.

Joe Garnie led the first wave into Skwentna. The hard-driving Eskimo from Teller trotted into the floodlights set up on the river at 3:14 A.M. Sunday, March 3. Being first counted for more than bragging rights. Garnie had won the "Dodge Dash," a special Iditarod promotion, and the prize was a $15,000 Dakota pickup. With the keys to his new truck in hand, Joe vowed to set fire to his old truck.

Within 2 hours, 15 teams were camped on the river below postmaster Joe Delia's cabin in Skwentna. This was the Iditarod's elite. They fed their dogs and traded stories about the first day of the race, all the while eyeing each other warily, waiting to renew the chase.

The shiny new truck was nice, but Garnie's sights were set on the arch waiting 1,050 miles north. By half past noon, his sled was packed near the checkpoint tents at Finger Lake, 45 miles farther up the trail. Barve was again second, followed by Adkins, Swenson, Tim Osmar, and Jonrowe.

Seventeen teams reached Finger Lake before Butcher. Everyone was camping when Susan arrived at 6:01 P.M. The Butch had other ideas. She dallied just 15 minutes before ordering her 18-dog team onward toward Rohn. Iditarod's defending champion was leading for the first time in the race.

As the front-runners maneuvered for position, Mowry burned up phone lines from his hotel in Dawson City, Yukon Territory. According to race headquarters, I had checked into Knik at 6:02 P.M. Saturday and I'd never left. Mowry knew that was probably misinformation. But what if I'd lost a dog? What if the team was sick? What if . . . It was maddening.

The Coach's strategy called for me to reach Skwentna by noon on Sunday. Forty-nine mushers managed to do that; I wasn't among them. Mowry called every few hours. New teams kept showing up on the river below Delia's cabin. More than 60 teams had registered at Skwentna by 7 P.M. on Sunday. The checker's log also showed one scratch: Englishman Roy Monk.

His dogs' feet were too sore to continue. Team number 2, meanwhile, remained listed "in Knik."

The Poodle Man passed Daily on the river, roughly ten miles from Skwentna.

"Give the devil his due," Daily grumbled to himself, watching Suter pass. God, those poodles are clipping right along, looking good.

Tom couldn't say the same about his own team. Both of his high-priced leaders were a bust. The seed of suspicion planted during the Klondike had blossomed into an ugly reality. These dogs needed better conditioning. He could only blame himself for that. Relocating to Alaska had burned up a lot of time, but it didn't excuse the training deficiency. And Daily was haunted by the memory of his sponsors' unconcealed disappointment. There goes the free ride.

Reality, as so often happens, had arrived with a vicious bite. Reaching Skwentna a full hour behind the damn Poodle Man, the musher gloomily declared his 24-hour layover. The dogs needed a breather.

Since the day he signed up, Daily, an old hippie, had been reveling in the prospects of celebrating his thirty-ninth birthday mushing the Iditarod Trail. That day had arrived, and he wondered what he'd done to deserve such karma.

The river was crisscrossed with trails. Each intersecting alternative appeared better to Chad, who kept dodging between them. The general direction was right, so I let Golden Dog pick his own way. He performed reasonably well until we caught up with the *Anchorage Daily News* snowmachines late Sunday afternoon. Jim Lavrakas and Craig Medred had parked a few yards off the trail. Chad made a beeline for them. He flopped at the

journalists' feet, bringing the team to a dead halt. I had to get off
the sled and drag him back on course. From there, his confidence
shrank with each step. Before long, I banished Chad to wheel,
inserting Harley in single lead.

Intertwining trails didn't faze the monster. Given a choice
between trails, Harley never agonized. He barreled forward,
flopping his ears up and down with each step.

Relieved of his pressure position, Chad pulled like a demon.
Muscles rippled in his shoulders. His head bent downward; this
time from joyous effort, not discouragement. Watching the
transformation, I shook my head. What a basket case.

Nearing Skwentna, I put the White Rat up front with
Harley for better control. The combination worked beautifully. The wafting scent of woodstoves was as good as a dinner
bell to an old sled dog like the Rat. She blazed ahead, displaying energy she normally concealed. In training, the Rat always
ran fast enough to keep pace, but not so hard that she might
have to work. In that respect, the Rat was the least honest
dog in the kennel, and her calculated deceit infuriated the
Coach.

When you prodded her, the white dog's tug line would
tighten, but the effort only lasted until you stopped watching
her. Like most leaders, she had an uncanny memory for trails.
But given any chance, she'd strike out for home. It didn't matter
whether the team had just left the lot. Cutting corners was her
goal in life. I didn't care. The dog might be lazy, but she knew
commands. And I enjoyed her games at mealtime.

Every day, without fail, she would stash her pan in the deep-
est possible corner of her house, which happened to be the
longest house in our lot. Our game grew more demanding with
the onset of blizzards in December. I had to lie on my belly to
reach the pan through her tunnellike entrance. The Rat ap-
plauded my cooperation with frisky hops. Then she'd squat on
her haunches, lifting both paws in a begging motion.

"The Rat, the Rat," I'd sing, filling her pan. "Queen of All Dogs."

The Coach commented on an unintended consequence of my affection. "Rat is getting fat, O'Donoghue. Quit giving her seconds!"

I loved the conniving White Rat, and she paid me back tonight, guiding Harley toward Skwentna's sagging checkpoint banner. It was a few minutes before midnight. Made it by 12, only it was the wrong 12.

The postmaster appeared holding his clipboard. More than 20 hours had passed since Delia had first checked Garnie's sled for required gear. He was groggy.

"How many teams are in, Joe?"

Delia shrugged. "Lost track," he mumbled, handing me the clipboard for my signature. "C'mon up to the cabin when you get settled."

Where does the time go? First I bedded the dogs in straw. Then I picked up my four-gallon pot and searched for water. Other mushers directed me to a hole chopped in the thick river ice. You had to reach way down to scoop the water out with a coffee can. Filling the pot took a little longer than I expected. That set the tone, I guess. Everything took longer than I expected. Four sacks of supplies were waiting for me. Fetching those 50- to 70-pound sacks required several trips. That took more time.

Sack number 1 contained my most pressing needs at Skwentna, and every other checkpoint: whitefish for the dogs; new batteries; dry gloves; and several toilet-paper rolls for the stove. I threw each dog a chunk of whitefish—starting with Harley, of course.

Iditarod provisioned each checkpoint with dozens of cases of bottled Blazo alcohol fuel, or a similarly flammable equivalent. I collected my share of fuel bottles and carried them back to the team. Placing a roll of toilet paper in the cooker's bottom pan, I dowsed it with fuel. A flick of a Bic lighter sent blue flame jetting from the toilet paper, which served as the wick for the fuel pooled in the pan. Next, I inserted the pot, suspended several inches above the roaring torch.

Boiling four gallons of frigid water took a good half hour. While waiting, I chopped meat and mixed it with dry food in two 16-gallon coolers. After pouring in the hot water, I resealed the coolers and let the meaty stew soak.

After feeding the dogs, I checked their feet and dabbed ointment on any that looked sore. Rainy's feet were unblemished, but I wrapped her sensitive wrist in a special rubberized wrap to keep the joint warm and loose. Foot care alone probably consumed 45 minutes to an hour, a routine that would be repeated at almost every stop on the trail to Nome.

I was tired but pleased as I climbed the hill to Delia's cabin. Hadn't been that many years since I had climbed this same hill to interview others. This time this adventure was mine. Inside the warm cabin, I grabbed a bowl of chili and sat down with Delia and Iditarod photographers Jim Brown and Jeff Schultz.

Brown, a graying Iditarod mainstay, greeted me with a twinkle in his eye. "I'm tired of chasing the crybabies in front," he declared. "This year I'm going to follow the teams in the rear. That's where the good stories are."

The bodies of sleeping mushers and race officials were scattered across the cabin's floor. The man responsible for all of this was snoozing in a chair: Joe Redington—a slightly shrunken 73-year-old grandfather, with rumpled clothes and a gray day-old beard.

I remembered interviewing Redington in 1988, down on the river below this cabin. People had been saying that he ought to give it up. That the race was too tough for a man of his age. For three years running, Redington hadn't been able to prove them wrong. Twice in a row he had scratched with injuries. The year before Old Joe had finished, but thirty-third place was quite a comedown for a three-time fifth-place finisher, and the man said to own the best racing dogs in the world.

Redington looked terrible that day. He was leaning on his sled, sipping hot Tang with a sour expression. It wasn't the juice—he swore by that sugary powder. It was his head. " 'Fraid I'm coming down with a bad case of the flu," rasped Old Joe, who didn't believe in fooling with aspirin and those other pills.

The front-runners, indeed, most of the field, had cleared out of Skwentna hours earlier, postponing their required 24-hour layovers for another 100 or 200 miles, and eliminating the risk of a storm sealing off Rainy Pass. Redington was left nearly alone on the Skwentna River with Herbie Nayokpuk, another aging legend. Both men were taking their extended break here, out of necessity: Old Joe, hoping to recover from the virus; Herbie, praying that his coastal dogs would bounce back after wilting in the first day's heat.

I spent a long time talking to Redington. I figured the chances were good that he wouldn't make it much farther up the trail, and I had a lot to learn about the Last Great Race and its founder.

Tonight I was ready to discard another illusion. Getting all of my dogs to Nome was a fantasy I couldn't afford. Not if I wanted to make it more than a mile between tangles. I filled out the paperwork required for dropping Gnat and Daphne from the team.

Written explanations were required for each dropped dog. Mushers were supposed to note any medical problems or special instructions about handling, such as "This dog bites strangers." I provided a detailed account of Gnat's mishap with the tree in Anchorage, the comments from vets, and his whimpering behavior after Knik.

My explanation for dropping Daphne was not so sympathetic. "Queen of tangles, never pulls, chews harnesses by the box."

Reading the form, the Skwentna veterinarian chuckled. "So why did you bring her?"

"Been asking myself that question for a hundred miles."

During my 12-hour stay in Skwentna, I napped just two hours. Sunrise found me on the river, changing my runner plastic and repacking. Four hours later I was busying myself with the sled. My dogs were getting anxious. Raven and Spook were barking. Digger was leaping in place. I had my back to the sled when the team jerked the hook free and bolted. The team dragged my empty sled about a hundred yards before Redington and two other guys caught the dogs.

"I don't think they need more rest," Old Joe said.

Barry Lee had been warned: Expect a long 45 miles from Skwentna to Finger Lake. "It doesn't look like it, but it's all uphill," Bobby told him. "You're rising toward Rainy Pass."

With his brother's comments in mind, Barry tried to ignore his team's plodding pace, but disappointment was gnawing at him. Though his dogs acted happy, the team was just crawling.

I caught Lee right after he finished changing booties. Aware that my dogs were faster, he ordered his team over to a parallel snowmachine path, clearing the way for me to pass.

Behind me, Lee's dogs broke through the crusty side trail. While he struggled to pull the team back to the packed snow, many of his dogs took advantage of the distraction to kick or pull off the booties that had just been placed on their feet with painstaking care. Politeness had just cost Barry another 20 minutes of work.

Early Monday afternoon Joe Redington, Sr. completed his required 24-hour layover in Skwentna. I had my dogs off to the side and was tossing out snacks when the old racer barreled past.

"Go get 'em, Joe!"

He flashed a familiar weathered smile.

Sparks shot upward from a roaring log. Heat had melted a circular wall, six feet high, in a surrounding snow drift. Dewey Halverson, his face lit by flames reflecting off the glassy walls, had the other Finger Lake volunteers in hysterics with his impressions of other mushers.

The checkpoint consisted of a cluster of tents in a clearing between tall spruce trees. Accommodations for mushers were sparse. We had a floorless tent, heated by a small sheet-metal stove. Spruce boughs served as bedding.

After tending my dogs, I headed for the tent carrying a fat ice wad of used booties. Most were castoffs from other teams, which I'd snagged en route. My own booty situation was approaching a crisis. The icy trail had already shredded several hundred, wiping out my reserves. Examining my frozen assortment in the mushers' tent, I picked out several dozen booties in good shape and burned the rest.

Alan Garth, Chase, and I talked by the stove, which hissed with drying gloves and booties. Mark Williams was sleeping soundly nearby.

Chase mentioned that he had never, in all his Iditarods, drawn a decent starting position.

"Yeah," I said, "I got lucky, but I didn't know what to do with it."

Herrman was off in the woods by himself. He couldn't bear for others to witness his distress. First it had been the heat. Now his dogs were sick. Only 11 dogs left, and 9, NINE, had bloody diarrhea. It looked to Sepp like they had swollen tonsils as well. The German had a theory about the cause. Living at his remote cabin in the Brooks Range, his dogs hadn't been exposed to the viruses common in populated areas. They had never had a chance to build immunity to the diseases carried by the other teams. Up north, the trapper depended on no one but himself. He didn't need or want any help now. Those nosy Iditarod officials could just mind their own business.

For 36 hours Sepp kept the fire going under his cook pot as he camped near Finger Lake. Using snow melted by the gallon, the trapper nursed and hand-fed his poor sick puppies.

Despair was overwhelming Barry Lee. Twelve hours had passed since he had set out from Skwentna on the 45-mile run to Finger Lake. He wasn't absolutely sure, but he doubted anyone was behind him. Every team in this race was faster, and nobody was wasting as much time. What was I thinking of taking so many naps? he asked himself. Yet he felt tired even now. Bone weary. Oh, what was he going to do? This wasn't just wilderness; it was an emotional wasteland. Tears ran down the musher's cheeks.

Suddenly Lee sensed a light over his shoulder. Stopping his team, he slowly turned, expecting to see the headlamp from an approaching musher. The light came from no earthly source. A corona reached across the heavens. Shimmering bands formed an arching circle in the sky, reminding the musher of a great circus tent. The lights were an intense, dynamic presence. And so beautiful. Barry divined a message in the display: God had staged this Northern Lights show to let him know everything was going to be OK.

Anchoring his team with two snow hooks, Lee lay on his back in the snow, reveling in the glorious celestial fire. Tears again streamed down his face. This time, tears of joy. "Thank you, God," whispered Barry Lee, staring up at the wondrous colors.

He was still rejoicing when a real headlamp appeared from behind. It was John Ace, a thick-bearded, barrel-chested musher from Sutton making his sixth run to Nome.

"How far in?" Lee asked.

"Oh, not too far," said Ace. "Two miles, maybe three."

Trailing the other musher through a thick stand of tall spruce, Lee sensed a change within himself. Whatever else happened, however grim the situation might get, he would never again feel so low. He had company on this, on any trail. His faith was confirmed. How could it be otherwise? At the moment of Barry Lee's greatest need, a message had come.

CHAPTER **5**

Storm on the Mountain

Leaving the campsite at Finger Lake, I mushed into an inky void. The Northern Lights had faded, and clouds must have rolled in, because there wasn't a single star shining. Despite new batteries, my headlamp merely poked at the darkness with its narrow, ineffectual beam. Maybe my eyes were shot from staring at the bonfire, but the night was blacker than black. So it was that I had a blind man's grip on the sled—when my dogs plunged over the edge of an invisible chasm.

Worst hill I'd ever run with a dog team. Couldn't see the bottom. Fresh from their rest, the dogs sprinted down the slope, while I teetered on one slippery runner, stabbing for the brake with my free foot. As unexpectedly as it began, the blind fall ended. The void leveled out, and I continued onward, feeling my terror give way to anger. Someone at the damn checkpoint could have mentioned the killer hill less than a mile ahead. Guess they didn't want to spoil my fun.

The torture of the unexpected was becoming a familiar theme. Entering the race, I thought my reporting background would more than compensate for my mushing inexperience. I could list Iditarod's famous hazards: Rainy Pass, the descent into Dalzell Gorge, and the brutal Farewell Burn. I had a general idea of the geography from flying the route, something few other rookies could claim. But aerial observations made at 100 miles an hour were meaningless here on the ground. And writing secondhand stories was no substitute for real life.

Uncertainties were in full swing early Tuesday morning, as I approached the infamous canyon at Happy River Valley.

"Happy River's got less than half the usual snow," race manager Jack Niggemyer had warned us at the prerace musher's meeting. "The steps are in pretty good shape, but they're narrower than usual. Just be cautious. It's not a death ride, but it won't be as easy as last year."

Barry Lee had heard that he should unfasten the tug lines before attempting the steps, so the dogs couldn't pull quite as hard on the downhill chutes. He had shared the tip while we camped at Finger Lake. It sounded like a good idea, but I had a feeling—mushing through tonight's void—that I wouldn't know I was close to Happy River until the team dragged me over the edge. So I ran all night with the tugs disconnected and a tight grip of my handlebar, expecting to whip into another dark hole any second.

Light was breaking through the trees when I saw a handmade sign nailed to a tree. "SLOW!" it proclaimed, over a sketch of a dog team running down a 75-degree slope. "Hill next four steps."

If only I'd known the canyon was marked with a traffic hazard sign.

Terhune took the plummet the afternoon before my own descent. The three steep drops, cut sideways into the canyon, were tricky, but he managed to steady himself, sliding on one heel, while holding his sled tilted toward the wall, as veterans had warned him to do. Indeed, Terhune wasn't finding the canyon all that scary, and he relaxed as the team leveled out on what he assumed was the canyon floor. But this year Iditarod's trailbreakers had tried to ease the descent into Happy River Valley with not three, but four sideways steps down the wall. The final switchback took the musher by complete surprise.

Terhune hung on as his sled tumbled down the side of the canyon, dragging the half-dozen dogs in the rear of his team. The sled rolled six times before slamming to a stop against small trees and bushes. Several dogs were pinned underneath. Terhune was scared to look.

A television crew from ABC's *Wide World of Sports* was strategically positioned at the bottom of the canyon. The cameraman recorded Terhune's mishap, then rushed over to get a close-up of the musher's reaction.

Jon was sprawled on his back when the cameraman leaned over him.

"How would you like that thing shoved up your ass," cried the infuriated former paratrooper as he jumped to his feet.

The cameraman hastily retreated. Footage of the spill showed up in the network's Iditarod broadcast, minus Terhune's commentary.

The dogs were unscathed. Their master was the one hobbling out of the canyon. Terhune had twisted his back. His fingers began tingling and soon became numb. Before long, the gentlest of bumps sent pain shooting through his spine.

Climbing a steep, bare riverbank on the far side of the canyon, Terhune's sled became stuck. The crippled musher lacked the strength to free it. He wasted 30 minutes extending his gang line, hoping to improve the leverage of the dogs. But the sled remained wedged. He was struggling with the problem when the Hot Dog Man arrived on the scene. Munoz helped Terhune muscle the sled up the hill, and the pair mushed together into the Rainy Pass checkpoint late Monday afternoon.

Spreading straw for the dogs, Terhune lay down in his

sleeping bag next to his leaders. He placed his windup clock under his ear, with the alarm set for three hours. He figured the clock was broken when he awakened eight hours later, but there was nothing wrong. Bells had sounded until the spring ran down; Terhune had just never heard them.

Dozens of teams had wiped out on the steps before I ventured into Happy River Valley. Their mishaps cut grooves in the snow, turning the short, steep drops into suicide chutes. My sled launched into the canyon on three of the four descents. Twice I stayed aboard and, leaning toward the wall, managed to keep my sled from rolling as it skidded downward, coming to rest against bushes and trees rooted on the side of the canyon. A few dogs were dragged over the edge with me, but most dug in, holding firm as they waited for new orders from the boss.

"All right! All right. Go ahead!" My sled weighed at least 300 pounds. The total load had to be closer to 500 pounds with me added. Displaying the formidable power of 15 dogs, the team easily hauled sled and driver back on track.

I thought my sled-handling was improving when I made it down the third step unscathed. Right. My sled went completely airborne on the fourth, and I let go. For the first time ever, I consciously let go of a dog team. The sled landed in a bushy tree about 15 feet down the canyon wall. The dogs in the front of the team crouched low, hugging the slope. Down below, Cyrus looked around frantically, acting more bewildered than hurt. His partner in wheel, Skidders, was already on his feet, calmly shaking himself off. Feeling guilty, I clambered down to retrieve my sled.

"I wouldn't do the dogs any good with a broken leg," I told myself, but the words sounded false.

"Denali" is an Athabaskan word meaning "great one," or "high one." Local Indians gave the peak towering over the Interior that honored title long before 1896, when prospector William Dickey stuck the name McKinley on North America's tallest mountain. The traditional name is preferred by most Alaskans over Dickey's tribute to an Ohio politician who never set foot in Alaska. Indeed, just about every musher has a big dog named Denali, and I was no different.

Wide-shouldered with peaked ears, weighing about 45 pounds, my Denali was muscled like a canine bodybuilder. The young male, a month shy of three years old, should have been coming into his prime on the Iditarod Trail. He and his litter-mate, Screech, shared a striking physical resemblance. But that was all they had in common. Whereas she was a hard-working sweetheart, he was surly and constantly growled at the other males. And he wasn't keen on putting those rippling muscles to work. His tug line drooped whenever I looked away.

Maybe the others were fed up with Denali's laziness. Mushers talk about veteran dogs nipping young slackers in the ass. Perhaps the young male made a move for dominance within the team and was rebuffed. I heard a quick growl, then the other dogs turned on Denali as a group, fangs bared, and began tearing into him from every side. I've seen big males square off, but the curl in tiny Cricket's lips as she sunk her teeth into Denali's left haunch was more menacing. There was no mistaking her intent, or that of the other assailants. It was a pack judgment.

I jumped into the fray as Harley circled back to get in on the action. Throwing myself over Denali as a shield, I elbowed and kicked his attackers away. Then I unclipped the victim from the team and tied him behind the sled.

Blood oozed from bites on his nose and ears, but Denali didn't appear seriously harmed. I was debating what to do with him when I saw Raven nervously watching from the woods nearby. The sight gave me a chill. Lose a dog and I'd be out of the race. At home, I wouldn't have worried, since our escapees never strayed far. But I couldn't take anything for granted with a spooked dog in strange surroundings.

"Here Raven. C'mon little princess," I said, gently coaxing her. The tone of my voice was all she needed. She dashed over with her tail between her legs, trembling, shaken by the violence.

"That's OK Raven," I said, stroking my delicate black beauty. "Everything's all right."

I placed Denali in wheel, where I could keep him under closer watch. If there were lingering animosities, they were soon forgotten. The dogs, including Denali, perked up their ears and leaped to their feet at the familiar rustling sound of the snack bag.

The trail to Rainy Pass rolled and snaked through a forest of thin alders. When they set trail earlier in the winter, Iditarod volunteers had trimmed these fast-growing trees. Unfortunately, the snow pack dropped during a warm spell that followed, subjecting dog teams to a gauntlet of jagged sticks and stumps projecting eight inches or more from ground level.

Plowing through mile after mile of the battering sticks, I kept wondering if we were on the right trail. But the markers were unmistakable. My sled was taking a beating. Sticks kept snagging the chains connecting a piece of snowmachine track between my runners, which I used as an extra brake. Sometimes the impediments stopped the team, throwing me against the handlebar—but only for an instant, until the stick, or whatever it was, gave way under pressure, launching my sled forward as if from a slingshot. On one sharp dip, I tasted utter disaster as a stump snagged my sled bow. Under pressure from the dogs, my sled bent in what seemed to be an impossibly tight arc. I braced myself, dreading the "crack" of runners snapping. Thankfully, the bow clamps burst first. My sled popped loose, sporting a busted nose, but sliding.

I almost never drink hard liquor, but I had left Knik packing two bottles of Jack Daniel's. It was Jack Studer's idea. The larger quart-sized bottle of whiskey was strictly for trading purposes. Out in the villages, a bottle can buy you a freshly laid snow-machine trail, said Studer, who understood better than anyone the misery of plodding to Nome on snowshoes.

I was also carrying a pint of Jack for personal use. Studer advised me to take a quick belt as I approached each check-point. He said it would soothe my transition from the serenity of the trail to the madhouse atmosphere of checkpoints.

The seal on that pint of Jack remained unbroken through Eagle River, Wasilla, Knik, Skwentna, and Finger Lake. But I was ready for a sip as I neared Rainy Pass late Tuesday morning. The bottle felt light as I pulled it out. Hardly a drop remained inside. At first I was baffled, but then I noticed a tiny hole in the cap, where the booze had leaked out. A broken bottle I could understand—but what were the odds of this happening?

Groping inside the sled bag to see if there were any other surprises, I pulled out a handful of plastic splinters: the remains of my spare headlamp reflector. That was no biggie. Though headlamp bulbs burned out fairly often, I had never, over the entire course of training, cracked a headlamp reflector. Those things were as tough as steel.

Parking on a gentle snow-covered slope below Rainy Pass Lodge, I felt bruised and disoriented. Like a mugging victim, assaulted in a beautiful park. My hips and knees were sore from being dragged God knows how many times. Raising my right arm was extremely painful. It humbled me to think that Redington was mushing this trail in his seventies.

And what about Colonel Vaughan? He was already 70 years old in 1975, the first time he attempted Redington's Great Race. He didn't make it to Nome that year. Or the year after, when he took a wrong turn in the Alaska Range and spent four days lost before being rescued. Friends and race officials tried to discourage the colonel from attempting the Iditarod again. Vaughan didn't listen. He returned for the 1978 race, and that time he made it to Nome. Over the next 11 years, the colonel ran the Iditarod eight more times, notching his fourth official finish in the 1990 race at the ever-ready age of 84.

The first time I met him, Vaughan was stretched out on the ice at a checkpoint, crawling from dog to dog, inspecting each paw, rubbing in ointment and placing on booties. He used the belly-down approach to compensate for his bad knees. The colonel wasn't about to let a slight physical disability force him into retirement. Not Norman Vaughan, the only U.S. airman to earn battlefield honors by dog team, by retrieving a top secret instrument from a downed plane in Greenland during World War II. Sixty years after dropping out of Harvard to handle dogs on Admiral Robert Byrd's expedition to the South Pole, Vaughan was Alaska's ageless adventurer.

Contemplating my bruised thirty-five-year-old body, I knew the colonel was tougher than I'd ever be.

I was strongly inclined to take my 24-hour layover at Rainy Pass, a scenic horse ranch overlooking a lake high in the Alaska Range. But the lodge was closed to mushers this year, and the checker wasn't encouraging.

"This really isn't a good place to stay," he said. "There are no facilities. Not even a tent. Yesterday it snowed and rained on the mushers."

It was day 4 of the race. I'd slept a total of about six hours since leaving Anchorage, and I wasn't thinking clearly. I badly needed a nap. Climbing a mountain pass in this foggy state sounded crazy. Yet I couldn't rest. There was talk of a storm on its way. I didn't want to get caught on the wrong side of the range. Rainy Pass might stay blocked for days, and my race would be over right here.

I packed and repacked, agonizing over whether to move on. Medred came over to interview me. It was so bright out that I had to squint to bring the reporter into focus. Finding his questions difficult to follow, I answered with grunts.

Ace was camped nearby. The veteran said he was going to try to beat the storm over the pass. That sealed my decision. We agreed to rest our dogs a few hours, then pull out about 6 P.M.

Mushing the Iditarod Trail, it was tempting to think that the dogs and I had cut all ties to our lives back in town. But the mundane world hadn't forgotten me. A personal check for $145, written in payment for Dr. Leach's veterinary services, arrived Tuesday at National Bank of Alaska. Last-minute supplies and unexpected expenses, like the vet bill from Rat's fight with Daphne, had pushed the total cost of my participation in the Iditarod over $16,000. My personal account was already overdrawn by $3.56. All my bank accounts, including the special Iditarod account, were tapped out. The check written to Dr. Leach was returned unpaid. An overdraft notice was mailed to Deadline Dog Farm.

Ace came over to talk while I was getting ready to break camp.

"I don't want to scare you," he said, stroking his thick beard, "but take a little extra food, a little extra fuel, and prepare yourself in case we don't make it."

Ace spoke from experience. His first race he had weathered a long night in the pass, trapped mere yards from a shelter tent that had been rendered invisible by the storm.

I had 15 dogs, which meant that I had 60 paws to prepare. The situation was not helped when Rat and Cyrus pulled their booties off. Ace mushed out of the checkpoint. It took me an additional 45 minutes to get ready. Several veterinarians came over and helped guide my team out of the checkpoint. The dogs looked good, including Denali, who had been treated for his bites. I sensed that the vets were more concerned about my own haggard condition and blatant incompetence.

Despite the rumored storm, it was bright out, with hardly a cloud in the sky and a calm, warm 20 above zero. Trail markers led us to a steep hill, perhaps 150 feet high. Rainy and Harley tried to climb it, but slipped right back down. Bathed by the evening sun, the snow was too slick for their new booties.

Damned if I was going to strip off those booties. Not after the hassle of putting them on. I ran up front, grabbed my leaders by the neck line, and began pulling them up the slope, kicking steps in the soft snow with my bunny boots. The dogs seemed amused to see the boss working on the front end of the gang line. Together we crept up the slippery hill.

Looking virtually straight down at my 64-foot-long string of dogs, I wondered what the hell was going to happen if the sled tipped, or I lost my footing. But the sled remained upright, incredibly enough. One step at a time, the team and I neared the top.

Lavrakas spotted us climbing the hill. It reminded him of a scene from the gold-rush days: a miner making a superhuman effort as he hauled supplies toward an unknown camp. The incline was so steep, however, that the photographer rather doubted I was on the right trail.

The light was starting to go. Lavrakas roared to the bottom on his snowmachine. Alas, he was digging in his camera bag for the right lens when I crested the top of the hill.

I mushed toward the pass with growing dread. The landscape was barren, completely inhospitable. The surrounding mountains were jagged and cruel, casting an ominous air over the basin I was ascending. As dusk settled in, I caught Ace cross-ing a windswept plain. He was having trouble with his leaders and waved me ahead.

It grew darker and the wind picked up. Snow began falling. The trail was rising with no end in sight. I sensed that we'd lost our race with the storm, but there was no turning back.

Seeking a spiritual boost, I popped a tape in my Walkman. The band was Los Lobos. I enjoyed the tune until I actually lis-tened to the words: "There's a deep dark hole, and it leads to nowhere. . . ."

Lavrakas reappeared on his snowmachine, shadowing my team. Several times he speeded ahead and positioned himself to get pictures of my dogs bursting through the flowing snow. His flashes added a surreal dimension to my predicament.

I was warm enough, but the wind and snow were definitely getting worse. And I was mushing up into Rainy Pass, elevation 3,400, the highest point on the 1,150-mile Iditarod Trail. Red-ington once faced 100-below-zero conditions on this same stretch. I was thinking about that. And I was thinking about the warning from Ace.

When I got the chance, I flagged down Lavrakas and asked him if he knew how far it was to the survival shelter. He raced back to confer with Ace, then zoomed ahead, vanishing in the storm. About 30 minutes later, the photographer returned.

"I went quite a ways ahead and couldn't find the shelter," Jim said, looking grim.

I was reluctant to part from my speedy messenger in the storm. Lavrakas's face had taken on a guardian angel's glow. I think we both suspected I wasn't ready for this. But my dogs were straining to go. And the trail wasn't getting any better.

"I'm strapped to an engine with no reverse," I shouted over the snowmachine's throb. "Tell Ace I'm going ahead."

The shelter was supposed to be on the edge of a lake, near

the top of the pass. In the tunnel vision created by my headlamp, I was lucky to glimpse the dogs, much less the landscape. Visibility was so poor, we could be within ten feet of the shelter and I might not see it. New snow was already piled a foot deep, and it was coming down hard.

Rainy was in her element, acting strangely buoyant. She and Harley were leaping, leaping into the swirling soup, splashing through the flowing drifts. I was so tired I could hardly stand. The snowflakes streaking toward my goggles reminded me of the way stars appear when the starship *Enterprise* shifts into warp drive. Were we moving uphill or was it down? Did the trail really tilt sideways here? I felt so disoriented, I couldn't tell.

Rainy seemed to know where she was going.

"Have you been here before little Rainy? Is this where you got your name?"

Our records about the lesbian's racing history were inconclusive. Coming from Knik, Redington's Iditarod-crazed training grounds, it could be that she was drawing on memories of the Great Race. The sport's history is full of such stories. Emmitt Peters, an Athabaskan musher from Ruby, had a revealing experience in his first Iditarod. His leader, Nugget, kept stopping the team in odd places along the trail. The musher didn't know what to think when the lead dog ignored a village checkpoint and confidently steered the team to a stranger's house. Then a local woman mentioned that the dog had slept in that same spot before, the year Nugget guided Carl Huntington's team to victory. Peters realized that the leader's puzzling pauses were nothing but familiar rest stops. With Nugget's help, the rookie went on to win that Iditarod, a feat that earned Peters the nickname Yukon Fox.

Then again, Rainy might be sniffing out a mountain-goat path, leading us toward a cliff. There was no way to know.

This had to be Harley's first trip. Minto, the big dog's village, boasted champion sprint mushers, but no one that I knew of from the village had ever attempted this trail. Harley supplied the engine that night, but Rainy held the steering wheel. I wondered how far I dared trust the little lesbian.

I was glad when Ace finally caught up. With my team leading, we continued for about another hour, until the veteran, too, had doubts.

"We should have found that shelter by now," he said.

Bowing to the elements, we hastily made camp. The dogs immediately pawed cozy niches in the snow. I staggered up the gang line, plowing through waist-deep powder, and tossed each dog a chunk of beef and a six-inch piece of Kobuk sausage fat. Not much of a meal, but it was too windy to fire up the cooker, and the dogs needed something. Right now, navigation was the problem. There was no telling what this storm might bring. Or how long this forced shutdown might last.

I flipped my sled on its side, dumping the contents. I'd packed everything in stuff bags with just this sort of emergency in mind. Placing the sled upright, I stripped off my snow-machine suit, shook it off, and stretched it across the bottom of the toboggan for insulation. Next, I unpacked my sleeping bag—a Tangerine Dream expedition-quality bag from North Face, supposedly warm to 40 below zero—and laid it across the suit. Kicking off my bunny boots, I slipped into the sleeping bag. Sitting with my back to the stanchions supporting the handlebar, I took off my headlamp and clipped it to an inside pocket, angling the beam to light the sled's interior. Almost done now, I grabbed the open flap of the sled bag and pulled it overhead. Then I pressed the Velcro strips together and sealed myself inside. My sled bag had become a survival cocoon.

Wedged inside the tight shelter, I congratulated myself for buying sledmaker Tim White's extra-long-model Iditarod toboggan. The situation would be far, far worse, I told myself, if I had skimped and bought White's standard sled, which was six inches shorter. Focusing on the small triumph was more comforting than dwelling on the big picture.

At the beginning of the race, two scenarios scared me: falling through ice into open water on a cold night, or getting nailed by a storm in an exposed section of the trail. I wasn't even a quarter of the way to Nome and already I felt like a lamb tied to the dark gods' altar.

Living on the Lower East Side, the biggest threat from the environment had been being mugged. I always left the cab garage on Ninth Avenue with a camera bag slung over my shoulder, and $75 to $100 cash tucked in my right sock. I worked too hard to stuff $8 in another cabbie's pocket. Instead I caught the subway at Times Square, which was still a lively place at five o'clock in the morning.

Over time, I grew careless. Trains were few, and long delays were common at that time of the morning. I began to stray farther and farther from the protected area near the token booth, seeking more comfortable places to sit, with better light for reading the newspaper. My favorite spot became the fourth or fifth step of an unused staircase at the far end of the lower subway platform. The staircase led to a closed section of the station. The top of the stairs was sealed by a fence.

One morning, a voice intruded on my reading.

"You know it's not very safe here," said a young black man, standing so close I could have reached out and touched the gold chains around his neck. He smiled, introduced himself as "The King," and welcomed me to his dominion.

Two of his friends quietly approached from opposite sides of the platform as the King and I bantered. I calmly stood up and stretched, taking stock of the situation. The platform ahead of me was empty. Standing on the staircase I had the advantage of height. But I was also cornered by the hand rails and the fence behind me.

"What's in the bag?" The King said, pointing at my camera

bag. The bag contained three Olympus 35-mm camera bodies, several lenses, and a powerful flash—my entire life, or so it seemed at the time.

Instead of answering the King, I smiled. Not because I saw a way out. I smiled because I was an idiot, because my back was to the wall in the confrontation every city dweller fears, because there was no avoiding any fate, and because, mainly because, surrender wasn't an option.

The King and his friends sauntered away.

My breath was loud inside the sled bag. So was the ticking of my watch. The wind was a divine fist, rocking my sled with each blow. Each gust sent tiny jets of snow through gaps in the Velcro. Illuminated by my headlamp, snow crystals rained down on my sleeping bag in shimmering streams. I pried the Velcro strips apart and squeezed them together more carefully, shoring up my defenses.

Madden had talked me into buying a dozen packets of processed salmon. He swore that it would taste like candy on the trail. And the salmon is so oily that it remains soft enough to eat, regardless of the temperature.

Two packets of the salmon were stowed in the sled bag's inside pocket. I dug one out and cut it open with my folding Buck knife. The fish was cold and stiff, but it crumbled easily into bite-sized bits. I chewed slowly, savoring the intense flavor. Then I licked the greasy wrapper clean. Madman knew what he was talking about.

Carefully opening the sled bag, I checked the dogs. Those I could see were curled in tight balls, mostly covered with blankets of snow. Resealing the cocoon, I dug my toes into the sleeping bag and wiggled inside. Then I switched off the headlamp and huddled in the dark, listening to the wind.

Strange to say, I felt peaceful stuck on top of Rainy Pass.

There was no escape. I was again cornered. So what? I wasn't beaten. And I wasn't close to surrendering. This was a delay. Nothing more. For the first time in weeks, there were no decisions to make, and no schedules to keep. The storm had me in its grip, and all I could do was ride it out.

Iditarod's leader was furious.

Instead of taking his 24-hour layover in Rohn, Nikolai, or McGrath, where the other front-runners halted, Terry Adkins kept his dogs on the march, gambling on his mountain-conditioned dogs' ability to grab an insurmountable lead. The veteran's strategy hinged on two factors, both of which were beyond his control. To delay the pursuit, he needed a storm, preferably on the 90-mile trail to Iditarod, the ghost town that gave the race its name. He also needed the support of Iditarod's trailbreakers, the volunteer snowmachiners who open the lead musher's trail. The timing of their work was crucial. If the snowmachines got too far in front, their work could vanish in drifts. If they weren't far enough ahead, the trail might not "set," or harden, in time for the lead musher's passage.

Adkins got his storm, but the trailbreakers were running too far ahead. He battled drifts in the final miles leading to Ophir. Continuing on alone was out of the question. He filed an official protest with race officials. He angrily told reporters that he might even scratch. The mushing Montanan, with more Iditarods under his belt than anyone else, vowed to make this race his last.

"It's like living with a woman for 17 years and finding out she's unfaithful," Adkins told the *Anchorage Daily News*.

The complaints and threats were meaningless. Adkins knew it. Words weren't going to part the white sea blocking the race leader's trail.

When I poked my head out of the dark cocoon, the sky was clear, and the terrain was nothing like I expected. Ace and I were not, as I had thought, camped on a downward slope. Our teams rested in a flat, exposed bowl.

Ace could hardly believe his eyes. The survival shelter stood a few hundred yards away. I was more surprised when I looked at my watch. Nine hours had passed!

The dogs, and the gear I'd tossed out, were cemented around the sled in white mounds. There was no trace of a trail. But the route ahead was clearly defined by a line of fluorescent orange strips waving from bushes in the gentle breeze. I looked up the line of markers to the notch at the end of the bowl, perhaps a quarter of a mile away. The pass.

I turned to Rainy. "You knew right where we were last night. Didn't you girl?"

She yawned, leisurely stretching and sunning her tight white belly.

A thin skin of snow clung to the rocks at the top of the pass. Watching Rainy and Harley scrambled over them, I braced for a wild drop. But the slope was gentle, and I could see my whole team cresting the ridge. It was too cloudy to see much of the valley beyond. Dalzell Gorge was saving her secrets.

It was a grand morning on the Iditarod Trail. A hundred yards from the pass, I stopped the team, throwing my sled on its side for an anchor. Pulling out the pocket camera I wore around my neck, I shot pictures of Ace descending the mountain.

The gorge was nothing like the icy roller coaster I was warned to expect. The storm had dumped over two feet of new snow. Rainy was swimming in powder deeper than she was tall. Harley's head wasn't covered, but he was swimming just the same. Repeatedly he looked back at me, eyes crying out for a rescue. Tough going. The team kept bunching up, tangling every few feet, and breaking through the soft crust into concealed pools of water.

"Those dogs do like to tangle," said Ace, chuckling as he watched from behind.

Struggling though the deep soup, I thought back to something Mowry had told me on our final test run. We were crossing an open field. Tiny six-inch drifts were on the march, riding the rising wind.

"This is probably worse than anything you'll see the whole way to Nome," the Coach shouted. He gestured at jets of snow raking sideweays across the back of his legs. "Compared to this trail, Iditarod is a highway." In two trips up the Iditarod Trail and one Quest, representing over 3,000 miles of long-distance mushing, Mowry liked to brag that he had never even unpacked his snowshoes. I shook my head as I reached for mine.

I broke trail for an hour or two, gaining perhaps half a mile as I wallowed in powder and sweat. Progress was steady, albeit at a snail's pace. It was sweet finally hearing the whine of engines echoing from the ridge. It was Medred and Lavrakas. The journalists were traveling to Rohn by snowmachine. Like cavalry to the rescue, they flew past Ace and me, leaving a new trail in their wake.

Two teams, driven by Mark Williams and Tom Cooley, came loping down the gorge behind the snowmachines. My dogs were in snow-plow mode, and a traffic jam developed. Waving Ace and the others by, I stopped my dogs for a snack break.

Our subsequent run through the gorge was exquisite. The new trail provided footing for the dogs yet remained soft as a cushion. Team and sled glided through thickening trees, skirting pools of open water. I was enjoying life when I spied Medred and Lavrakas up ahead, suspiciously perched on a rock. Rounding a curve I confronted the photo opportunity: a narrow icy bridge over an open creek.

There was no dodging this. As my sled skidded sideways on the ice, I flipped it on one runner and steered it by the open water, trotting alongside like a pro.

"You're the first one to make it," Medred called out, sounding surprised.

Lee came through an hour later. His sled whipped into the creek, becoming wedged under the bridge. Lavrakas got a shot of Lee grimacing as he stood in the frigid water.

Could have been me. Would have been me if I hadn't spotted the media stake out.

Covering the race for the *Frontiersman,* I hadn't dared visit Rohn. Access to the remote checkpoint, near the junction of the Tatina and South Fork Kuskokwim Rivers, was mostly limited to charter flights, which I couldn't afford on our budget. If the weather closed in, a person could get trapped for days waiting for a flight out. And that just wouldn't do at all, because Rohn didn't even have a phone from which to feed stories back to the office.

In the gold-rush days, miners traveling the Iditarod Trail found a roadhouse waiting in Rohn. Now the only structure standing was a small 1930s-era cabin, maintained by the Bureau of Land Management. It was reserved for race officials and veterinarians. There was a wall tent, equipped with a stove, where mushers could sleep; that was it for services. Rohn's drawing card was solitude. Off in the spruce forest, away from most reporters and the excitement present in most villages, sled dogs got more rest.

Perhaps a dozen teams were camped at Rohn when I checked in at the cabin at 3:20 P.M. on Wednesday. I immediately declared my 24-hour layover. Over the next few hours, Lee, Daily, Alan Garth, Bill Peele, and, shortly after 8 P.M., Sepp Herrman, mushed into camp. No one remained on the trail behind us.

The mushers tending dog teams bedded in the sheltering spruce here represented Iditarod's broad spectrum. We had experienced dog drivers such as Ace, Daily, and Herrman—three men who had shared their lives with sled dogs. And we had mushing adventurers like Peele, a 55-year-old pharmaceutical company employee from North Carolina, and Garth, a social worker from England. They were each driving dog teams leased from Old Joe's huge kennel 90 days or less before the race.

Fetching water from the river with the help of a rickety camp ladder, I served my dogs three hearty meals during our leisurely stay in Rohn. I amassed a huge pile of surplus booties from the camp refuse heap. The checkers also allowed me and the other stragglers to dry personal gear over the cabin's wood-stove.

On the advice of veterinarian Bob Sept, I gave each dog a foot massage, rubbing ointment into every paw. After 275 miles on the trail, three of my dogs had troublesome cuts or splits in their pads. My sore-footed trio—Screech, Cyrus, and the White Rat—had possessed iron paws during training. Therein lay the cause. They weren't used to wearing booties and, Cyrus especially, kept pulling them off.

I was really worried about Cyrus. The young dog had stopped pulling on the final miles up to the checkpoint, and he seemed listless, quiet even. It was possible I might have to drop Rattles's poor puppy.

"Could sore paws alone account for such a personality change?"

You bet, said the vet, who gave me a small vial of ointment for the cuts. I dabbed the goo on those sore paws every few hours, placing booties on afterward to keep the dogs from licking their toes clean.

A time adjustment was factored into each musher's 24-hour layover. Since I had mushed the first dog team out of Anchorage, my mandatory stop was extended by 2 hours, 43 minutes, which boosted my layover to almost 27 hours. That accounted for the rude surprise I found waiting Thursday morning on the checker's time sheet. Though I had beat five teams into Rohn, they were all scheduled out ahead of me.

By noon, everyone was scrambling to go, including the checkpoint staff. The musher's tent disappeared before I took a planned nap. Flames danced over roaring trash barrels as vets and checkers burned everything nonessential. The crackling fires and smoke gave the scene an apocalyptic edge. I was anxious to get moving.

Lee and Garth were the last out before me. As I helped guide Lee's dogs to the trail, I kidded Barry that he had better push his dogs for all they were worth, because we would be coming at him like a steamroller. He laughed. We both knew my dogs were faster. And I didn't plan to carry that damn Red Lantern any farther than I absolutely had to.

I was required to stay until 6:03 P.M. It was closer to 6:30 by the time I pulled out of the camp. The checkpoint staff turned out in force and cheered my departure. The last sled in Iditarod's 70-team field was again on its way.

I had Chad in single lead. He and the other dogs were supercharged by their 27-hour rest. Maybe 200 yards from camp, a bump threw the sled sideways in the air. I landed flat on my chest and got the wind knocked out of me. The team dragged the overturned sled and me about 75 yards, spewing a trail of cassette tapes, brownies, batteries, and juice containers from the rear sled-bag pocket. I finally stopped the dogs in an icy section, which offered little for the snow hook to bite into. I looked longingly at the snacks and tapes scattered behind me. Those cassettes represented tunes carefully selected for the coming run through the Burn. A Miles Davis tape, which I had been saving, lay in the center of the trail, perhaps 7 feet back.

Raven was chirping like a poodle. Spook was baying. Harley and Cyrus were jerking the sled forward, inch by inch.

"Sorry, Miles," I said.

I shifted my foot, and the brake sprang free. Chad felt the

release and leaped at the trail ahead. The team whipped my sled with mad zeal.

I did what I could to hold the dogs to a reasonable pace, but paws were flying as we entered a narrow tunnel in the spruce. The sled glanced off several big trees without incident. Then, with a sharp "crack," my right rear stanchion nicked a small tree and splintered. The handlebar felt like a limp noodle.

Snow was falling, each flake lengthening the gap between my team and those ahead. I tied the team to a tree and examined the damage. Didn't look that bad. A few hose clamps should do the trick. In less than 40 minutes, I was back on the trail, aiming to close that gap on Barry Lee.

"Nothing to it," I thought, pleased with my ingenuity.

The patch job held for about 15 minutes, until I smacked another tree, further busting up the stanchion and a rear support bar.

The light was fading as I chopped down a small tree and lashed it over the stanchion like a splint. The repair job made for sluggish steering. I traveled a few miles before an abrupt dip in the trail sent me nose-diving into the runners. Pieces of my head-lamp reflector fell when I lifted my head. The bulb was still burning, but it cast a splotchy light. Looking at my sled, I blinked a few times, unwilling to accept the truth. The splint had held, but now the companion rear stanchion was broken.

"No longer funny, guys," I said, using a tone that caused the dogs to perk up their ears.

I couldn't believe it. Snow was pouring down on us. Flakes sizzled on the bare bulb of my crunched headlamp. The next checkpoint, Nikolai, was at least 75 miles away, and I had a broken sled.

First priority was the headlamp. I pieced together shards and formed a crude reflector, which I attached to the bulb bracket with first-aid adhesive tape. The patched reflector threw a frag-mented beam, but light of any kind was precious. Then I chopped down another thin tree and fashioned another splint. The overhaul took 90 minutes and turned my sled into some-thing more suited to Fred Flintstone than an Iditarod musher.

Only traces remained of the tracks ahead, but the trail re-mained obvious through dense groves of spruce and snow-covered tussocks. Navigation got tougher as we entered the Post River Valley, where the trail crossed gravel bars and zigzagged through driftwood piles. "Chad," I whispered, "you're follow-ing something out here, but where are the markers?"

I heard later that a number of mushers had got lost in the area, including Runyan and Swenson. That might explain why Chad confidently charged down several blind alleys. Trouble was brewing as I turned the team around several times. But I had ground to make up, and Golden Dog was still my fastest leader. I tried to erase the disappointments with quick snacks, but it wasn't Chad's night. The third or maybe fourth time I second-guessed his judgment, Chad's ego crumbled. He buried his head in the snow and refused to budge.

This was no place to argue. Placing Rainy and Harley in lead, I drove the team hard for several hours. I couldn't detect the trail myself, but we passed enough markers to maintain my confidence in the lesbian. Our luck ran out on the edge of a large lake. Rainy charged into the white expanse, but her clues ended at the shoreline. She swung the team right, then left, searching for a bearing. Then she looked at me, but I couldn't help. From what little I could see through the white soup, the broad lake's white surface was seamless and perfect.

Throwing the sled on its side, I halted the team on the snow-covered ice and ran up to Rainy. She shied, as always, but looked at me as I knelt down beside her. "It's not your fault, little girl," I whispered. "Not your fault at all."

Pulling the dogs off the lake, I bedded the team in a clump

of bushes. It was snowing again, blowing loose powder anyway. I dug a pit to shield the cooker from the wind. After serving the dogs a hot meal, I emptied my sled for the second time and climbed inside. I slept fitfully, haunted by the knowledge that I was alone—in last place—at least 800 miles from Nome.

CHAPTER 6

Alone in the Burn

In the grey light of dawn, I rejoiced.

Out in the center of the lake—a solitary marker pole greeted me. My fine friend, the trail marker, was an inch and a half wide, stood two feet tall in the snow, thin as a reed, but capped with fluorescent orange tape that blazed wonderfully against the lake's broad sea of white.

Rainy and Harley made a beeline for it, plowing through six inches of new snow. I was heartened, but worried nonetheless. The powder wasn't deep enough to stop the team, but it was bound to slow us down, which meant that Lee and Garth would increase their lead.

A traffic jam clogged the trail out of Iditarod, 250 miles north. Early Friday morning, March 8, Susan Butcher had mushed out of the darkness into the glare of the TV lights set up by the banks of the Iditarod River. Three thousand dollars in silver ingots was waiting for the first musher to reach the ghost town of Iditarod, but Butcher refused to claim the prize. She told race judge Chisholm that she wanted to wait for Dee Dee.

"We mushed eighty miles together, and I want it to be a tie," Susan said. Her request was rooted in anger. The run from Ophir had taken 25 hours, twice as long as usual because the front-runners had had to break their own trail. The Iditarod's defending champ was seething.

Race marshal Kershner had seen this coming. Following the debacle with Adkins, he had intercepted the trail-breaking team on the Yukon River and ordered them back. Kershner wanted them to blast through to Ophir, but the snowmachiners had backtracked only as far as Iditarod before turning around.

According to Butcher, she, Jonrowe, Adkins, Osmar, Buser, Barve, and King had traded off the front position, sharing the burden placed on lead dogs cutting a new path through the drifts. Although Swenson and Runyan had arrived at Iditarod along with the others, their names were noticeably absent from Susan's honor roll.

"What a bunch of crybabies," responded Swenson.

Runyan ducked the name-calling, saying that he was just running at the best pace for his dogs.

The newcomer to Iditarod's front pack, Jeff King, cast the dispute in strategic terms. "This isn't a Boy Scout trip. It's a race," he told reporters. "You don't get in the ring and grease Muhammad Ali's gloves for him."

As the sun rose Friday morning, Runyan mushed out of Iditarod in first place. By noon, a front pack of 18 teams was on the trail to Shageluk, with Jonrowe and Butcher bringing up the rear.

Back in McGrath, Lynda Plettner was peeved. That damn Urtha had Abdul, her best leader. After the experience of watching him struggle through the Klondike, Plettner had made sure that the rookie's entire Iditarod team was first-rate. All Urtha had to do was feed those dogs and hang on. She was the one driving the kennel's puppies. So WHERE was he?

Urtha Lenthar had appeared to be in good shape when Plettner left him in Rohn. Checking the time reports, she noticed he was a little late getting out. Linda could understand that. But it didn't explain his interminable delay in the Burn. The pups had hauled her across in ten hours. Urtha had the better team, so he should have mushed into Nikolai hours ago.

Plettner mushed on to McGrath, where she spent more long hours waiting and hounding officials for an explanation. Word was finally relayed that Lenthar had RETURNED to Rohn after getting lost. What was happening out there?

Urtha finally reported in at Nikolai. Plettner got him on the phone. It was a troubling conversation. The schoolteacher sounded extremely discouraged.

"Look," Plettner said, growing impatient. "Like, I've been sitting here an enormous amount of time. So I'm going to, like, casually move over to Takotna. Call me there when you get to McGrath."

Leaving Rohn, Bill Peele was concerned about his lead dog. Most of the team looked frisky and refreshed, but that darn Charlie had been acting up again. Peel stopped his team near Farewell Lake, intending to shift his ornery leader to a less critical position. The cunning dog sniffed an opportunity. He twisted out of the novice musher's grip and dashed off into the surrounding stunted spruce. Charlie didn't stray far, but he refused to come back.

Peel offered Charlie food. He tried hiding behind his sled, hoping the escapee might draw in close enough to catch. He wasted hours trying to coax that dog back. Nothing worked. At a loss, Peele decided to drive his 15 remaining dogs to Nikolai, where he could consult with Iditarod officials. Charlie howled and howled as the team pulled away. As Peele crossed the Burn, those mournful cries haunted the kind-hearted musher from North Carolina.

Traveling just ahead of me was Barry Lee. Babying his dogs was paying off. During the first three days of the race, he had limited runs to an easy three hours. He was "sweetening the team," as he called it, for harder driving later. Now, after a daylong layover in Rohn, his team was supercharged.

Lee had invested three hours fixing the snowmachine track he used as a primary brake. Streaking out of Rohn, the hefty musher put that drag track to use, trying to hold his dogs to a reasonable pace. But the jury-rigged brake snagged on a stump and tore loose.

Lee had grown up driving crazed sprint dogs. He didn't use a brake then. He decided he didn't need one now. Skills polished 20 years ago on the track in Anchorage came back as Lee jockeyed his sled past trees, rocks, and other encroaching hazards. The sled ricocheted through the ruts carved by local buffalo, catching air as the runners skipped across frozen mounds of overflow. This was mad, just mad. Barry loved every moment of it.

Lee kept an eye on his watch, and, exactly five hours after leaving Rohn, he shut his team down for a well-deserved meal. Based on his brother Bobby's geographic clues, Lee reckoned he had covered at least 45 miles, putting the team near the start of the Burn, which sounded like a good place to tackle in the daylight.

The stars were bright as Barry Lee climbed into his sleeping bag. He felt good. His whole life had built toward this moment when he would rest alongside honest dogs on the Iditarod Trail.

Snow began falling. It was coming down hard when Lee

awoke four hours later. Alan Garth had passed by during the night. The Englishman's tracks were already covered by half a foot of new snow.

As Lee resumed the chase, the dogs—so puffed up with excitement upon leaving Rohn—deflated before his eyes. Watching them slog through the thickening snow, the musher grimaced. He had his old team back—that wretched bunch from the Klondike 200.

There were tracks and evidence of a camp. Clearly another team had rested here overnight. The discovery, after 14 hours of traveling solo, provided a major boost to my entire team. Tails high, my dogs excitedly sniffed the campsite. Rainy appeared more alert and quickened her pace. I was thrilled, but tried to keep it in check. The team ahead probably had a lead of several hours, and it didn't seem likely we were gaining much ground.

The deep snow knocked a couple miles an hour off our speed. Weighted down by the twin tree-splints, my sled felt sluggish, and I couldn't do much pushing on the hills for fear the handlebar would break.

Under a gray sky, I followed the trail through thinning strips of spruce. Before too long, I mushed past the last of the living trees and entered a charred land of the dead. I knew this place, if only from legend: Farewell Burn.

Pictures of the Burn didn't capture the desolation left by the huge forest fire that swept the area in 1977, charring 360,000 acres. Fourteen years later, the land remained a graveyard, littered with rotting stumps and a spider web of skeletal trees.

It got colder as I entered the dead zone. A breeze soon picked up, and I rode with my back to the cutting wind, fiddling with face masks, seeking a magic combination that might keep my face pink and alive. Above all, I wanted to avoid the Aussie's fate.

I'd been in Ruby for several days, covering the last teams passing through the checkpoint. I was booked to depart on the next mail plane out when the call sounded over the checkpoint radio. A rescue was in progress.

The injured musher was shivering, drenched in sweat, and bundled in a blue sleeping bag when he arrived. It was Brian Carver, a soft-spoken farmer from Melbourne, Australia, who had been thrust into the race after a musher friend had suffered a training accident. I'd written a funny little story about Carver's last-minute search for an Australian flag so he could show the home colors when leaving the starting chute.

Traveling in the back of the pack with Mowry and Peter Kelly, the Aussie had proved a game, if quiet trail companion. In retrospect, his companions recalled that Carver had, perhaps, acted unusually listless when they camped the night before the accident. He hadn't bothered to change his socks and gloves like the others. He wasn't hungry. The Aussie had just puffed on his cigarettes and watched the others.

The temperature was falling. Kelly realized that from the way his glasses kept frosting up. Mowry reckoned Carver must be tough to bear the temperature, wearing nothing but those thin glove liners. None of the rookies knew exactly how cold it was, but they agreed it was bad, maybe 20 below zero.

The next morning Carver, moving with zombie precision, abruptly broke camp and mushed straight through to Sulatna Crossing, the next checkpoint. Volunteers at the remote tent camp were appalled by the musher's condition as he struggled to sign in: three of Carver's fingers and several of his toes were frozen solid.

It was obvious to them that the Australian was in need of immediate medical attention. Carver wasn't so sure. His chalk-white digits weren't pleasant to look at, but the injury wasn't painful, not in that frozen state. He clung to the hope that he might yet tough out the race.

Ham radio operator Rich Runyan, then working his first Iditarod, patched through a call to a doctor at Providence Hospital in Anchorage. After a hurried conference, the doctor read the musher a medical report over the radio. The Aussie's determination faded as he listened to the clinical analysis of the miseries— starting with potential amputations—he faced if any of his frozen parts thawed and refroze out on the trail. Carver reluctantly scratched.

Mowry arrived at Sulatna shortly before Carver boarded the plane for Ruby. He was shocked by the other musher's injuries.

"Don't you do it, mate," the Aussie told him.

Carver's frostbite was thawing by the time he landed on the river below Ruby. The internal blood fire had begun, leaving him feverish and helpless, with that left hand jammed under his right armpit and his knees hunched in the sleeping bag. Throwing off my camera bag, I helped the two pilots carry him from one plane to the other. The musher groaned when we bumped his feet against the door frame.

Carver recognized me and pulled himself together to answer a few short questions.

"They say it was forty below," he whispered quietly. "I had no idea it was so cold. It was a great Iditarod until this happened. I just had no idea it was so cold."

"Are you guys racing or what?" The caller was Madden. He sounded nervous, as if this morning's Two Rivers' Tune-up represented his serious racing debut instead of mine.

It was a cold November morning, but I didn't have time to worry about it. I was running in and out of the house, loading Mowry's old utility truck. Any concern I might have felt about the sting of the air was dispelled by the thermometer dangling outside our cabin door. Twenty below zero. Nothing to it, I thought. Training in Fairbanks, we dealt with temperatures in that range all the time.

My gear seemed unusually stiff. The lines weren't pliable. Normally limp harnesses were kinked and had to be stretched apart. But I was too busy to pay attention to that since I had drawn the first starting position.

I was running eight dogs. Rainy and Casey were leading, with Pig, Bo, Screech, Beast, Betsy, and Raven filling the spots behind. It wasn't our best team, but one selected to minimize surprises. I hadn't given much thought to my personal gear, placing faith in my familiar motorcycle suit, a trusted 14-year-old memento of my days as a photo-lab delivery driver. I had a balaclava covering my head, but it wasn't tucked in, leaving most of my neck and face exposed.

Leaving the field, the trail joined Pleasant Valley Road. As soon as I made the turn, I felt the wind burning my cheeks. I gritted my teeth and concentrated on keeping the dogs rolling. Other teams were following at two-minute intervals. I'd started first and, so far, I was leading. If they were going to beat us, let 'em earn it.

No one caught us until we were well past the river, on the return loop. Dipping up and down with the trail, I heard a scraping sound and glanced backward. If a musher coming from behind called for the trail, I would have to pull over and let the sled pass.

A team was breathing down my back, all right, but the sled had no driver! The ghost team belonged to Jeff Boulton. About three miles into the race, his lead dogs had tangled. Boulton stopped, straightened them out, and was reaching for his sled when his excited dogs jerked the hook loose.

Rainy hesitated when she saw the crowd waiting at the finish line. Mowry clapped his hands and, coaxing her, ran with the team. People were clapping. For a few minutes I dared to dream that I might have even won. I even had Mowry scared.

"I didn't want you to win the first time out and wind up with an unruly student on my hands," the Coach said later.

He didn't have to worry. All but two other teams completed the course faster. I finished fifth, beating Boulton and another musher who was delayed by a huge dog fight.

At the finish line, Kathy Swenson mentioned that she had planned on racing, but didn't think it was worth it at 40 below.

Forty below zero. She had to be kidding! But it was no joke. Heat escaping through our cabin door had produced a false reading on our thermometer at home.

As we waited for results to be announced in the steamy convenience store, the winner of the race, Paul Taylor, slapped me on the shoulder.

"Pretty cold out there today," he said, mentioning that he'd wondered if his lips were freezing in the breeze.

"How's your face?" Taylor added, frowning.

Now that he mentioned it, my face felt sort of strange. My cheeks were rock hard to the touch, and cold. That's odd, I thought.

Back at the cabin, Madman, Mowry, and Studer were fooling around in the kitchen when I finished feeding the dogs and came inside.

"Man, what happened to you, O'D!"

It wasn't my imagination. Something was wrong. I had frostbitten my cheeks, a chunk of my neck, and both earlobes. My face was just beginning to swell. Within a few hours I puffed up like the Michelin Man. By morning, my mouth was framed with a pair of angry-red apples, and I had a pink golfball in place of my Adam's apple.

"First-degree frostbite," said the doctor, quickly assessing my predicament as he put on his coat for an emergency trip to

the hospital. "That area will be extremely sensitive to the cold."
He prescribed a simple treatment: Avoid outdoor sports for at
least three weeks. "Sooner than that and you might have scar-
ring," he said.

"Doc, you don't understand. I'm in training."

"You better train inside."

I shook my head. Train inside? Not for the Iditarod.

My face was funny-looking, but the situation wasn't. Even
after my face had healed, the new skin remained more vulnera-
ble. I fought back against nature, accumulating a new arsenal of
cold-weather gear. The old motorcycle gear was scrapped for a
$98 Refridgiwear snowmachine suit, sized triple extra large, al-
lowing me to layer additional clothing underneath. Penny Wake-
field, a local clothing designer, made me a lambskin hat and a
face mask with fur sewn on the inside. My face mask collection
soon threatened to crowd us out of the cabin.

"Just smear your face with Vaseline," said Studer, compar-
ing the trick to a swimmer rubbing on grease before attempting
the English Channel. I was skeptical, but I began routinely glob-
bing it on before tending to chores in the dog lot. It actually
made a big difference.

I dressed for each run like a commando suiting up for a mission. The outfit started with long underwear, top and bottom,
covered by polypropylene snow pants, and a thick, hooded
pullover from Apocalypse Design, a local expedition outfitter.
For foot protection, I used a $175 pair of huge white bunny
boots, the U.S. military's gift to the Arctic.

Despite my careful preparations, pieces of my body kept
dying. Mowry would return home from a run sweating like a pig.
I'd retreat to the bathroom to survey the expansion of bloodless
white areas on several fingers, already tipped by deadened blisters.

"You're hopeless, O'Donoghue," the Coach said of my
mounting scars.

I bought more gloves. And I bought more chemical hand

warmers, which I clung to like talismans, rarely leaving the cabin without stuffing another handful in my pockets.

The warmers were neat little things. Tear open the plastic wrapper, shake the tea bag–sized sacks contained inside, and the warmers usually produced steady heat. I say "usually" because those warmers, which cost about 50 cents apiece, had a high failure rate. Roughly one in three was a dud.

I also experimented with larger fluid-filled heat pouches. These were miraculous, providing a 20-minute burst of intense heat when you flexed a metallic disc floating inside the clear fluid. Unlike the dry chemical warmers, the pouches were recyclable. If you placed a stiff white used one in boiling water, the contents liquefied and cleared, becoming as good as new. Alas, the pouches proved worthless. Routine jostling in the sled triggered them. They were always dead when I wanted one.

In Alaska, nothing takes the place of field-testing.

My biggest success against the cold came from dietary changes. Stuffing myself with bacon, buttery muffins, and cheese before training runs — that helped quite a bit. Even more important was drinking before, after, and during runs. Sipping a thermos cup of warm Gatorade, soup, even a beer, as I cruised down the trail, pumped more heat through me than a suit lined with chemical warmers.

The dead forest grew cold, then colder still. I had a full thermos, but it was difficult to tap into while jumping fallen logs and weaving between old tree stumps. More hot Gatorade spilled than reached my cup, leaving my fingers burned then chilled inside swiftly crusting gloves.

The snow is often thin in the unsheltered Burn, but recent storms had helped me out. Our trail was adequate, and a steady line of reflectors gleamed from the skeletal trees ahead. The wind ebbed and finally died by early afternoon.

I knew I was 93 miles from Rohn and Nikolai, and that it should take about 16 hours, an hour less than I'd already spent, to make the crossing. But statistics didn't tell me anything about my own wretched progress, not after camping, the repair jobs, and riding my shattered sled. I realized that I had no handle on the actual size of the Burn. Somehow that had never come up when I covered past races, nor in my conversations with the coach.

Cresting each mound in the barren ruins, I searched the horizon for signs of life. No escape came into view. I was looking off in the distance as Rainy and Harley followed the tracks of a previous team and disappeared. Instinctively, I braced. Too late. The sled launched off a cliff, and I was looking downward at the dogs.

Frantic to avoid crushing anybody, I rolled to the left. The sled thudded to the ground on its side, missing the dogs by scant inches. Or so I thought, until Skidders bellowed in pain. The old wheel dog had a nasty slice on his right rear leg, caused by a glancing blow from a sled runner. Skidders quieted as I examined his wound. I swallowed hard and pretended to be calm. This looked bad. It was a deep slash, wide open to the muscle, right above Skidders' ankle. At least it wasn't bleeding much.

"Sorry, old man," I said, digging into the sled for my first-aid kit.

The injured dog calmly watched as I greased the cut with antiseptic salve and bandaged it. I tried loading him in the sled bag, but Gnat's burly father wiggled free and leaped out. Shaking himself, he yawned, sniffed the bandage, and seemed ready to forget the whole incident.

"All right, tough guy."

We resumed our march. Skidders, at nine the oldest dog in the team, fell into rhythm with the team's pace without so much as a limp.

A solitary figure appeared in the distance. It was a person, on foot.

"Jesus," I whispered, trying to figure out which musher might have lost his team.

Drawing closer, I made out a man pulling a small sled. What was anybody doing out here on foot? The riddle was answered when I spotted the rifle slung over a shoulder—a hunter. The man greeted me warmly, and I halted the team. Like two astronauts meeting in a dead lunar basin, we talked in the middle of the Burn. I was cheered more than I would have expected by the human company.

The hunter whipped out a pocket camera. "Mind if I take a picture?"

The distraction provided by the hunter was brief. Hour after hour, I pressed on, bouncing over partially buried trunks and old stumps. In midafternoon, the sled slammed to a stop, nearly flipping me over the handlebar.

"Son of a bitch!"

The chain anchoring my snowmachine track was caught on a small, firm stump. I couldn't lift my sled over it. And I couldn't slide the sled backward—not with 15 dogs straining forward on a downhill slope.

"Son of a bitch!"

We weren't going anywhere unless I cut off the stump. Double-anchoring the team with both of my snow hooks, I grabbed my axe.

I'd been trapped on a mountain in a storm. Dragged off a cliff. My sled was busted and patched with trees. Now I was playing logger in a dead forest.

"Un-" I cried, swinging at the stump, "stoppable!"

I repeated the mantra with each bite of the axe, feeling stronger with every blow. "Un-stoppable! Un-stoppable! Un-stoppable!"

The stump gave way. The team surged, popping both snow hooks as I leaped aboard the runners.

"That's right," I shouted at the dogs. "We are un-stoppable!"

Plettner was doing just fine, thank you. Those pups zipped right over to Takotna. She couldn't praise them enough. It was Urtha who had her worried. Her mushing student's situation was growing worse with each phone call. Plettner hardly knew what to say anymore.

"The dogs won't go right," Urtha complained. Hansel, one of the leased team's key leaders, "wasn't performing," he told her.

"Is he mentally or physically having problems?" Plettner asked.

"Well, I sure don't know."

Plettner instructed Lenthar to find a vet and have the dog checked out. He did, and the examination proved inconclusive. That settled matters as far as Lynda was concerned.

"Look Urtha," she said, "take a break, but not much of a break, because you're going very slowly and those dogs AREN'T TIRED. Then get over here to Takotna. I'm going to wait for you."

The stray had to be a team dog. That much was obvious from the harness. And who else would be traveling the Burn this time of year besides Iditarod mushers?

Then again, Doc Cooley wasn't an official entrant himself. The debonair mushing vet from Wisconsin was Iditarod's so-called "trail sweep," conducting tests on sled-dog metabolism while providing veterinary backup for teams traveling in the rear of the field. It was a new concept, something Cooley, 44, had thought up after years of frustration watching apparently healthy Iditarod dogs collapse from undetected heart problems. Doc suspected electrolyte imbalances might be the cause. The race offered the perfect opportunity to test the hypothesis.

Cooley tried to lure the stray within reach, offering the dog chunks of meat. Darting between trees, Charlie remained out of reach, barking at the unwelcome intruder's team.

Not far ahead of Cooley, John Ace barely clipped a tree with his knee. Though only a glancing blow, it came at a damaging angle. It was as if a grenade had exploded under Ace's sled, which tumbled down the hill. He felt like his face got the worst of it. He didn't notice the throbbing in his leg until later.

Dawn was breaking. Ace figured he could tough it out to Nikolai. Not that he had any choice. The burly musher drove onward. The pain in his leg steadily increased, as did the swelling. Before long, Ace was precariously hunched over the sled, unable to help his dogs on the hills, and enduring terrible pain as he repeatedly capsized.

The team dragged its injured driver into Don and Catherine Mormile's camp in the Burn. They took one look at Ace's leg and ordered him to lie down. The leg might be broken, they warned. Ace, a former Vietnam medic, wasn't entirely convinced. He held out hope of finishing this, his sixth, Iditarod. But he welcomed their help feeding his dogs.

Cooley arrived on the scene and lent his voice to the Mormiles'. Ace's condition was indeed grave. On a bitter night like this, Doc told the musher, he risked losing that leg, because swelling magnified the risk of frostbite. The veterinarian convinced Ace to take shelter in his sled bag and wait there while he mushed to Nikolai for help. Just to be on the safe side, Cooley confiscated Ace's boots, leaving him no choice but to stay put.

Race Judge Al Marple and Jeff Stokes, a local EMT, returned several hours later on snowmachines, equipped with a rescue sled. In a bumpy ride, punctuated by the musher's groans, they hauled the crippled musher to the village. Ace was flown to McGrath Friday afternoon. X rays revealed a hair-line fracture in his leg just below the knee. He and his dogs were headed home. This incident brought the total number of race casualties to eight.

Tom Daily found the Burn oddly fascinating. He passed through the skeletal forest at night, his favorite time for mushing, chasing the tracks of a fox in the fresh snow. The team's joyride ended at Sullivan Creek, where his dogs balked at crossing the open water. The creek was about 15 feet across. Trailbreakers had built a temporary bridge for the race leaders, but the jumbled logs and sticks looked dangerous now. A dog killer, Daily decided, after scouting the crossing.

Bridge or no bridge, the rushing water had to be crossed. After a few abortive attempts at ordering the leaders across, the musher took matters into his own arms. One at a time, he picked up his dogs and carried them to the far side, wading through freezing water well above his knees. The chore delayed Tom Daily three hours, and turned his space-age foam boots into huge clumps of ice.

Lee and Garth were studying Sullivan Creek when I arrived. My timing couldn't have been better. We teamed up for the crossing. I rode sleds to the edge of the creek, holding the dogs to a crawl as Lee threw reluctant swimmers into the water. Garth was positioned on the far shore, coaxing the dogs forward, and ready to yank foundering critters to safety. Soggy though they were, the dogs pulled our sled across upright and dry. Between the three of us, we forded the creek with minimal delay and no accidents.

I was the last one across, riding my runners all the way and sending spray flying from my bunny boots.

Sunlight was stabbing through clouds as we stopped on the far bank and snacked our soggy dogs. I took a picture of old Skidders holding his head high, impatient to go on again. Incredible dog.

Lee grinned at the sight of my taped headlamp and the trees lashed to my sled. "I wondered what was holding you up."

Judging from Kershner's comments before the race, I knew I could probably arrange for Mowry to ship replacement stanchions and anything else I needed to McGrath, a large village 50 miles from Nikolai. But that might take days! After what I'd just been through catching up, there was no way I was going to let Lee and Garth leave without me. After McGrath, the next likely place for a commercial air shipment was Anvik, over 200 miles north. Could the patched sled make it that far? It seemed like a hell of a gamble.

Garth's leaders were tiring. Lee asked if I wanted to take the lead. I nodded, and he slowed his team so I could pass.

"Catch this," I said, tossing Lee an imaginary gift as our sleds met.

"What's that?"

"The Red Lantern!" I shouted.

Barry Lee laughed.

"You want somebody to work on that?" said the Nikolai checker, eyeing my patched sled.

Did I? I could have kissed the guy. He sent me to Nick Petruska, an Athabaskan sledmaker.

"I have a little birch," Petruska said, studying the damage. "I'll see what I can do."

I tied the team alongside Petruska's house, pulled out the

cooker, then unhitched my sled from the gang line. The Athabaskan pushed it across the yard to his work shed.

In little more than the time it took to prepare the dogs a hot meal, Petruska duplicated the shattered parts and rebuilt the back end of my sled. I was amazed. It felt stronger than ever. The quiet villager didn't ask for it, but I gave him $100. I was back in the race. Unstoppable indeed. Catching the Poodle Man would be merely a matter of time.

I walked Skidders to the checkpoint and rousted the veterinarian from bed. Though bleary-eyed, the volunteer from the Deep South grabbed his medical bag and immediately set to work, cutting off the bandage with a pair of scissors. The dog's pasty white cut looked awful to me, but it wasn't infected. Sealing the gash with some sort of medical staple-gun, the vet wrapped the paw.

"Have the bandages rechecked," he said, gently rubbing Skidders's neck, "but there's no reason that dawg can't run all the way to Nome on that foot."

A race judge and several villagers were talking about Bill Peele. The rules were clear. The musher couldn't continue without his missing dog, which several mushers had seen haunting the woods near the Burn. Peele couldn't even officially check in at Nikolai. He had two choices: scratch or find Charlie.

After consulting with the judge, Peele arranged to rent a snowmachine, which he had absolutely no experience driving, and he hired several snowmachiners from the village. The motorized posse was supposed to leave in the morning.

Leaving the checkpoint, I ran into Steve Fossett, another rookie who was getting ready to pull out after completing his 24-hour layover in Nikolai. Lean and slightly balding, Fossett, forty-six, was a classic adventurer. The president of a securities firm in Chicago, he wanted to add the Iditarod to his already impressive list of mountain-climbing and ocean-swimming achievements. He was mushing a team leased from Canadian

musher Bruce Johnson, an Iditarod veteran and winner of the
1986 Quest. But Fossett's hired dogs weren't cooperating.

Crossing the Burn, the dogs repeatedly quit, forcing Fossett
to camp for hours each time. It was a dismal repeat of his experience on the Kusko 300, when the canine work stoppages caused
him to scratch. His faith in the Iditarod investment was eroding.
The best gear and dogs money could buy wasn't worth much
without cooperation between the team and its driver.

"I haven't got any leaders at all," Fossett said, sounding
deeply discouraged.

I beat a hasty retreat, leaving Fossett to stew about his fate.

Plettner was appalled. Her leased dogs were fine, but Urtha
looked just pitiful. He was shivering and had a pasty, exhausted
pallor. Plettner was glad she had waited for him. Takotna was a
quiet little village; there wasn't a better place on the entire trail
for an emergency overhaul.

She steered her rookie inside the checkpoint, entrusting the
local volunteers to stuff him full at their bountiful table. Later,
while Urtha slept, Plettner arranged for him to borrow a plain
snowmachine suit. It was 20 below outside, and the forecast
called for colder temperatures in the days ahead. If the schoolteacher was in trouble now, he'd never make it unless he ditched
that idiotic parka of his. Urtha had one of those fancy new coats
that probably felt good in the store, Plettner judged, but left a
musher encased in frozen sweat.

While I lingered overnight in Nikolai, where I used Petruska's
phone to file my first *News-Miner* trail report, four checkpoints
and some 260 miles ahead of me Jeff King was working up an
appetite. He snuck out of Shageluk about ten-thirty that night,
managing to leave the other front-runners behind. Four hours

later, King mushed into Anvik, where he claimed $3,500 and the gourmet dinner waiting for the first musher to reach the Yukon River.

The intense musher from Denali Park played down the significance of his surge to the front. The big prize was, after all, more than 500 miles away in Nome. "But I am the one who gets dinner," King told reporters.

Using a two-burner Coleman stove, a chef from the Clarion Hotel in Anchorage swiftly dished up a seven-course dinner, consisting of an appetizer plate of assorted seafood, chicken consommé with garden vegetables, sautéed shrimp in gin and vermouth, the hotel's own black raspberry sorbet, Caribbean lamb medallions, a fresh fruit and cheese plate, and ice-cream tarts. Three types of wine were served—Domaine Chandon Blanc de Noirs, Robert Mondavi Chardonnay, and Kiona Merlot. And for dessert there was chocolate mousse and coffee.

As he dined under the glare of television cameras, surrounded by a huge crowd of villagers, waiters, and the media, King confessed that hunger wasn't the only motivation behind his bold breakaway. "I wanted a chance to say hi to my kids on TV."

A single six- or seven-hour push, with one or two short snack breaks: that's how long it took most Iditarod teams to cover the 48-mile run from Nikolai to McGrath. Fossett, the securities firm president, had the same goal when he mushed from Nikolai late Saturday night. But his leased dogs had their rookie figured out. No more than an hour or two outside the village, the team quit again. Fossett fed his dogs a hot meal and gave them a long break. He eventually got them moving, but his leaders soon called another strike. The workers had seized control and were playing fetch with the boss.

The sled dogs toyed with Fossett for 15 hours before pulling his sled into McGrath. The frustrating experience convinced the stockbroker to sell short and take his losses. Turning the uncooperative dogs back over to Johnson, Fossett scratched, becoming the ninth entrant to do so in this year's race.

CHAPTER 7

Story of the Day

Leaving Nikolai, the trail followed snowmachine routes west through lakes and marshes to the Kuskokwim River. Past traffic had carved a fast, smooth alley for dog teams. Chad was in a cooperative mood, displaying the speed and command response that had made him our number one dog throughout the fall. Barry Lee had left two hours before me, but we caught him without even trying.

My key chain thermometer read zero. The sun's low angle created blue shadow dogs, bounding in perfect harmony, touching paws with every step.

Roughly midway to McGrath, a TV crew from Anchorage intercepted me on a snowmachine. Chad veered off the trail, ran to the reporter, and lay down by her feet.

"How does it feel to fall so far behind?" the reporter asked.

I fielded several similar questions about my troubles, while swapping Harley and Raven to lead in place of Chad. He accepted his demotion with joy. Freed from the pressures of leading, he was whining to go again. So were Digger and Cyrus. "Listen," I told the TV woman, "if you want, the cameraman can ride on up front for a bit. But I've got to go."

Daily passed us during the media ambush. Bidding the cameraman good-bye, I gave chase, steadily gaining ground as the trail twisted through sloughs and spindly shoulder-high spruce.

Nearing the Kuskokwim River, I saw a cluster of weathered shelters. Seeing the pole racks overlooking the bank, I guessed it had to be an old fish camp. The place looked deserted now, but in a few months those racks would undoubtedly sag under the weight of drying salmon.

"Who are you?" The voice came from the trees.

I blurted out my name.

"Great, I've been looking for you." A photographer I knew from the *Anchorage Times* dashed out from behind the camp. He fell in behind the team on a snowmachine.

As we approached McGrath, the trail snaked through thick woods then abruptly dropped onto the Kuskokwim. Daily, taken by surprise, dumped his sled coming off the hill. When my team piled into his, dogs were sprawled everywhere. The photographer grabbed a shot of us as we straightened out our dog teams in the glow of the setting sun.

A *Times* reporter was waiting for me when I parked the dogs in front of Rosa's Cafe. "How does it feel to go from first to last place?" he asked.

God, we're such lemmings. I remembered being in this same place, asking similar predictable questions. Joe Runyan was the first musher to reach the Kuskokwim village that year, followed by Babe Anderson, the local favorite. Like the other reporters pestering the leaders that day, I hadn't grasped the real story.

Neither Runyan nor Anderson had yet taken their required long break. They had chosen to push their teams through the Burn, all the way to McGrath, before starting the 24-hour clock. Consequently, their lead was illusory. Most of the other mushers in the race that year were, at that moment, in the process of completing their layovers at checkpoints en route. The incredible part was—they, too, were even then falling behind.

"The real story is behind us," Runyan said. "Joe Redington, he's your story."

From Skwentna to Rohn that year, the front-runners had pushed each other, exhausting their dogs as they slogged through miles and miles of soft snow. Temperatures had dropped while Redington was nursing his flu. The trail, packed by the plodding race leaders, hardened to a racing glaze, perfectly timed to catapult Old Joe and Cannonball Herbie Nayokpuk once more into the fray.

"I feel like an old fox chased by fifty young hounds," Redington said later that night, stomping his hook into the snow outside Rosa's. Redington's astonishing leap into the lead, 400 miles into the race he had founded, made for a good story, but no one considered him a serious contender, not at 70 years old.

Nayokpuk commanded more respect. The Inupiat musher from Shishmaref, then traveling close behind Redington, hadn't been a threat since undergoing a heart operation several years before. But his announced retirement hadn't lasted, and Herbie ended up finishing a respectable eighth in his comeback attempt. His overall record boasted finishes in every top-five spot—except first. At 54, Nayokpuk remained a long-shot contender.

Two hundred miles later, the Old Fox was even farther in front. By then, the story about his effort was assuming gigantic proportions. Could Redington pull it off? Debates raged in every cabin, seafront bar, or urban office in Alaska. An enterprising songwriter released "The Ballad of Smokin' Joe," which got heavy play on Alaska radio stations. Everyone was pulling for Joe.

Redington remained the leader in Ruby, the gateway to the Yukon River on the Iditarod's northern route. Adults in the village cheered, and their children ran alongside the sled as Smokin' Joe's team trotted up the hill.

As the first musher to the Yukon that year, Redington earned the feast, which became a great media event. Photographers and cameramen jostled for position as the unkempt, wind-burned musher picked up his dainty fork.

In the middle of the dinner, Ruby's checker pushed through the crowd carrying a fat beaver carcass. Seeing the beaver in Emmitt Peters's hand, Old Joe set aside the fancy silverware and jumped to his feet. Digging into his pocket, he pulled out a handful of crumpled bills. Redington had a dog that wasn't eating right, and he figured that beaver, a flavorful high-energy meat, might be the cure. So Redington had asked the checker to find a trapper. Mission accomplished, the Athabaskan known as the Yukon Fox knew better than to wait on ceremony.

Leaving Ruby, Redington's team met an incoming musher.

"Brother," Old Joe shouted, raising one hand.

"Brother," said Nayokpuk, returning the gesture. "Hurry," he added. "Get out of here before they catch you."

The trail to Nome was wide open. But Redington's team balled up outside the village on the frozen Yukon. His leaders weren't in the mood to hurry away from the cozy village. Redington trudged up front and switched leaders. The team ran a few feet and balled up. He again switched leaders, producing another few yards of progress, then another tangle. He switched leaders again, and again, and again. Dogs were never going to beat Old Joe—a musher for 40 years—in a test of sheer will.

Nearly 45 minutes elapsed before Redington's team regained momentum. I got a picture as Smokin' Joe's team rounded a big rock wall, finally leaving Ruby behind. The Old Fox was still in front, but those young hounds were gaining. I had my first taste of the woes created by reluctant leaders.

None of the press realized at the time—and Redington was

too protective of his race to point it out—but his amazing drive had already been sabotaged by a race organization screwup. Whereas Adkins complained because his trailbreakers sped too far ahead, allowing the trail to blow in, Smokin' Joe had the opposite problem. Loping like the wind, Redington's dogs actually overtook the snowmachines charged with clearing the front-runner's path.

To the uninitiated, that wouldn't appear to be such a bad thing; snowmachiners could surely repass dogs, even the fastest dogs, at their leisure. Perhaps. But such developments inevitably damaged the front-runner's chances.

Nayokpuk had earned his nickname, Shishmaref Cannonball, in a telling incident. Leading the race in 1980, Herbie overtook the trailbreakers in Rohn. Unwilling to slow down, he barreled alone into the Burn, where he wasted half a day, lost in the charred forest, because of the lack of trail markers.

Redington's problem was the snow. Where he caught the snowmachiners near Cripple, the halfway checkpoint on the Iditarod's northern route, the snow was deep and powdery. Old Joe pulled into the checkpoint holding a six-hour lead on the young hounds. While others reveled in the hoopla surrounding his arrival, which earned him $3,000 in silver coins, Redington was appalled at the volunteers' casual attitude. Nome remained his goal—to get there first, the Iditarod's founder needed a good trail punched through.

An argument erupted, leading to a further delay. The trailbreakers finally left, but time had run out. It was a sunny day, and the trail was soft, too soft. When Redington tried to leave, still comfortably ahead of the pack after a five-hour rest, his dogs sunk to their armpits, awash in the mushy powder. Old Joe wisely retreated to the checkpoint, giving the trail more time to set. Butcher, Buser, and the other young hounds arrived during the delay, smelling blood for the first time.

"Good to see you so upbeat," said race Judge Bill Bartlett.

"Why not," I said. "This is fun, and it sure beats working.

"I'm not staying long," I added, grinning through the ice clinging to my beard and mustache. "I'm picking up a head-lamp, getting a beer at McGuire's, and then I'm out of here."

The time had arrived to execute the Coach's strategy. Mc-Grath, population 550, was a big noisy village. Iditarod teams seldom get much rest here. And the town has so many distrac-tions that mushers inevitably waste a lot of time. So Mowry's plan called for giving the dogs a short break, then pushing on to sleepy Takotna, about 25 miles ahead.

Bedding the dogs near the airstrip, I went shopping for a new headlamp. The prospects weren't good. Alaska Commer-cial, McGrath's main retail store, had already closed for the night. Checker Chris O'Gar came to my rescue. She fetched the manager, who graciously reopened the store and sold me a $32 headlamp. It was a cheap toy, producing a feeble, unfocused beam. But you take what you can get.

A package was waiting for me at the checkpoint: a box of chocolate chip cookies, baked by Shelley Gill, my old *Frontiers-man* boss. "Congratulations," read her note. "You've survived the hard part. The rest is a breeze."

Terhune had planned from the start to take his layover in Mc-Grath. The decision was dictated by his poor eyesight, which ne-cessitated his using extended-wear contacts. Terhune hated the feel of the damn things, but glasses and mushing don't mix. He could hardly walk outside in his heavy gear without fogging his thick glasses. The choice boiled down to wearing contacts or mushing blind, and McGrath was the first stop where he knew he could count on finding a cabin warm enough so that he could disinfect the lenses without freezing them solid.

As in most villages, families signed up to host Iditarod mushers. Famous mushers such as Butcher, Runyan, Swenson, or Redington, were coveted guests. Most veterans had friends they stayed with year after year. Terhune, an unknown rookie, landed in a house overrun with three mushers, more than a dozen Iditarod pilots, vets, and judges, and an even larger complement of dogs. Though exhausted, he couldn't sleep. The noise and clatter left him feeling bitter: big-name mushers wouldn't put up with cramped conditions like this. Terhune continued brooding until the final tick on that 24-hour clock.

McGuire's Tavern holds an illustrious place in Iditarod lore. In years past, when locals such as Eep or Babe Anderson had a shot at winning, loyal friends sought to derail the competition by offering them free drinks. Iditarod has become so competitive that top racers seldom risk visits to McGuire's anymore. But I claimed a bar stool with pride.

The bartender greeted me with a bowl of chili. Another Iditarod supporter sent over a free beer. I stayed for about an hour, soaking in the warmth and conversation. Walking to my sled, I tap-danced in my bunny boots.

At 9:30 P.M., precisely two hours after our arrival, I yelled, "Get up!" Dogs that weren't already standing rose and stretched. Little Raven began barking. "All right," I cried, reaching for the hook. "Let's go get the Poodle Man!"

The sled slipped forward. Ahead of me, the dogs trotted toward a gleaming string of markers, leading into the darkness.

Takotna was supposed to be a short 23-mile hop. Three hours out of McGrath, I cursed all map makers and their unholy spawn. This trail climbed forever, bumping over snowmachine moguls, with no end in sight. At last, I saw a cluster of lights.

The promised land beckoned. Tiny Takotna was famous for greeting every Iditarod team, from the first to the last, with hot water for the dogs and a hearty meal for their driver.

The checker, a local musher, was apologetic. "We didn't expect anyone before morning," he said.

Five days had passed since Butcher had led the first wave of teams through the village. With a lull expected tonight, the fire under the water barrel was left unattended. A skin of ice covered the surface of my complimentary "hot water."

The walls of the community center were lined with a neat gallery of mushing photos. I found a huge spread of food waiting, and several nice locals eager to host a tired musher. Did I need anything? Anything at all? What did I think of the race so far? Afterward one of the women guided me to a quiet library, where I bunked out on the carpeted floor.

I was awakened, as requested, at 6 A.M. The dogs, after more than four hours of rest, would be primed. I felt worse off for my own 90-minute snooze. My body was rebelling, but I staggered to my feet. The race clock was running again.

The Coach's strategy called for bolting from Takotna, thus sealing my lead over the teams still napping in McGrath. The concept—so exciting in the kitchen at home—felt awful in the flesh. Before lying down to rest, I had asked the Takotna women for booties I might salvage and for a needle to patch the chewed harnesses in my sled.

"I wouldn't use thread on those harnesses. Use dental floss, it's tougher," one woman told me.

Six hours after arriving, I left Takotna, packing a box lunch prepared by the checkpoint volunteers, a big bag of salvaged booties, and a dental-floss dispenser with several needles tucked inside. The Coach's plan had vaulted me a dizzy three or four spots ahead in the standings, past Lee, Garth, and Daily. Not to mention Peele, who finally captured sly Charlie in the Burn that very morning. Mushing for Ophir, I traveled in sole possession of sixty-second place, approximately 30 hours behind the next teams.

Little Cricket limped terribly on the road out of town. I checked her over, but found nothing wrong. If the mysterious malady had shown up in a bigger dog, I would have turned around and dropped it at the checkpoint. Cricket was so small that carrying her, if it came to that, wouldn't be a problem. Watching closely, I left her in the team. She limped for about two miles, then straightened up. Over the 35 miles that followed, Cricket was her old self, keeping a taught tug line and briskly trotting with no hint of strain.

I was also watching Cyrus with considerable concern, but that wasn't a new development. He hadn't looked good since his foot problems surfaced at Rohn. Rattles's pup was a changed dog, and not for the better. He was listless. His ears were down, and his tug line, running in wheel, was often slack. He wasn't even ripping off his booties anymore—the one good sign since I had devoted a lot of time to keeping his paws medicated.

The Coach would have dropped Cyrus in an instant. "Remember, O'D, you're only as fast as your slowest dog." I was not sure why, but I wasn't ready to give up on Cyrus yet.

The 38-mile trail to Ophir followed a closed seasonal road through a valley flanked by savage mountains. "Weight Limit" signs were posted at several small bridges, specifying tonnage restrictions for various vehicles. I snapped a picture of my dog team trotting by one of the signs.

The morning was cool and clear. The team made good time behind Chad and Raven, our fair-weather duo. Despite an increasing number of cabins alongside the road, the valley was marked by a disturbing stillness. No welcoming smoke rose from the cabins here. They were entombed, cold and lifeless. The eerie spell was broken by a hand-painted sign taped to a trail marker: "Ophir, 5 miles," framing a sketch of a smiling coffee cup.

The Ophir checkpoint pulsated with life. Inviting smoke rose from a cabin nestled in a grove of tall spruce. A neat line of supply sacks rested outside the cabin, near an assortment of snowmachines, freight sleds, and a small mountain of trash and surplus gear. The checkpoint was staffed by veterinarian Mary Hoffheimer, a radio operator, and the owners of the cabin.

"I was beginning to wonder if you would ever get here," said Mary, whom I knew from covering past races. She frowned with mock indignation.

The veterinarian carefully examined Cricket, feeling for sore spots and manipulating her legs. Like me, Mary couldn't find any cause for the limp. The dog's leg might have been asleep, she said, or possessed some other kink that worked itself out. There was another possibility, Mary suggested, smiling. My little Cricket might have faked the whole thing—in hopes of hitching a free ride.

"Could you also check that bandage on Skidders?" I asked, and went on to tell her about my harrowing plunge off the cliff in the Burn.

"Wait a minute," she said, peeling the bandage from the staples. "I've heard about this dog. You're the one!"

Hoffheimer said she'd run into the vet who treated Skidders in Nikolai. He'd described a semihysterical rookie who had dragged him out of bed to treat an old dog who was mending just fine. "I put in a few staples," the vet told Mary, "more to calm the musher than anything else."

"That rat bastard!" I said.

We compared notes on the race as Mary changed Skidders's bandage. Working this, her third Iditarod, the New Hampshire veterinarian had the opportunity to watch the entire field pass through checkpoints. The general condition of dogs appeared excellent, she said, in teams traveling in both the front and the back ends of the race field. But the vet was appalled by what she had seen in several of the middle teams.

Inside the cabin, Mary raided the checkpoint supplies and heated me a bowl of stew. I studied the checker's log while I ate. Four teams had departed Ophir within three hours of my arrival: Linda Plettner, Urtha Lenthar, Mark Williams, and Gunnar Johnson. But those mushers had all rested here for at least 13 hours, and most had stayed closer to 19 hours. Worse, the Poodle Man was reported already out of Iditarod, meaning that he had a lead of at least a hundred miles. But Suter's speed was deceptive. The fool hadn't yet taken his 24-hour layover, a strategy that had the vets increasingly concerned. The damn poodles hadn't beat us yet.

I could have used a nap, but I didn't plan to linger long in Ophir. I was in a hurry, determined to press on before Lee and the others caught up. Such foolishness shaped my thinking as I rushed into a series of stupid mistakes.

King was sleeping off his big dinner. Butcher mushed into Anvik, paused just 12 minutes, then led a wave of veteran teams up the Yukon River.

By the time King resumed the chase, three hours later, Butcher was resting at the next checkpoint, Grayling, with eight other mushers on the way. The front pack held no surprises to those familiar with the race: Barve, Jonrowe, Garnie, Buser, Tim Osmar, Runyan, Swenson, and Matt "the Miner" Desalernos from Nome.

Butcher paused six hours in the village of Grayling, resting her dogs through the heat of the day. The champ then set the pace again, leaving on the 60-mile trail to Eagle Island at 3:20 P.M. on Saturday.

Adkins mushed into Grayling as Butcher pulled out. The Montanan paused just five minutes and then gave chase. By dusk, ten teams were streaking up the Yukon behind Butcher, with half a dozen others preparing to follow.

The forecast called for a blizzard with possible temperatures of 30 below on the windy river. "I'm just going to wear everything I've got," former champion Rick Mackey told reporters.

The predicted storm didn't materialize, but strong winds and drifting powdery snow slowed Butcher to a crawl.

At 11:30 A.M. on Sunday—at approximately the same time I mushed into Ophir, 200 miles south—Joe Runyan parked his dogs in the ravine below Ralph and Helmi Conatser's cabin on Eagle Island. Coming from behind, Runyan had beaten Butcher, Barve, and Quest veteran Kate Persons to the remote island checkpoint by nearly half an hour.

Nome remained more than 400 miles away. No one wanted to break trail to Kaltag, a tough 70 miles farther up the Yukon. Front-runners bedded their dogs in the snow, built crackling wood fires, and nervously eyed each other, daring someone, anyone, to make the first move.

Ralph Conatser had checked in 23 teams before the first musher left. The deadlock was broken at 6:30 P.M. on Sunday by Jeff King. Within an hour, the chase was resumed by Barve, Runyan, Buser, Swenson, Jonrowe, and Butcher—whose 18-dog team remained the largest and best rested among Iditarod's lead pack.

Logic was left out of the equation as I repacked for the 90-mile haul to Iditarod. I was obsessed with cutting weight in the sled.

Speed. Speed was all-important. With that goal in mind, it was time to improvise. For the upcoming run, one of the longest in the race, I sought to maximize speed by carrying less dog food than I had originally planned.

Checkpoint volunteers were sorting the surplus left by other teams, salvaging what they could, burning most of the rest. As I dragged over a sack filled with spare bags of lamb, liver, and beef, an uproar broke out over another musher's castoffs.

"Eels?" cried one of the volunteers, dropping the bag and jumping backwards. The exotic fare was left by Chase. The light-traveling Athabaskan had passed through Ophir the previous morning.

The sun remained high. My dogs had only been resting about three and a half hours. They were groggy as I put on their booties. Most recurled and fell back asleep as I moved down the line.

Then I heard the word I'd been dreading: "Team!"

It was Daily.

I began chucking my gear in the sled, preparing for a fast getaway.

Mary stood on the brake as I guided Harley and Chad over to the trail. The dogs were balking; none were happy about leaving so soon. I lifted Screech, Scar, even Rainy, off the ground by their harnesses and stood them upright.

"You're leaving?" said Daily, parking his team nearby.

"That's right," I said in a false, bright tone. "These dogs smell poodle meat."

Mary didn't say anything, but the vet side of her must have been appalled watching my team wobble out of Ophir. The dogs moved stiffly. I'd never seen them looking so discouraged. Even Raven hung her head, uncharacteristically quiet. Life in a chain gang obviously wasn't something she cared to bark about.

Roughly halfway to Iditarod was an old uninhabited shelter known as Don's Cabin. My plan was to push straight through to it. The distance was about 45 miles. We had clear weather, and I figured the team could do that in six or seven hours, easily.

Cutting short the team's rest backfired on me. Any benefits of leaving early were sapped by traveling for hours in the blazing sun. The team's speed faded in the heat. Thirsty Harley led the crew in gulping snow at every opportunity.

By midnight, there was no sign of Don's Cabin, and I was losing the battle to stay awake. We had covered plenty of ground. That was evident from the changed landscape. The trail was rising over a barren dome of tundra, rock, and ice. This was a harsh and menacing place, a desolate end-of-the-earth setting. And if I thought it was bad—outfitted in my space-age gear, driving dogs fueled by the best nutrition money could buy, tapping caches of supplies flown in for my convenience—what must it have been like in 1910? Those cheechakos, stampeding toward the new strikes reported at Iditarod, had protected their hands with rags and had stuffed newspapers under their coats for insulation.

Redington's Great Race was often billed as a tribute to a 1925 serum run. I've always considered that story a farce. Dog teams were used to rush diphtheria vaccine to Nome, but the serum was transported in a 675-mile relay from Nenana, hundreds of miles off the Iditarod Trail. One musher, Leonard Seppala, had mushed more than a hundred miles to collect the precious package, then carried it 91 miles. But the other eighteen serum-team drivers weren't involved in anything comparable to the modern event. I had more admiration for the forgotten miners and mail carriers who had chanced this desolate passage without glory or a crisis to drive them.

Few markers remained standing in the thin, wind-blasted snow covering the barren hills. I followed what I took to be the paw marks of previous dog teams. The tracks were strangely grouped, covering a broad swath across the biggest dome. Only later did I discover that I was mistakenly trailing a caribou herd other mushers had seen in the area. I kept dozing, repeatedly catching myself in the process of falling off the sled. Part of me whispered "stop," but the forbidding countryside spurred me onward. It would be hard to find a worse place to get caught in a storm.

At last the trail began descending. Steering the team toward a line of scrubby bushes, I made camp. Moving like a zombie, I threw all the food I could find together and cooked the dogs a hot meal. Then I crawled on top of the sled, not bothering with the sleeping bag, and slept.

Dawn was reaching over the moonscape when I awoke. It was cold. Shivering inside my clammy suit, I hustled to get the dogs ready. In ten minutes, max, the team was on the move. Guiding the sled with one hand, I ran alongside, pumping my legs to generate heat.

Perhaps two miles beyond where we had camped stood what had to be Don's Cabin. Dogs started barking as we approached. Someone was home. It was Ralf Kuba, a German adventurer making his second attempt to travel the Iditarod Trail on skis. A year earlier, he had set out on the same mission, using two German Shepherds, Cessy and Sagus, to pull his pulka, a small light sled. He had made it as far as Takotna before the remote checkpoints ahead closed.

This year Kuba had beefed up his small team with Trapper, a veteran Iditarod husky, and he had set out three days before the start of the race. I found him in a depressed mood.

"It's no good," he said. "The dogs are sick and weak."

The German's dogs looked pretty lively to me. And fat.

Checking out Don's Cabin, I decided that anyone would become depressed in that rat hole. The place was falling apart, with broken windows and a thick layer of ice spilling inside. This was the proverbial last resort; that it was described as a shelter confirmed my worst suspicions about the weather in this area.

I pinned a note to the front door urging Barry Lee to hurry up. The trail was starting to get lonely. Kuba was miserable, but he assured me that he wasn't in trouble. I left him there, promising to advise the checker in Iditarod about his difficulties.

Another clear bright day. By midmorning I was sweating and began stripping down, shedding first the snowmachine suit, then the thick bibs. The heat was tough on the dogs, but I kept pushing. My foolishness had thrust us into a different sort of race: the dog food was gone. What mattered now was reaching Iditarod before my dogs crashed, or another storm rolled in. Getting pinned down out here would mean the end of my race.

I wasted precious time putting up with Chad's antics, figuring he set the fastest pace. A lead dog's speed is moot when he squats in protest every hundred yards. I finally came to my senses and put Harley and Rainy in lead, two dogs I could count on to keep us moving forward. To pick up the dogs' spirits, I cut up my two remaining personal steaks—the last food left in the sled—into 15 small bites and passed those out. I'm not sure it was helpful, particularly for Harley, whose hunger was fanned by this miniature appetizer.

With his insatiable appetite, Harley had never been good about passing anything edible on the trail. With the sun beating down and an empty belly gnawing at his concentration, the big dog was far too hungry to pay attention to a musher holding an empty snack bag. Following his nose, Harley began dragging the team off the trail into each and every campsite left by the 62 teams that had passed this way before me. He was determined to scarf every shred of food those other teams had left behind, and I couldn't really blame him.

We slowed to a crawl behind Harley's meandering quest. Hungry Boy was as oblivious to my shouts as he was to the lesbian's attempts to mount him from behind. Screech, meanwhile, had picked up an old glove and was sucking on it like a Lifesaver.

"Hey, there's a letter for you," Kuba told Daily as the musher stopped outside Don's Cabin.

Daily wondered if he was hallucinating. Who was this German with two fat shepherds? The musher relaxed when he read my note and realized it was addressed to Barry Lee. Daily was encouraged to hear that I wasn't more than a few hours ahead. Not because he wanted to beat me. Tom wasn't seriously racing this year. He didn't need to, not with his two-year sponsorship deal. No, Tom Daily was getting lonely.

Lavon Barve lead a group of seven teams off the Yukon River into Kaltag early Monday morning—day ten of the Iditarod—but these front-runners weren't hanging together for the company. Barve, Butcher, Runyan, Buser, Osmar, Swenson, and King were forcing the pace, pushing each other toward Nome, 350 miles ahead.

"This is rumble time," Buser told a *Times* reporter. "When somebody pulls the ice hook, you've got to go."

For the second year in a row, Barve made the first move in Kaltag. The hefty Wasilla printer mushed out of the village at 8 A.M., bound for the coastal town of Unalakleet. Butcher, Buser, and King gave chase within the hour, with Runyan and Swenson not far behind.

"Right now, it's Susan, Lavon, Rick, and Runyan," said Butcher's husband, Dave Monson. "We should know by the end of today."

Most observers gave the edge to Butcher. The defending champ's 16-dog team remained the largest in the front pack. She was a superb athlete herself, famous for running behind her sled, providing an extra boost climbing hills. Butcher's compact frame and slight build also gave her team a substantial weight advantage over those of the larger contenders, Barve, Swenson, Buser, and Runyan.

The weight differential had long obsessed Barve, who carried as much as 240 pounds on his own burly frame. He wanted a rule linking the number of dogs in each team to the weight of the team's driver. According to Barve, "jockeys," such as Butcher and the bantam-sized King, ought to be restricted to smaller teams of, say, 13 dogs instead of 20—to keep the race fair. He left Kaltag with 14 dogs, grousing to reporters about the difficulty of competing against Butcher's larger team.

As he prepared to follow, Swenson had more on his mind than dogs. His wife Kathy had called to resume an argument that had led the musher to order her away from an earlier checkpoint. Race judge Chisholm was present when Swenson took the phone call. "Afterward," he said, "Rick was possessed."

Late Monday afternoon, I spied Daily's team in the distance. Watching him close the gap, it was as if my sled was being pulled by a string of Arctic turtles. I felt crushed and defeated as he passed me with a friendly wave.

Daily halted about a hundred yards ahead and planted his snow hook. He turned to me holding a carved pipe. "Do you smoke?" he asked.

Alaska was no longer a pot smoker's haven. As a result of the recriminalization measure adopted during the November general election, possession of small amounts of marijuana was now punishable by a $1,000 fine and up to 90 days in jail. But

cops weren't patrolling the Iditarod Trail as Daily and I shared a
few puffs on the crest of a barren hill.

Looking out over the desolate valley before us, I wondered
again at the madness that drove the gold seekers to bet their lives
on the harsh country ahead.

"Let's go home," I said as we neared a cluster of deteriorat-
ing buildings. Rat and the other dogs broke into a full lope—the
very effect intended when the Coach and I had begun using
those words in the final mile of training runs. Over the course of
the race, the phrase was becoming ever more powerful. "Let's go
home" tipped the dogs that a checkpoint, rest, and food lay
within the team's grasp.

The McGrath vet blamed Rock's hair loss on stress. The dog's
condition certainly wasn't serious, he said.

Barry Lee wasn't so sure. Rock was shivering under her thinning coat, putting the dog at risk if the weather turned bad. Figuring he had nothing to lose, Barry paid a visit to the store and
bought Rock a child-sized sweatshirt.

Rock sported her souvenir sweatshirt as far as Ophir, but it
wasn't doing the trick. It was getting colder. Watching her shiver
on her bed of straw, Lee knew the dog had given him everything
she could. Rock was headed home.

Crossing the barrens near Don's Cabin Monday night, Lee
found most of the trail markers had been blown down by the
wind. Where he could, Lee jammed the markers in the ground,
standing them upright for Garth and Peele, who were still bringing up the rear.

Sleep deprivation overtook Lee as he descended the hills. He
kept dozing, and hallucinated that he was running over his
wheel dogs. Before that became a reality, the musher made camp
in an exposed spot with nothing to break the wind. Lee was
cold, very cold, in his cheap sleeping bag.

He was awakened by a dog team.

"I'm shattered, simply shattered," Garth whispered to Lee before continuing toward Iditarod.

Shivering in his sleeping bag, Lee pondered the Englishman's strange remark.

Daily mushed up the river into the ghost town at 6:30 P.M. on Monday, March 11. I trailed in ten minutes later. Passing Iditarod's skeletal buildings, I studied the broken windows for ghosts. I didn't see any, but the ruins had a presence to them.

Most of the race staff had already flown north, leaving Rich Runyan, a ham radio operator, to serve as the checker for us stragglers in the rear of the field. A veterinarian was also left at the checkpoint. He was packed and itching to get out as soon as Iditarod's air force could rescue him.

Doc Cooley, the mushing vet, had his leased dogs bedded down nearby on the frozen beach. They were a feisty bunch of champion-caliber sled dogs, the same ones Minnesota musher John Patten had recently mushed to victory in Montana's 500-mile Race to the Sky. Cooley wasn't traveling fast enough to tire the dogs out, and they continually snarled and scrapped amongst themselves. Despite the hair-curling growls, blood was seldom, if ever, spilled. The fighting was largely for show. The snarls amounted to trash talk among a team of highly competitive athletes. Daily and I nicknamed his dogs "Doc's wolf pack."

My dogs came alive as I dug through my checkpoint supply sacks for whitefish. I had to anchor Harley's neck line with my second snow hook to prevent a mob assault on the rations. I threw the team frozen slices of liver and chunks of lamb.

A hole was chopped in the river ice for water. But the water was stained dark yellow from the area's high mineral content.

Yuck. So, using melted snow for dog water, I pumped hot stew into the dogs until even Harley shied away from his bowl. As they slept off the feast, I cooked a second meal to dish out in the morning. My team wasn't budging for at least 12 hours, and not until I heard the dogs barking again. I wanted to erase all memory of that last hard march.

After ten days on the trail, my feet were rotting inside those clammy bunny boots. If I didn't dry them out, I might as well just grab the axe and start amputating.

Daily shunned cabins. He much preferred to sleep under the stars. Leaving us to share the warm cabin floor, Tom stretched out near the dog teams, looking forward to a peaceful night.

The first disturbance was Garth. Lurching to a stop at 3:30 A.M., the Englishman staggered off his sled and headed inside the cabin, leaving his dogs to fend for themselves in an exhausted pile.

I was sewing harnesses when the Englishman threw open the cabin door and plopped down in a chair by the stove.

"I'm shattered, simply shattered," Garth announced. The crazy Englishman had made the 90-mile trip from Ophir in a scorching nine hours.

Flipping on his headlamp at the second disturbance, Daily confronted a dazzling apparition. It was Kuba, nicknamed "the German from Mars," owing to the array of reflective tape on the adventurer's gear.

The bleary-eyed musher's patience eroded as Kuba turned his own dogs loose. The three newcomers pranced through the camp, sniffing everything and sending our four teams into a frenzy. Several members of Doc Cooley's wolf pack got loose, and a new round of fighting erupted.

Enough was enough. Daily stomped into the cabin and roused Cooley. "Doc," he demanded, "you've got to come and stop the killing."

Cooley yawned, staggered outside, and grabbed his loose

dogs. He tied the team off to a flimsy stake and trudged back to the cabin. Daily heard the wolf pack renew its bickering, but he was too tired to care anymore.

My dogs had chewed a total of three harnesses in seven months of training. I figured I was being cautious packing five spares and shipping three more harnesses to various checkpoints. By Skwentna, Daphne alone had shredded three harnesses. The chewing epidemic was just beginning. Other dogs, particularly Rainy, suddenly acquired a taste for harness webbing. By Iditarod, the spares were all in use, and at least half the team was sporting harnesses with patches made from other harnesses beyond repair.

Doc and Daily left Iditarod Tuesday morning. My own departure was derailed by a sudden outbreak of chewing. So it was that I was polishing my seamstress skills in the cabin, 40 minutes later, when a dog team came trotting up from the river.

"Barry, I've been waiting for you."

Lee was mortally tired. You could tell by his puffy red eyes. But his smile was as wide as ever. We talked for a little while, and then I had to go. My team had had 15 hours of rest, and the dogs were getting antsy.

The 65-mile trail to Shageluk was demonic enough to satisfy my wildest masochistic desires. From the crest of each hill, I'd see another, sometimes several more hills, unblemished save for tiny white scratches rising to the sky through trees and brush. Each faint white streak represented the trail climbing yet another distant hill. There was no end to them. Some of the upward slopes were so steep that I could have done chin-ups on the handlebar. On the descents, the dogs spilled down the powdery gutter in a cloud of paws and fur.

Doc and Daily were barely two hours ahead, but the wind had largely erased their tracks on the hilltops. And most of the markers were down. I didn't have too much trouble following the surviving clues in the daylight, but I worried that Lee would be traveling blind after dark. So I made a point of grabbing fallen markers as I passed them, and replanting the reflective sticks in the snow, much as Lee was doing for Garth and Peele. With Iditarod's front-runners nearing the coast, the doorway to Nome was closing on those of us in the back of Iditarod's field. We each had to do what we could to keep it open.

The lesbian was acting strangely. She kept stopping and freezing, with her head cocked as if she was listening. At first it alarmed me—I kept waiting for a moose or a bear to rise out of the brush. But nothing happened. Her pauses had a trancelike quality, as if she was lost in thought. Yelling had no effect.

"Earth to Rainy. Earth to Rainy," I said, wondering if she was having a mental breakdown. The thought was scary. The lesbian was our main navigator. Without her, Harley would be impossible to control. Chad, Raven, and the Rat were good for fill-in duty, but that was about it. I needed Rainy. So I waited, and watched, and wondered what the bossy little dog was seeing in her mind's eye.

I caught up with Daily about nine that night, near another deserted fish camp. It was a woodsy stretch and, for a while, we lost the trail in deep snow. But within thirty minutes, the markers led us out of the trees and into a village street. A crowd of children escorted us to a building decorated with an official Iditarod checkpoint banner. The building was closed and dark. Daily and I were trying to decide what to do when checker Arnold Hamilton roared up on a snowmachine. He steered us to a field behind the school, where Cooley's team was already resting.

"You're the reporter," Hamilton said as he returned on the snowmachine. The checker's son was now aboard. The boy handed me a bucket of hot water. "I read your stories. You're my pick to get the Red Lantern."

"What!" I cried. "How can you say that? I'm miles ahead of Lee and Garth."

Hamilton laughed.

"I'll find some way to disqualify them," he said.

Villagers in Unalakleet, 265 miles ahead, lined the ten-foot-high snow banks of the street cheering the first teams to reach the coast.

Susan Butcher had reclaimed the lead on the 90-mile trail from Eagle River to Kaltag. Her dogs were fed and resting before Barve trailed her into the village 45 minutes later. Another 25 minutes passed before he was followed by Buser, Osmar, and Swenson.

Butcher now held a commanding lead in her bid for a record fifth crown. Nome was a mere 200 miles away, and the performance of her dogs on the windy coast was legendary. The temperature in Barrow was 30 below and falling. Snow flurries were moving south from the North Slope, and the wind was gathering off the Bering Sea Coast.

A skinned beaver dripped blood in a bucket as it thawed. Welcome to the bush. It was about 11 P.M. as I sat down at the dinner table with Hamilton, his wife, Carolyn, and her son, Keith.

Hamilton quizzed me about my impressions of the land I'd just crossed. The Athabaskan said he knew the area well. On his return from Vietnam, he had spent a year out there alone, running traplines out of a remote cabin. "It was a good place to think," he said.

Gesturing to the beaver, the villager explained that he was teaching the boy to live off the land, as he had, practicing the lifestyle known as subsistence. After dinner, Keith showed me a litter of pups, which he hoped might someday pull a sled in the great race. Then Hamilton steered me to a bunk where I grabbed a quick nap.

Because we were traveling so far behind the race leaders, the condition of the trail worsened with each passing day, but it was paved with hospitality in Iditarod's villages.

Peele wasn't a quitter. It cost him more than $700 in gas and wages, but he and his Nikolai posse tracked Charlie down. He did not begrudge the money. The dog's harness was snagged on a bush when the searchers found him. He would surely have died without their help. But the ridiculous incident burned up more than 48 hours.

It was Sunday night before Peele mushed into McGrath, driving what was now the unrivaled last-place team. Garth and Lee, the only mushers even close, had left McGrath at least eight hours before, and both had given their teams long breaks in the busy checkpoint.

A reasonable man might have been discouraged. Except for Takotna, which hardly counted because it was so close to McGrath, Peele was headed into no-man's-land. Snowmachines rarely traveled the 215 miles between McGrath and Shageluk, and a single storm could easily bury the trail, transforming his race into a trek for survival.

But Peele didn't have much in common with other middle-aged men. On two different occasions the tall Southerner with the shaggy white beard had stood on top of 20,030-foot Mount McKinley. He was the driven sort, a man who took up mushing in Alaska less than a month after undergoing major knee surgery. He had borrowed $40,000 from his retirement fund to pursue this Iditarod dream. The holder of the Red Lantern might have been stubborn to the point of foolishness, but you couldn't call him a quitter.

The weather held as Peele pushed across the barrens toward

Iditarod. He didn't find many markers left standing, but scanning the horizon with his field glasses he picked out enough to stay on course. He pushed himself relentlessly, limiting his breaks to the absolute minimum needed for the dogs. The effort seemed to be paying off when he mushed into Iditarod within four hours of Lee's departure.

The old geezer looked ragged to the lone race official left in town. But who wouldn't? Radio operator Rich Runyan decided that Peele was holding up pretty well for a guy traveling alone out here—some 400 miles behind the leaders.

CHAPTER 8

O Mighty Yukon

"Happy Trails Brian O'Donoghue." The sign was nailed to a tall spruce. The forest was plastered with Iditarod greetings, but it was comical seeing my name sharing the same trunk with Jeff King's, who was more than 300 miles ahead.

Leaving the forest, the trail descended along a frozen slough, spilling into an immense white plain, interrupted only by distant folds of ice, jutting perhaps eight feet high. I sucked in my breath. This had to be the Yukon River.

Close ahead lay the Athabaskan village of Anvik, yet the only hint of man's presence was a string of tiny trail markers skirting the massive river's edge. Farther out, a solitary line of trees grew from a small island, pointing like a spear at the vast white expanse.

I felt small.

Skidders had me concerned. My old wheel dog was limping. He was favoring a front paw, so the problem was unrelated to that cut on his rear leg. I stopped and examined him, but couldn't identify a cause. His tug line remained taut, so I left him in the team. The old stud was still pulling—on three legs— as I mushed the team off the river into Anvik, passing the church where a bell had heralded King's arrival four days earlier. It was Wednesday at 3:30 P.M. A crowd of shrieking children chased us to the checkpoint at the community lodge.

Cooley's wolves were bedded on straw outside the checkpoint. I found him inside. The vet was itching to get to Grayling, the next checkpoint, a mere 18 miles farther up the Yukon. Gunner, Williams, and Lenthar were still there, he said, waiting for us. That was great news. But I wasn't budging from Anvik for at least two hours. My dogs were due for a break. I also needed to go shopping again. My folding Buck knife was still resting on a chair at Hamilton's house. Replacing it was essential.

I was mixing dog food later when the checker approached me. "A musher's got to have a good knife out there," said Norman McAlpine, handing me a Swiss Army knife. "Take mine."

Doc diagnosed Skidders's limp as resulting from a sprained toe. "I'd take him to Grayling and see how he does," said Cooley. "It's not far. We can look him over again before the long haul to Eagle Island."

I was already dishing out dog food by the time Daily showed up. Tom's lips were unusually pinched. Bogus, his last dependable leader, was showing signs of mutiny.

"I don't think Bogus wanted to run the Iditarod again," Daily said sourly.

Cooley tried one last time to convince Daily and me to leave with him. We declined, promising to follow before dark.

Sixty teams had already passed through the village, accompanied by a sizable contingent of race volunteers, hotel caterers, and media people drawn by the "First Musher to the Yukon" feast. McAlpine told us to help ourselves to whatever was left from that earlier invasion. Daily and I pigged out, frying an entire pound of bacon.

The checkpoint's bounty included a shipment of my

mother's booties and a card from Iris, who wrote that everyone was rooting for me. Hearing from her—wow, that took me back.

The bewitching Israeli artist was one of my favorite dance partners at the Howling Dog Saloon, Fairbanks' rough-hewn summer showcase. Iris paid the rent by designing outdoor clothing at Apocalypse Design, a local manufacturer of expedition gear used by Butcher and other top mushers.

One summer night during a break in the music at the Dog, Iris and I ducked outside into the bar's big fenced yard and began talking about the gear she could make me for the race. I figured I could get away with a single custom suit. Iris argued for layered clothing.

"What you need ees a beeb," she said.

"A beeb?" I said, baffled by her Israeli-accented purr.

"A beeb for the legs. A pile vest to keep your chest warm. You're too thin, you need the protection," Iris said, laughing. "You should place your order now. It gets very beesy in winter."

I dragged Iris back toward the dance floor. It seemed much too soon to be ordering cold-weather gear. It was 70 degrees out. Volleyball games continued past midnight under the rosy midnight sun. Winter seemed a million miles away then. Now I inhabited a hostile cold world, wearing those "beebs" like a second skin.

While the dogs snoozed, McAlpine entertained Daily and me with stories from his own 21-day Iditarod saga. The tempo of the villager's race had been set on the first day, when he lay down for a quick nap and didn't stir for 14 hours. It was a blunder Daily and I could well appreciate. McAlpine, for his part, understood what it was like to hunt trail markers at the far end of the Iditarod's field. He made his 1983 trip in the company of Colonel Vaughan, who's never been known for speed.

"The colonel was so polite he tipped his hat to every tree," the checker said.

Barry Lee had ground to make up. He didn't want to tackle the Yukon River alone, and Peele was too far behind. Feeling pressured, he hurried out of Iditarod in the early afternoon on Tuesday.

Garth had an hour's lead. Considering the Englishman's mad dash the night before, when he mushed his Redington dogs 90 miles without a break, Lee wasn't at all confident that his team could close that gap. He was, at first, happily surprised when he found Garth camping roughly midway to Shageluk. But something about the scene disturbed Barry Lee. He paused to check on the Englishman's condition.

"I'm OK," said Garth, peering from his sleeping bag. "I just need to sleep."

"Are your dogs still moving?"

The dogs are fine, the sleepy musher assured Lee.

Barry shrugged and continued on. He came across Kuba, a few miles later.

"What about the other guy?" the German asked. "He seemed to be in pretty bad shape. And his dogs won't run."

Lee was perplexed. Should he go back? Garth said he was all right, and he was in his sleeping bag. It was not as if he was collapsed on the trail back there. Barry Lee mushed on.

Fresh snow was blowing. The team's speed slipped as Lee's dogs plowed through half a foot of powder. The musher's low-budget approach was also costing him. He had tough white plastic on his sled runners. The white-coded material lasted longer than the softer black or orange plastic favored by most racers; it was optimum for traveling over bare, rocky terrain. In these conditions, white plastic created friction, which made Lee's sled harder to pull. Most racers would have changed their plastic, but Lee had long ago used up the few spares he had bought in Knik.

Barry wasn't packing much dog food either. He didn't plan for a dinner stop on the 65-mile run to Shageluk. Forced to camp, the musher tossed out snacks. His dogs would just have to hold out until Shageluk for a full meal.

The checkpoint was closed when Barry mushed into the village on the morning of March 13. He found a veterinarian, but the volunteer's plane was already revving for departure. The vet made no effort to hide his eagerness to get to Nome for the finish of the real race.

Lee's anxiety was heightened by the Iditarod official's impatience. Catching Daily and me was becoming absolutely urgent, or so the musher decided. Making a snap decision, he scrapped plans to cook his dogs a meal here and—minutes after arriving in Shageluk—Lee bolted for Anvik. Barry thought the Yukon village lay a mere 18 miles ahead. But he was confusing the upcoming run with the short hop to Grayling. The distance to Anvik was closer to 30 rugged miles.

Up and down the Iditarod Trail, Lee and other weary mushers were making costly mistakes. The grace period was over. Alaska, ever remorseless, indifferent to mortal ambitions, was about to remind us that the games played here are hers alone to call.

Peele found the cabin at Iditarod stifling hot. He slept poorly, wishing he could speed up dawn's approach. He, too, felt rushed. But it didn't make sense trying to leave the old ghost town in the dark. Late in the second week of the race, the tape on the trail markers was often so frosted that it was no longer reflective, or it was torn off entirely by the wind. Assuming, of course, that a particular marker was standing at all for the Iditarod's Red Lantern musher.

Morning brought the light Peele wanted. It also brought wind, and the team smacked into drifts soon after leaving Iditarod. Seeking a boost, Peele dug out his personal stash of caffeine tablets. "This is worth one or two cups of coffee," the musher told himself, swallowing the first pill.

Radio operator Rich Runyan was supposed to close down the checkpoint at Iditarod, then follow the last team over to Shageluk on a snowmachine, towing a sled packed with his electronic gear. He was going to accompany the rear teams through to Unalakleet, a distance of about 350 miles.

The plan had sounded reasonable back at race headquarters. The radio operator from Anchorage hadn't given it much thought while mushers were still on the way to his remote post. His attitude changed after Peele had mushed away Wednesday morning. Listening to the wind, Runyan felt growing flickers of dread. He was alone. Left behind out in the wilderness. Runyan knew his fears were foolish. If he needed to, for any reason, he could fire up his generator-powered radio and talk to the world. This knowledge wasn't enough to dispel the camp's eerie silence, or the whispers from the dark corners of his mind.

By late afternoon, the demons were gaining strength, adding urgency to the volunteer's packing. He keyed the big snowmachine to life. After an agonizing second, the engine caught. Rich Runyan savored that beautiful roar. His confidence surged as he quickly overtook Peele a few miles from the checkpoint. Though his team was crawling, Peele appeared in reasonably good spirits, or so it seemed to Runyan, who gladly accepted the musher's offer of fruit juice. After a brief pause, the radio operator bid the musher and his dogs good-bye and took off, his big snowmachine cutting a new trail through the mounting drifts.

During his second trip up McKinley, nearly a decade before, Peele had frozen his hands so badly that several fingers had turned black. None had to be amputated, but he lost a good deal of feeling, and his hands remained more sensitive to cold weather. Peele wasn't thinking clearly in the hours after Runyan left him. Fatigue and determination combined to induce a sort of madness in the musher. Battling to stay awake, he kept popping caffeine pills. And the musher took off his gloves, figuring that the pain of gripping his icy handlebar would keep him alert.

In the front of the pack, Susan Butcher weighed the risk. A ground blizzard was raging over the ice ahead. These were extreme, life-threatening conditions. Sixty-mile-per-hour winds and temperatures to 30 below combined to produce a wind-chill factor in the 100-below-zero range. Rather than attempt the exposed 40-mile crossing to Koyuk, Iditarod's leader took refuge in a shelter cabin below Lonely Hill, the last finger of land overlooking Norton Bay.

Butcher had mushed from Shaktoolik holding a 45-minute lead over Swenson. He, Osmar, Buser, and Barve caught her at a shelter cabin, where she spent six hours waiting for the wind to drop.

King and Jonrowe left Shaktoolik together, about four and a half hours after Butcher. The storm, moving inland, made for slow going. The pair hadn't got far before they were overtaken by Joe Runyan, whose swift, strong dogs were refreshed after a long rest. Jeff and Dee Dee spurred their teams to chase the tall musher from Nenana, but his team was faster and vanished into the swirling tempest. The storm intensified, at last forcing the pair to turn back.

Joe Runyan spied the camping teams as he approached the shelter cabin at Lonely Hill just before dark. If I can slip by here, he thought, I just might take it. He quietly crept past. For a moment, the wily former champion thought that he might actually escape unnoticed, but then he saw someone—probably from a news agency—running for the cabin door.

Out on the exposed ice, Runyan's breakaway was hampered when his headlamp blinked out. The musher shed his gloves to fix it. Wind instantly burned his moist bare hands. He knew he had to watch it or he'd get frostnipped. Cursing himself for such unprofessional carelessness, Joe put his gloves back on and dug out a spare headlamp. He beat the others to Koyuk, but Joe Runyan's appetite for risk was tempered by that close call.

Nature was keeping the game close. But Susan's team remained unquestionably the strongest. The Butch led the pack out of Koyuk at 7:30 A.M. on Wednesday.

The storm rolled backward along the Iditarod Trail. John Barron left Unalakleet in eighteenth place, behind the same pair of young leaders who had guided his team to victory in the balmy Klondike 200. In the village whose Eskimo name means "where the east wind blows," his leaders were overmatched. Frightened by the gale, they swung his team back toward the shelter of the village, spinning his sled in a circle. Barron's fourteenth Iditarod ended with that futile dance in the wind, less than 300 miles from Nome. This was his best dog team ever, but the dogs' coats were just too thin for a storm like this.

Barron grew protective when a reporter asked for the names of his reluctant lead dogs. "I don't want to say their names," he said. "Put John Barron. It's John Barron's fault. Dogs don't make mistakes. The dogs don't quit. It's always the musher. If there's a problem, it's me."

The radio operator found Garth still wrapped in his sleeping bag. The Englishman hadn't budged since Lee had passed the previous day. Garth had been stuck in the same spot more than 36 hours and accepted that his race was finished.

The Englishman assured Rich Runyan that he wasn't in any immediate danger of dying. But he was critically low on dog food, and his team still wouldn't budge. A previous snowmachiner had promised to send back a rescue party from Shageluk. Garth asked Runyan to make sure that the word got through.

The radio operator pulled back on the throttle and shot into the darkness. He was tired and hungry, but Shageluk couldn't be more than a few hours away.

It was blowing in the hills, covering the trail with loose snow. Runyan repeatedly strayed off course. Each time he got lost, he circled in a widening arc until he found new markers or some sign of the packed trail. It was hard work. The radio operator grew sweaty muscling his big machine through the soft snow. But he was, at least, making progress. Then he smacked a deep, soft drift, firmly planting the nose of the big machine in the snow. The radio operator settled down to await the rescue party Garth had summoned earlier.

Wind, snow, more wind, Peele felt that he was holding his own—until the weather went completely crazy. Rain suddenly poured from the sky. It lasted about 30 seconds, ending as the temperature dive-bombed from zero to 20 below in the time it takes to flip a coin.

Peele was dripping wet, exhausted, and feeling feverish—not to mention cold. His hands were stiff. He couldn't make them work. He was beaten, temporarily at least, and tried to unzip his sled bag, intending to climb inside and warm himself. The zipper was jammed with ice. The musher realized he had to get out of the wind. The only shelter available was the sled itself. Huddling on the sled's lee side, Peele wondered if he was going to die. Getting out the tape recorder he carried in his suit, Bill Peele recorded a message to his wife.

"C'mon, Barry, it's only eighteen miles," I told Lee. "Come with us."

Lee could only wish. He knew too much about sled dogs to risk pushing his exhausted, dehydrated bunch any farther. Daily and I weren't planning to leave Grayling before morning. Lee figured that gave him time to rejoin us for the long Yukon passage. Daily wanted to stay longer, but felt that he had better run for it while there was a strong team ahead. He'd lost all faith in Bogus.

"Can I follow you?" he asked me. "The only way I'll get to Nome is behind you."

The temperature was above zero. Cool, but nice. The gray light was dimming as Barry pulled Rainy and Harley by the neck line toward the street.

"It's supposed to be blowin' pretty hard out on the river," a villager said, while Lee waved good-bye to us.

I was wearing the snowmachine suit over my bibs and about three inches of inner vests and pile garments. The warm layering was standard procedure by now. My parka remained stowed in the sled. The Burn was the only place I'd needed the heavy coat. Leaving Anvik, which was nestled between sheltering hills, there didn't appear to be any cause for taking unusual precautions. Night was approaching, but I didn't notice so much as a breeze.

It was as if the Yukon sensed our presence. The wind rose like an angry grizzly and howled in our faces. Harley and Rainy dropped their ears and looked for a place to escape. The entire team sagged under the wind's terrific onslaught. My dogs were on the verge of curling into balls. Running to the head of the team, I threw Harley, then Rainy, into the wind.

Steeled by my demands, Harley clawed forward on the rock-hard snow, dragging along his more reluctant comrades. Rainy did her part as well, nudging the big dog toward the faint marks left by previous teams. The short 18-mile run became a hellish five-hour march. When I wasn't terrified by the weather, I was appalled by Skidders's torturous limp. The old dog never let up for an instant, pulling like a champion, but at what cost?

At least it wasn't snowing, or the trail would have vanished in drifts. And, thank God, it wasn't any colder. Smarting from windburn, I parked my team across from the Grayling community hall. Daily skidded to a stop close by and staggered from his sled. It was near midnight. There was plenty of straw from the earlier teams. My dogs sniffed through it, pawing together satisfactory nests, then plunked down. In seconds, most were calmly licking their paws. I was reeling myself. That tiny chunk of the Yukon had beat us up, and we faced 130 more miles on that river. The thought made me shudder.

The only Iditarod team in the village belonged to Doc. Williams and Lenthar had apparently left Grayling at roughly the same time that we had pulled out of Anvik. Well, let them go. I'd seen all I wanted of the river that night.

Cooley was ensconced on the carpet of the local kindergarten classroom, one of his perks as an Iditarod official. He was disappointed to hear that Lee had stayed behind. The three of us were rooting for Barry to catch up, but we knew his chances were slim against that wind.

I dragged Doc outside to examine Skidders. Afterward, the veterinarian advised me that the veteran sled dog's minor toe-sprain wasn't necessarily cause to drop him. "Maybe so, but it's killing me to watch him." I petted him as he licked that sore foot. "You got me to the Yukon old man, I think you deserve a vacation." I resolved to ship Skidders home in the morning.

Back in the community hall, Daily stoked the barrel stove until the room resembled a dry sauna. Gear steamed from the rafters. I stretched out on a bench table and soaked in the heat, trying to absorb every possible calorie before our next scheduled bout with the Yukon.

Daily had the blues. He wasn't sure he could face that wind again. He considered scratching. Why be macho about it? He and Fidaa could be in Hawaii right now. With such thoughts on his mind, Tom went out to check on his dogs. He struck up a conversation with a local musher, an Athabaskan who bragged he'd been raised on a dog sled. The Indian was a bitter man. He'd dreamed of running the Iditarod himself, but he said he couldn't find sponsors.

Daily was convinced that the villager was wrong. Any musher supporting a twenty-dog kennel ought to be able to scrape together the extra cash to run the Iditarod. Get that race experience, he told the man, and then shop for sponsors. The villager wouldn't listen. He wasn't interested in merely running the race. He planned to be a contender. Money was all he needed, the villager was sure of that.

Daily left the musher stewing in his bitterness. The conversation reminded Tom how lucky he was. Bring on the Yukon, Hawaii could wait.

Two players were left in the Great Game.

As the defending champ prepared to leave Elim, another dog team was visible on the horizon. Butcher told KTUU's television crew that she hoped it was Swenson. "I think it would be nice. We're both going for our fifth. Why should I race against Runyan? I don't respect him the way I respect Swenson. It's fun to see Rick coming strong."

The odds favored Susan. Rick hadn't won the race since 1982. That was a different era, one in which the Iditarod's champ could confidently boast to Shelley Gill that he would eat his sneakers if a woman ever won the race. But in this year's race Swennie was fighting to the last mile. He was the driver on the horizon at Elim. He pushed through the checkpoint there without stopping and, 26 miles later in Golovin, he was still tracking the Butch like a crazed wolf stalking a polar bear.

For seven years running, the Iditarod had been won by the

first musher into White Mountain, where teams rested a mandatory six hours before sprinting for the finish line, 77 miles ahead. Butcher was poised to make it eight straight as she checked in at 7:30 P.M. on Wednesday night.

Her last challenger, losing ground, didn't reach White Mountain until 8:38 P.M. Asked by a TV crew if he still had a chance, Rick Swenson snorted with disgust. "You guys have got to be realistic," he said. "Christsake, you got a team that's way stronger than mine, and I'm an hour behind her. Only a lightning bolt or something is going to allow me to catch her."

Butcher, camped nearby, radiated confidence as she evaluated her team against the competition. "I'm faster and I'm stronger," she said. "The dogs are happy. They love the coast."

Midnight was approaching in Anvik. Leaving the village, Barry Lee's dogs trotted along briskly. They were refreshed by their five-hour rest. It was the musher who wasn't ready for the raging wind that met his team on the dark river. Barry's cheap parka wasn't the greatest. And the blowing powder reduced visibility to almost nothing. The trail would sure be easier to find in the morning. That decided it. Awarding this round to the Yukon, Lee returned to Anvik.

To us, waiting in Grayling, the news of Barry's retreat seemed like a death knell to his chances. The gap was only 18 miles, but we couldn't risk further delay. Outside, a blizzard was forming.

"Are you absolutely sure about this, Doc?" I shouted, mushing from the village.

The wolf pack was breaking trail. Daily's team held the rear. My dogs were sandwiched in the middle. There was no wind, no sound, just torrents of fat flakes cascading from above, so thick I could hardly breathe.

Cooley laughed. "Oh yeah," he said. "We can handle it."

His leaders were amazing. "Gee, haw, gee, gee. That's right. Go ahead." Cooley directed the wolf pack marker by marker, and our three teams crawled ever deeper into a featureless white sea.

An hour out of Grayling, the snowfall was replaced by a series of wind storms. The sky would darken ahead. A churning white wall would then roll down the river and envelop us, and we couldn't see past the wheel dogs. As quickly as they came, the storms passed on. In the breaks between them, the Yukon stretched before us, a massive alley through the wilderness.

We traveled miles without seeing official trail markers. We relied on cut branches thrust into the snow with unnatural regularity. We guessed that snowmachiners had left these crude guideposts for the same purpose. There was no trail here. If one ever existed on this seldom-traveled stretch of the Yukon, it was forever lost now, buried by two to three feet of powder.

Daily had an old leader named Diamond. The dog was painfully slow and hadn't been much use on good trails, but he took orders with the precision of a marine—the perfect recommendation for this job. So Tom and Cooley rotated the point position. Mushing through the waves of changing weather and beautifully strange light, Tom felt cleansed of his recent blues. Thanks to Diamond, he had something to contribute in this stormy dimension.

It was my turn to feel useless. Neither Rainy nor Harley was much good as a command leader where trails weren't apparent. If I were on my own, it would have been snowshoe time. Rat was usually a good chaser. I put her in lead with Chad to give Rainy and Harley a break. It was warm, at least zero under a clearing bright sky. Cooley accelerated nearing a bend in the river, taking advantage of snow hardened by the wind. Rat kept bumping into Chad. He abruptly sat down.

Concealing my worry, I played with Chad until he decided to humor me. I moved down the line, petting heads and massaging necks until everybody was happy. "All right!" I yelled, catching the sled as it passed.

Both Daily and Cooley had vanished around the curve. As far as Rat was concerned, that canceled the chase. She quit next.

Watching the other teams pull away, I had almost cried out, "Wait, don't leave me!" Pride held my tongue, and now Tom and Doc were gone. I was alone on the Yukon fearing the arrival of another storm. Resisting panic, I calmly placed Rainy and Harley in lead. "All right." The team promptly lurched forward.

Rounding the bend I scanned the horizon. Tom and Doc looked like tiny centipedes far ahead. Again, I battled panic. Please, PLEASE let me catch them. It took us an hour to close the gap. And when I finally approached the others, something strange was afoot. Neither of the teams was moving.

Drawing closer, I made out two sleds, two dog teams, and no mushers. Coasting to a stop, I jammed the hook down and trudged to the closest sled. Doc was on his back, lying on his sled bag. Snoring in the midafternoon sun.

Barry Lee was warned before he left Grayling, where he had re-fueled the team during a four-hour stop. "There's decent trail for about ten miles, after that—nothing," said the checker, who'd surveyed the river on a snowmachine earlier that morning.

"Well, I got the snowshoes, and I gotta go," said Lee, feeling well rested and determined.

Two hours later, his confidence was ebbing. The trail ahead was swamped under two feet or more of loose snow. Lee strapped on his snowshoes. They were borrowed, of course, and he'd never tried them on. The homemade bindings were incorrectly attached. Each time he applied weight, the shoes nosed downward. Lee wore himself out trying to use them. After struggling for several hours, he returned to Grayling to regroup before trying again.

Daylight was going. Tom suggested we start looking for a sheltered camp. Doc wouldn't hear of it. He wanted to reach Blackburn's cabin, an unofficial rest cabin, which couldn't be more than ten miles ahead.

We were out in the middle of the river when the sky rapidly darkened. Gusts of wind slapped at my sled bag. Cooley ordered his wolves toward a bluff that would offer some slight protection. Joining him, we all decided to wait this one out, using the delay to feed our dogs. With any luck, the evening squall would skip past before we were done.

It got colder, and the wind steadily increased. It was 14 below the first time Cooley checked his thermometer. When he checked again, minutes later, the reading was 20 below zero and falling. "Watch your ass," he yelled.

Conditions felt deadly by the time I had water boiling in my cook pot. Standing with my back to the wind and my face shielded by the parka's thick ruff, I carefully poured the hot water inside the cooler. Next, I lined the pans out. Then I sat on the cooler with my back to the wind, letting the food soak.

"Thirty below, boys," Cooley shouted, chuckling.

Moving stiffly, I carried pans to the dogs, two at a time. The snow was soft, and I stumbled, splashing my gloves with the wet food. I felt my fingers burning, but it wasn't from heat. In the brief time it took to fill a pan with steaming food and carry it to a dog, a skin of ice had formed across the surface of the pan. My wet fingertips burned from the extreme cold.

As soon as the dogs finished eating, I collected the empty pans so they wouldn't lick them and freeze their tongues to the metal. Then I climbed inside the sled.

My hands were reduced to the functioning level of pincers as I pulled the sled-bag flap overhead. Yanking my gloves off with my teeth, I surveyed the damage. Seven fingertips were bloodless white. That was better than I had dared hope, nothing more than mild frost-nip. Huddling, I breathed on my hands until they throbbed with renewed life. I shucked the parka and unpacked my sleeping bag. Sealing myself inside the cocoon, I ate another packet of salmon, chewed on a carton of frozen juice, then fell asleep, feeling confident about my hard-earned survival skills.

As he had been for 1,000 miles, Barve, the burly 45-year-old printer, remained in the hunt, leaving Elim Wednesday night. Not that you could tell anything in the blizzard. Visibility was limited to about ten feet when Lavon halted his team to search for markers on foot. His frightened dogs yanked the snow hook. When the musher returned, they were gone. He didn't panic. He could find the damn dogs tomorrow. Survival came first, and it was goddamn cold. Lavon started walking toward Golovin.

On the other side of Elim, Garnie lost his team in similar circumstances, but his mitts were tied to the sled. Joe Garnie, an Inupiat from the coastal village of Teller, knew the enemy he faced. He dug himself a hole in the snow and flopped inside, facedown, conserving his body warmth as he waited for the storm to break. Whenever the creeping cold became unbearable, he ran in circles, waving his arms to get the blood pumping. Then he lay back down in his hole.

Garnie eventually made his way to a survival shelter, where he found snowmachiners tending a hypothermic Matt Desalernos.

On the ice between Shaktoolik and Koyuk, half a dozen mushers were lost for nearly 24 hours, including Barron's 21-year-old son, Laird. Pinned down by the storm, mere yards from a shelter cabin he couldn't see, the young musher's bid for rookie-of-the-year collapsed. All he'd take home from this rite of passage was a partially frozen foot.

Terry Adkins's bold ambitions perished out on the ice fronting Koyuk. He was reduced to huddling with fellow racer Gary Whittemore, who was shivering, badly hypothermic. Whittemore probably would have died without the Montanan's help.

In Shaktoolik, two race volunteers shared the suffering, frostbiting their eyelids loading dropped dogs on a plane. In Nome, Thursday's temperature was 20 below zero, with winds of 55 miles per hour.

Race marshal Kershner sounded beleaguered as he discussed the known injuries and reports of missing mushers. "I feel like a mother who's trying to gather her chicks," he told reporters.

Jeff Dixon fired up his snowmachine and left Shageluk on what he believed was a simple dog-food delivery mission. His duties kept expanding. First, he helped that fool from Anchorage, Rich Runyan, free his snowmachine from the drift. Next he found the Englishman with the starving dogs. Then Dixon had to go save Peele, whom he found sleeping on the ground outside his sled.

"You know those Iditarod people don't care about you at all," Dixon told Peele, shaking him awake. "They left you to die out here."

Runyan didn't spend long regrouping in Shageluk. He had ground to make up. At first light, he left for Anvik on his big snowmachine, towing the freight sled loaded with radio gear. Conditions worsened and, before long, Rich was lost again. Cruising atop a ridge, he glimpsed what appeared to be a marker in the valley below. Descending for closer inspection, he plowed into a deceptively large drift. He wrestled with it for a while, but it was no good. The snowmachine was stuck again.

Rich Runyan hadn't eaten for hours. It was miserably cold,

and hypothermia was becoming a definite threat. True, he still had that big radio, but he lacked the energy to assemble it. Unpacking his sleeping bag, the ham operator from Anchorage placed a call to the Lord.

Butcher's dogs were reluctant to leave their cozy beds of straw. The air at White Mountain carried an angry scent that night. The calm when she arrived had given way to a heavy wind blowing snow across the trail. It didn't bother Susan. She had an appointment to keep in Nome. At the precise minute her six-hour waiting period expired, 1:31 A.M., Thursday, March 14, she had her dogs on the march.

Iditarod's defending champion got off to a rocky start. Before her team faded from view, spectators saw Butcher jump off her sled several times to lead her team back to the trail. Her husband, Dave Monson, wasn't particularly concerned as he watched her exit. Dogs facing such a crush of media and fans had good reason to act skittish. His wife was still driving the best team in the race.

Minutes after the champ's departure, a snowmachiner roared into the checkpoint.

"You can't see anything out there," he said.

The storm rolled in as Swenson packed to go. It was 30 below, snowing and blowing hard, as he mushed out of White Mountain, one hour, seven minutes behind Butcher. The final chase was underway.

Joe Runyan was the third musher out. Susan had the fastest team. Nobody could catch her. Joe accepted that, but he fully expected to catch Swenson. And he did, passing far to one side of Rick's team, which had obviously strayed from the trail. That was understandable. Conditions were unbelievably bad. Runyan hoped the trail ahead was decently marked. His sled was stripped for a sprint to the finish line. He wasn't packed for camping.

Peele collapsed on the floor of the Shageluk village school.

"What do you want to do?" asked a checker.

"I can't leave, because I can't get my hands to work," the musher said, feeling morose.

Peele stalled through the day. He nursed his dogs, his aching body and spirit, hoping for a palatable solution where none existed. Forty-eight hours after limping into the village, the rookie from North Carolina signed the paperwork, adding his name to the scratch list, its numbers now having swelled to fourteen.

There was no uncertainty about Alan Garth's status. From the moment the Englishman had accepted a ride on the snow-machine, leaving his dog team behind, he had become subject to disqualification. To his credit, Garth joined the village rescue party that left Shageluk Friday and saved those Redington dogs.

Swenson didn't even see the other dog team. His leaders trotted straight through the string of sleepy, snow-covered sled dogs. He wasn't aware of the other team, parked crosswise blocking the trail near Fish River Flats, until his sled was nearly upon them. Then he wondered if he was hallucinating. That was Slugo he saw resting there—one of Susan Butcher's dogs.

A red suit with a dark fur collar popped out of the covered sled like a jack-in-the-box. It was Susan. Not sure what to make of this, Swenson shouted that he was continuing on. He got less than a mile before his headlamp gave out. Stripping off his gloves, the musher attempted to change the bulb, but had trouble seeing through his frosty eyelashes, and his hands instantly stiffened. His bare flesh couldn't withstand the wind, which carried a chill factor of 90 below zero. Appalled and angry at this careless injury, Swenson jammed his frost-nipped hands inside his snowpants to warm them.

Rick, helplessly stalled, saw another headlamp approaching from behind. It was Susan. She berated Swenson for leaving her without even checking to see whether she was all right. Butcher parked her team and helped Rick fix his headlamp. She explained that she had driven through here earlier trying to reach Timber, a sheltered area where the wind never blows, but that she'd turned back after losing the trail. The savage storm had engineered the unthinkable. Some 70 miles from Iditarod's finish line, Rick and Susan, the sport's celebrated rivals, agreed to stick together.

Swenson took the lead. The wind was so intense that he rode with his head turned to the left, protecting his face with the ruff. His leaders kept following the light to the side, and he repeatedly had to pull them back on the trail. Butcher was having the same troubles behind him. And then she was gone. No dogs. No headlamp. Swennie saw nothing behind him but swirling snow.

Cooley opened his eyes just in time. Daily's figure was shrinking in the distance. The musher was on foot, his dogs apparently abandoned. Reflecting on his own misery, Doc was seized by the conviction that Tom—gripped by a suicidal impulse—was marching to his death. The veterinarian leaped from his sled.

Sheltered by the river bend, Daily hastily squatted in the snow and attended to what was, indeed, a personal emergency. He was pulling up his pants when Cooley rounded the corner.

"Tom, . . . I thought—" gasped Cooley, panting from his sprint. Then he noticed the steaming evidence of Daily's vitality.

They both began to giggle.

Martin Buser was astonished. The shrewd Swiss musher had departed White Mountain at 5:30 A.M., holding scant hope of catching any of the four teams ahead. Yet, hard as it was to be-lieve, here was Susan of all people, emerging from the blinding gale, returning toward the checkpoint.

"Hey, you're going the wrong way, girl."

"It's not doable, Martin," replied Butcher, mentioning that she feared for Swenson's life. Lost as he was out there. "What are you going to do?"

"Well, I think I will give it a try," said Buser.

Tim Osmar and Joe Runyan materialized from the storm next. Like the champ, both were returning to White Mountain. They urged Buser to give it up. To take shelter at the checkpoint until the weather broke.

Declining the invitations, Buser drove onward. He'd waited for this chance at redemption, at erasing the memory of the opportunity he had blown the year Redington faltered.

In the 1988 race, Buser's young hounds had slowly but surely run down Smokin Joe's team. They nipped at Redington's heels all the way down the Yukon. The old musher's dogs remained swift, but he was having increasing trouble staying awake. Redington gave it his best, retaking the lead several times between Ruby and Kaltag. But he wasn't going to win.

The only one with a chance to stop Butcher that year was Martin Buser, an intense Swiss expatriate who was making his first appearance in the Iditarod's front pack. Swenson was root-ing for him, indeed, for anyone who could halt Butcher's drive for three straight wins. He sent word that Martin should go ahead and use the lightweight racing sled he had waiting on the coast.

Leaving Shaktoolik, Buser actually led Butcher by nearly an hour. The sun was sinking, throwing rosy shadows across the ice. Photographer Rob Stapleton and I followed Butcher out of town on a snowmachine. She was all business in her red jumpsuit. Her team looked strong. Her lead dog, Granite, owned this section of the trail.

Then a ground blizzard swept across the front pack. Buser became disoriented and was lost for hours in the whiteout. When it lifted, Butcher held a commanding lead.

"I've gotten sleep all over the place," she said, claiming the crown. "I don't even feel like I've been in an Iditarod race."

Looking haggard and disgusted, Swenson trailed her into Nome, saying that he "felt a little bad about beating Martin." Buser finished a distant third, his face a wind-burned mask of regret.

In the three years since that disappointment, Buser hadn't ever come close to duplicating that showing. Other mushers faulted his breeding program. Too much hound in those dogs, they said. The breed can't handle coastal wind.

Watching Susan and the others retreating, Martin Buser reeled from the opportunity now before him. Far from being frightened, he heard a magnificent, enthralling, victory song riding this storm.

Back at White Mountain, Butcher described how she had marked Swenson's last known location with an X in the snow, in case snowmachiners launched a search.

"If Rick's got a leader with the will to get him through, more power to him," she told a *Times* reporter. "I don't think he had much hope when I last saw him."

At the tail end of the field, Barry Lee made a deal. Two villagers in Grayling would bust a new trail to Eagle Island on their snowmachines, and he agreed to pay for their gas. The last musher in the field repacked for the Yukon with new determination. Next stop, Eagle Island.

Right off the bat, Lee noticed that his dogs looked feeble. The team's confidence was shot from the recent turnabouts. It was a dispirited bunch that stumbled out of Grayling along the familiar river trail. Barry resorted to the easy two-hours on, two-hours off, schedule he had used during the first days of the race. This time it failed to perk up the dogs. The team's progress remained dismal. Twelve hours of effort netted Lee barely 20 miles.

Less than an hour past our wretched Yukon camp, we found the cabin Doc had talked about the night before. The owners, David and Mona Blackburn, had amazing news.

"Have you heard? Swenson passed Butcher in a storm."

After they became separated, Swenson apparently figured that Butcher had made use of the blinding conditions to pass him. That suspicion seemed confirmed since his leaders soon regained their confidence, acting as if they were chasing another team. The wind faded as Rick neared the cabin at Timber, where the snowfall reminded him of flakes in a Christmas ball. The 12-mile trip from White Mountain had taken three hours. Now the musher was presented with a mystery. Eight inches of fresh snow rested on the ground, and it was completely free of tracks. How could that be? Swenson wondered. Was Susan lost?

After a brief rest, Swenson continued. Emerging from the sheltering trees, the trail reentered the wind. There weren't any markers to follow, and the team strayed into a willow patch. Swenson cautiously backtracked until he found a reflective marker. He was again on track, but the musher knew he had to be careful. Visibility was so bad he couldn't even see his own feet. None of his lead dogs could be trusted here.

Clipping together a handful of spare neck lines, the musher attached himself to the front of the dog team. He was the leader now. Advancing from marker to marker, Swenson led his dogs onward. The wind remained blinding. The dogs repeatedly knocked him down, surging forward faster than he could walk.

His driverless sled kept lurching into the team and causing tangles. Was this all worth it? the 40-year-old musher asked himself. Thoughts of his strained marriage and the years of humiliation provided him with his answer. Death on the Iditarod Trail would be better than giving in now, Rick Swenson vowed.

He was resting on the ridge, with his hood ruff flapping in the wind, when a bright light approached. He assumed it was Butcher and felt drained. But the light belonged to a snowmachiner.

"Where are the others?" Swenson asked the driver.

"They all turned back."

Twenty-three hours after leaving White Mountain, a slow-moving musher, with his parka collar sealed up to his nose, stood by the Burl Arch in a glare of floodlights, stiffly waving to the crowd cheering his arrival at the Iditarod's finish line at 1:35 A.M., March 15.

"I walked a long, long way leading the dogs," said Swenson, his weary voice amplified through a public address system. "It was cold. It was not a pleasant night." The musher's energy returned as he discussed Butcher's decision to turn back in the storm. "Maybe she's gotten a little bit soft with four victories under her belt," he said, prompting a whistling clamor on Front Street. The Iditarod's all-time champ wasn't finished. "She's going to have to get SIX now—if she wants to be the top dog."

The news of his victory staggered us. It wasn't so much the idea that Rick had beaten Susan. It was the sheer notion that anyone was in Nome—while we had another 450 miles to go.

The Blackburns treated our shock with a heavy dose of bush hospitality. Picking up a fork to eat breakfast, I felt as if I was dining at a resort. The sausage was spicy and charred, just the way I like it. The orange juice was thick and painfully tart. It was hard to believe the Yukon was right outside waiting for us.

It was a clear, starry night. The temperature on the Yukon registered 35 below as Barry Lee crawled into his sleeping bag. The situation was daunting, but he remained hopeful. Between the temperature and the prevailing calm, the trail ought to firm up by morning, and that might help a lot. A hard, fast trail would do wonders for his dogs' spirits.

A shrieking wind awakened Barry three hours later. "Oh, my God," the musher whispered, sticking his head out of the sled bag. It was blowing again. And it was warmer, much warmer out, maybe zero—a sure sign another storm was coming.

Lee got a rude surprise when he slipped on his bunny boots. The left toe was rock hard. A crack must have developed in the rubber vapor barrier. Moisture had seeped inside and frozen, destroying the borrowed boot's insulation.

Lee headed his team up the trail. He had gone two or three miles before the tracks left by the snowmachiners disappeared in new drifts. The powder was as deep here as anything he'd seen. The situation was spinning out of control. Barry figured that Eagle Island was 35 miles farther. He had cooked every bit of food he had the night before, gambling that full bellies would carry his dogs the distance in a single hard march. That plan seemed wildly optimistic now. Conditions weren't necessarily better on the trail behind him, where new drifts probably covered his path. Aware that a wrong decision here could prove fatal, Barry Lee turned to the one advisor who never failed him.

"God," prayed the musher, "every other clue up the line has told me to go on. What's going on here? Am I supposed to finish this race?"

Lee received an immediate response, a message sensed, rather than heard.

"No."

The answer was so emphatic, Lee decided that his personal fears were talking. He asked again. "Am I supposed to finish this race?"

"NO." He actually heard that. "YOU NEED TO GO HOME."

Barry turned his leaders around for the last time. It was 25 miles back to the village, and every step became a battle. Lee was soaking wet and shivering. His foot was cold. His dogs rubbed hair off their hind legs plowing through the crusty drifts, but the musher kept driving them. He had no choice. He had no food to give them, and they were weakening by the hour.

Four miles out of Grayling, Barry Lee emptied everything but his sleeping bag out of the sled. He wanted to shave every spare ounce. It was going to be close, he knew, but the dogs would make it. He was now confident of that much.

Oddly enough, the musher drew some comfort from the day's hardship. His unseen advisor was wise. This team never would have made it to Eagle Island. He had a season of mistakes to learn from. For now, retreat offered the only path toward salvation.

Doc's wolf pack was faltering. After Blackburn's cabin, the signs of stress were becoming unmistakable. Up and down his gang line Cooley's dogs flopped on their backs, squirming in the snow with each pause. Their snarls and squabbling showed that the dogs weren't fatigued in the physical sense. We weren't traveling fast enough to tire his leased champions. But even the best lead dogs can only take so much pressure.

Daily shared the trail-breaking duties on this warm, sunny afternoon. But his old leader was slower than a glacier. It drove Doc crazy following the other team. He couldn't take more than a mile of Tom's creeping pace before impatiently reclaiming the lead, and then Cooley's leaders would resume their games. At one point, Doc was trying to change his leaders in the deep snow when he tripped and fell, completely burying himself. The veterinarian popped back up, cursing, laughing, and almost crying as he spit out snow. My offer to put on snowshoes and blaze the trail myself didn't help.

"Snowshoes? God no," Cooley said, horrified. "We'll be out here forever."

In a deep section between two islands, we came across a half-buried bicycle. The powdery river had evidently defeated the specially rigged twin tires on each wheel. Judging from the tracks, the rider had continued on foot. We braced ourselves for the appearance of a body. Instead, we soon encountered an Athabaskan trapper traveling by snowmachine. Watching the winds the day before, the Indian from Grayling knew that any mushers left on the river had to be struggling. He'd come out scouting for us.

The trapper dug into his supplies, and, in short order, we three were sipping hot coffee and chewing strips of dried salmon. And the Indian had surprising news. A "whole bunch of teams" were still camping at Eagle Island, and the checkpoint lay little more than an hour away by dog team, he said.

I was famished and complimented the trapper on the salmon.

"You like them? Help yourself," he said, handing me a baggy filled with the chewy strips.

Gunning his snowmachine, the trapper looped around and streaked back toward Eagle Island, repacking our new trail.

Swennie's victory produced a weeklong orgy of front-page stories and special in-state broadcast reports. Elsewhere his victory was briefly noted, then the race swiftly faded from attention. The fate of the 50-odd teams left on the trail hardly rated a

mention. Even in Alaska, most of the sports-page ink was devoted to baseball spring training, now entering its meaningless
second week.

Four time zones away, television station WDCA played up Washington D.C.'s local Iditarod angle one last time. My participation
in the race had already been the subject of several local television and newspaper reports. Now WDCA combined their interviews with my family with a home video of the start and a
network story about Swenson's victory. Assuming the Iditarod
was over for everyone, the station erroneously reported that
Washington's musher had finished in sixtieth place.

As the newscast drew to a close, the anchors bantered about
the incredible sequence of events that had placed me—the son of
a once-prominent D.C. attorney—on a dog sled in Alaska.

"At least he's not a lawyer," anchor Jim Vance said.

CHAPTER **9**

The Kaltag Eleven

Dusk was near as I parked in the Iditarod village taking root in the slough. "HOW LONG DO YOU PLAN TO STAY?" asked Eagle Island checker Ralph Conatser, a hard look in his eyes. Dogs were sleeping or stretching over long beds of straw. Smoke rose from several campfires. Heaps of supply sacks and trash were scattered in the crusty, urine-stained snow.

The stormy 60-mile trek up the Yukon had taken us more than 30 hours. Conatser tensed as I described our ordeal, mentioning that the dogs needed a good rest. He relaxed as I added, "So we won't be pulling out until tomorrow morning."

"Oh, that would be fine, just fine," said the checker in a much warmer tone.

The scowl returned as Conatser gestured at the other dog teams scattered nearby. Terhune, Linda Plettner, Sepp Herrman, Don and Catherine Mormile had been camping on the island for the past three days. Mark Williams, Gunnar Johnson, and Urtha Lenthar had been in residence nearly that long. Friday's addition of Doc, Daily, and me brought to eleven the total number of dog teams crowding Conatser's peaceful retreat. He and his wife even had a visiting cyclist. After intercepting the three of us, the trapper had found Bob, the owner of the abandoned bicycle, struggling up the river on foot, through waist-deep powder. The amused trapper had given the failed Idita-cycler a lift to the checkpoint.

The crowd itself wasn't unusual. Twice that many Iditarod teams had jammed into the slough after Runyan lead the first wave last Sunday. But hardly seven hours had passed before King launched most of those teams on a new stampede up the Yukon. Mushers traveling in the rear of the field were different, said Conatser. They weren't racers. They were campers. Look at those wood fires burning in his slough! These damn campers would clear-cut his entire island if he didn't watch out.

"Some of these people act like they're never going to leave. They're eating us out of house and home. And we got one woman here who's driving me crazy."

"Daily and I have been chasing these guys for weeks," I said. "Don't worry. Now that we've caught up, we won't be sticking around."

The checker invited us to come by his cabin after we finished with the dogs. "Haven't got much left, but my wife will fix you something. I'm glad somebody here remembers the Iditarod is a race."

Jon Terhune hadn't forgotten. As Daily, Doc, and I arrived, the irritable Soldotna musher was tightening the straps, resealing his sled bag. Stuck in this lousy slough since Wednesday, Terhune was anxious to escape. He was sick of listening to Linda Plettner, sick of that Gunnar kid, the Mormiles, and those others. He thought they were a bunch of sorry whiners, every one of them. He planned to ditch them once and for all.

Earlier that afternoon, Terhune and the other seven mushers encamped at Eagle Island had pitched in $50 apiece and hired the trapper to break a new trail to Kaltag. They were unaware that Niggemyer, the race manager, had already cut a deal with the trapper, filling his snowmachine with gas for that same mission. The trapper kept a straight face as the mushers approached him with their request. They wanted him to wait until morning, but the trapper was impatient to get back to Grayling. The trip north was hundreds of miles out of the way. So the trapper struck out for Kaltag that evening, carrying his unexpected $400 bonus.

Another cold night was forecast on the river, at least 30 below. Plettner and the others resolved to wait until daylight, giving the trail more time to set. Terhune thought they were fools.

"Screw you people," he said, stomping out of the stove-heated mushers' quarters. "I'm leaving."

Plettner, Herrman, and the Mormiles felt differently. They were angered at Conatser's refusal to share supplies abandoned by previous teams, and his stinginess in doling out alcohol for their stoves. Several went so far as to accuse the checker of creating the shortage by bartering away his checkpoint reserves. They had complained to Iditarod as a group.

Before we arrived, Bill Chisholm had flown in to Eagle Island to sort out the dispute. The race judge had marching orders from Kershner to get the trailing pack teams moving. Accordingly, Chisholm not only backed up Conatser's decisions on supplies; he warned the mushers not to expect special help. The visit ended in a confrontation between Herrman and Chisholm, a neighbor of Swennie's who was familiar with the German's hard-ass reputation as a dog trainer and Brooks Range survivalist.

"Sepp," the race judge said, "I bet you never see the coast."

The comment infuriated Herrman, whose pride was already suffering from mistakes he had made early in the race. True, he hadn't pushed his dogs. He'd been playing nursemaid ever since the starting line. But Sepp no longer doubted that he'd make it to Nome, if only to spit in the judge's face.

There were hard feelings all the way around. I wasn't about to take sides. Herrman and the other mushers were foolish to ask for official help. I'd seen that lesson played out many times.

"From the moment Swenson crossed under that arch, we've been on borrowed time," I warned the group. "Iditarod is going to want to wrap up the race—any way they can. If we want to get to Nome, we have to take care of ourselves. Ask for food, fuel, anything—and you're risking disqualification. I've seen it happen."

The others seemed surprised. They weren't considering the logistics supporting our extended adventure. This was day 14. More than a dozen mushers were already in Nome celebrating with Swenson. The support network of veterinarians, pilots, ham-radio operators, and other volunteers was already fragmenting. The majority of these volunteers came from Anchorage or other urban areas. The thrill of providing us with 24-hour service, sleeping on hard floors, and eating camp meals was, by now, wearing thin. The big award banquet in Nome, due to start at about six on Sunday evening, marked the end of the race for most people involved.

Even so, our situation looked pretty good to me. We had Doc Cooley, our own private veterinarian. We could expect help from Iditarod supporters in the villages ahead, where our supplies were still waiting. Most important, within the group here we had the sheer dog power needed to break our own trail to Nome. Strength in numbers was something Daily, Doc, and I keenly appreciated after our hard-fought drive from Grayling.

"I can't BELIEVE they're waiting for us," Daily confided later, echoing my own thoughts. "But it sure is nice."

The Yukon swallowed the trail before his eyes. Terhune was discouraged, but refused to backtrack. Every mile brought him closer to Nome and farther away from those slackers in the slough.

Grueling hours later, the musher saw a light approaching. It was weaving like crazy, left and right, left and right. As it drew closer, the light straightened out, taking a direct line toward him. It was the trapper on his snowmachine. The man had lost the trail on the return trip from Kaltag. He was searching for it when he spotted Terhune's headlamp.

"You're the only one that came?" shouted the trapper, doubting the evidence of his own eyes.

Terhune shrugged.

The trapper's freight sled was loaded with extra cases of Heet alcohol fuel, which he was delivering to the checkpoint back at Eagle Island. He unpacked a handful of bottles and gave them to Terhune. The trail was open, the villager said, but he didn't think it would last. "Try and avoid the places where it goes back and forth," he added, "because I've been lost for an hour."

In the middle of the night, the trapper threw open the door to our warm room on Eagle Island and staggered inside. Clutching an open bottle of liquor, he stumbled over the mushers slumbering in his path.

"What're you all doing here?" he shouted, quite drunk. "Put inna trail alla way to Kaltag. You shoulda gone. Shoulda gone."

At the river's edge, the trail disappeared—no other word fit. Rainy cast about, perplexed. I ran to the front of the team and calmed her, searching for clues in the hard white crust. Nine dog teams had come this way in the last hour or so—channeled along the river through about eight winding miles of waist-high brush. Not a sign of the traffic remained. Wind whipping across the exposed flats had erased every scratch, every pawprint of their passage.

A churning white cloud swallowed the river ahead. It was a ground blizzard, a surface-hugging soup of wind-whipped powder. My team was perched on the edge of a gray-white limbo, violent and surreal. Our vantage point on the brink offered no refuge, nor did the scrubby bushes behind us. We were horribly exposed to the wind raking the frozen river. The dogs didn't like the looks of this. If I wanted to avoid a forced camp, we had to keep moving.

I took Rainy and Harley by the neck line, preparing to lead them by foot, when Daily's frightened voice cut through the storm.

"Wait, wait," he cried, halting his dogs behind mine. "My hand is frozen!"

Fresh out of the checkpoint, Tom had noticed his hands felt cold in those high-tech gloves. Stripping off the outer shells, he inserted a chemical hand warmer into each mitt. That effort was undermined by spindrift powder, which instantly collected on his thin polypropylene inner liners. With the shells back on, the snow melted, and Daily's hands became soaked, and his fingers became even colder. He forced the discomfort from his mind, waiting for the little chemical packs to kick in. That stoicism proved misguided; one of the warmers was a dud.

Coming up behind me, Daily rudely discovered that he couldn't even flex the fingers on his chilled hand.

My dogs were lying down in the wind. Not understanding his predicament, I angrily urged him to hurry.

"Give me five minutes."

"Make that two minutes," I snapped. "Tom, we gotta go!"

I ran back and helped Daily swap his wet liner for a dry one, slipping another warmer in the mitt. As the two of us fumbled, the dogs on both teams began digging in, instinctively carving shelters from the drifts.

"I think we should consider turning around," said Tom, flexing his stiff hand inside a mitt, uncertain whether it was damaged.

"We are NOT going back!" I declared, angry that he would even suggest such a thing. "We're two hours out—that's two hours closer to Nome."

If I had to weather another storm, I wanted to do it right there, without surrendering an inch. The situation was infuriating. After all the trouble we had gone through to catch those other teams, here Tom and I were in last place again, falling farther behind by the minute. And why? Patching harnesses might have cost me a few minutes, but that wasn't the main reason. It was because we sat on our asses and let the others get away—that's why! I'd be damned before I'd turn around.

Sensible as ever, Daily was equally adamant. This was a terrible place to stop. Dogs couldn't rest here. There was no way to feed them. What if the storm didn't break for hours? Or days? We risked weakening our dogs through exposure. It made more sense, he felt, to regroup in the shelter of the slough. He didn't mention his concerns about the hand; it stung, at least that was a good sign.

The two of us were going at it when Cooley unexpectedly mushed up from behind. The dog-driving veterinarian had been detained at the Conatsers' cabin, where he had used the couple's radio phone to confer with Iditarod headquarters.

"Why'd you stop?"

We hurriedly explained the situation.

Doc shook his head. "I don't do reverse!" he shouted, grinning through frosty whiskers.

With a sharp command, Cooley ordered the wolf pack on by, passing our already snow-covered dogs. Showing nary a trace of hesitation, his team marched into the shrieking void. Daily, whose hand was now wonderfully pliable, and I quickly roused our dogs and chased him.

Terhune followed wind-bent trail markers into a narrow slough. Something about the shape of the drifts here made him edgy. The snow was a bit too wavy, too sculpted. He didn't care to imagine the sort of wind conditions required to create this special effect.

Jon was aware that his dogs were nearing their limit. What about that deserted fish camp not too far back? The old buildings weren't much to look at, but they offered some shelter from the wind. He grabbed his leaders and turned the team around.

Terhune rested the dogs through most of Sunday, waiting for the wind to break. An opening finally came in late afternoon. He took advantage of the calm, but trail conditions proved awful. If a base existed under the waist-deep powder, the musher couldn't find it. He was angry at his bad luck, tired, and deeply depressed. Four hundred miles distant, Nome seemed impossibly far.

We caught Plettner's group by midafternoon Saturday. The sky was supremely clear. The Yukon stretched before us, a broad field of glistening white bordered on either side by tiny lines of trees. Our ten-team convoy slowly inched up the massive river's center. The place made the Big Su look like a racquetball court.

Daily and I remained at the caboose end of the convoy. It was an extraordinary scene. The chain of dog teams stretched a half-mile or more ahead, forming a line of brightly colored caterpillars crossing a desolate white prairie. From my sled runners, I banged off pictures of the procession, catching dog teams arrayed in an arc, stretching from my wheel dogs to the trailbreakers mushing across the distant horizon.

Sepp Herrman's team abruptly peeled away from the convoy. "I will catch you when I please," he shouted. Quickly and efficiently, the German made camp on the frozen river. The convoy had barely gained a mile before a wisp of smoke curled from Sepp's cook pot.

I'd left Eagle Island packing a full cooler of hot dog food. I fed the team a real meal during one of the convoy's many lengthy delays. It was an eat-and-run situation. I collected the pans as fast as the dogs finished their food. As I picked up Denali's, the ornery cuss bit my hand. Furious, I bopped him with the pan.

"You ungrateful son of a bitch! I saved your life."

Watching him slink away, I realized that the earlier pack judgment was right. I resolved to drop the ungrateful slacker the moment we hit Kaltag.

Late in the afternoon, Daily spotted Herrman's team closing in from behind. The trapper's reappearance drew an immediate reaction from the front of the convoy. Like the children's game of telephone, a message was relayed from musher to musher down the line: "Send up, Sepp."

"Gee," Herrman said, sending his finely trained leaders jumping out of the trench. "Haw." The leaders executed a neat left-hand turn and bounded forward, passing us with hardly a sideways glance. I whistled in appreciation.

"Now, that's a dog team," I told my own crew. "From now on that's the kind of performance I'm going to expect from you guys."

The summons to the head of the convoy marked a turning point for Herrman. The long break at Eagle Island had wrought a welcome change. Tails were up. His leaders were eager to go.

"I have a team back," Herrman mused, watching his dogs muscle through the deep snow. He mushed past Cooley and Plettner and kept moving straight up the Yukon. Within a few minutes the convoy lurched forward again, with a noticeable burst of speed.

Entering a slough, I saw a dog team on the side of the trail. Word passed back that it was Jon Terhune. I'd never met him before, but I noticed that the gaunt, bearded musher looked pained as the others loudly hailed him. Biting his lip, Terhune fell in behind Daily and me, driving the last dogs in line on the Iditarod Trail.

Call it the Yukon's farewell kiss. Rising from nowhere, a freak storm enveloped us. Even Herrman was impressed by the sudden unannounced blast. One second he was gazing at the lights of Kaltag. The next, he was battling a windstorm more intense than any he'd ever seen in the Brooks Range, a wilderness known for its extreme weather.

Sepp's trapline-tough dogs fought their way clear of the localized maelstrom. The rest of us slammed to a dead stop. Chaos descended on the convoy. Mushers were stomping around, yelling at their dogs and jerking lines. All for naught. Survival genes took over as the wind sent our dogs digging for shelter.

My brain may have been foggy from fatigue, but the storm seemed to sweep us into a different surreal dimension. It wasn't cold or frightening, just weird. Snow drifts reached out and engulfed our convoy like an advancing giant amoeba. Dogs and mushers were transformed into strange statues. Cyrus, still on his feet, whined and jerked on the gang line. My powerhouse pup didn't like the sea of snow rising around him. Daily hugged one of his dogs, and the two melded together. I slapped myself and rubbed my eyes, but the fantasy world remained.

Then, for the fourth time in the race, I dumped my sled and climbed inside.

Barry Lee slept on his decision to scratch. In the morning, he again prayed while attending the Sunday service at Grayling's Arctic Mission, but nothing was added to that "go home" message.

Lee's remaining doubts were resolved by a telephone conversation with Niggemyer in Nome.

"Barry," the race manager said, "there's a lot of guys getting belt buckles this year who are missing pieces of themselves. I can't help you back there."

Lee signed the damn papers and began dealing with the logistics of flying his dog team home from a Yukon River village. And what about that gear he'd abandoned on the river? The cooker alone was worth an easy $100. Lee, awash in the personal and financial ruins of his dream, couldn't afford to throw away anything valuable.

The musher tracked down Rich Runyan, who was recuperating before tackling the Yukon again. Coming out of Anvik, the wind had blown so hard, the radio operator had crouched down on the big snowmachine and barreled up the frozen river with his eyes closed. Closed! It was crazy, but he couldn't see where he was going anyway.

The sky was, for the moment, clear. Runyan felt sorry for Barry and agreed to help him with a salvage mission. The men disconnected the sled loaded with radio equipment and hooked Lee's empty dogsled to the snowmachine. Riding double, they buzzed out of the village.

The river cache was easy to find. From half a mile or more away, Lee could see two men digging his castoffs out of the drifts. It was the trapper and Bob the bicyclist. Their snowmachine had run out of gas returning down the Yukon. After walking nearly ten miles, the pair had found Lee's tracks, followed by odd pieces of wind-blown gear. They were in the process of searching the drifts for a sled and, possibly, a body.

Trading misadventures, the four Yukon survivors had a good laugh at each other's expense. Runyan's snowmachine could only carry one passenger at a time. Leaving Lee to repack the dogsled, Runyan ferried the trapper back to the village.

Bob was in no mood to wait. Vowing to hoof it to Grayling, he strapped on Lee's old snowshoes. Barry warned him about the screwy bindings, but Bob the bicyclist—showing the same spirit that had got him this far—wouldn't listen. The musher smiled as he watched Bob stumble several hundred sweaty yards before finally admitting defeat. The two waited together on the river for Runyan's return.

"All right, who's got my headlamp?" Terhune demanded, scanning the mushers slowly stirring in Kaltag's mushers' quarters.

No one paid him much attention. Most of us were bleary-eyed, struggling to collect our thoughts and gear following painfully short naps in the bunks upstairs.

I was depressed by the news that Barry Lee had scratched in Grayling. It was an ugly day. We hardly finished cooking dog food before the Kaltag checker, operating on orders from Iditarod, had advised us to leave using a tone appropriate for a sheriff delivering an eviction notice. Daily had called him on it, chiding the villager for being "a lackey for race headquarters." After traveling 18 hours in storm conditions, few of us were in the mood to be rushed. Cooley had bought us the nap time, telling Iditarod headquarters that, in his opinion as a race veterinarian, an afternoon of rest was essential for the dogs.

My first priority was to arrange for Denali's departure. Entrusting the ungrateful mutt to the checker, I took the opportunity to phone in my third trail column. "Forget what you hear about the Last Great Race being over," I dictated. "It's far from over. . . ."

The piece recounted my Yukon adventures, from the trek with Daily and Cooley to the convoy's night in the Arctic twilight zone. "Some people think traveling in the back of the Iditarod pack is a camping trip," I concluded. "This is an ordeal."

Back in the newsroom, the Coach—disgusted by my miserable progress to date—was pleased as he peeked in the file and read about my argument with Daily upon leaving Eagle Island.

"O'D might make it after all," the Mowth announced.

Even without my efforts, the large block of teams traveling in the rear of Iditarod's field was attracting notice. An Anchorage television station was referring to us as "the Kaltag Ten." The number was derived from the official standings released by race headquarters. We knew better. There were eleven Iditarod teams in our convoy. He may have ducked the hoopla in Anchorage, but Doc Cooley was an Iditarod musher now, or none of us deserved to make the claim.

By midafternoon Sunday, the dogs had had six to eight hours of rest, which meant that nap time was over for the mushers. Weather reports carried a strong argument for haste. Another storm was coming.

From the Yukon, the Iditarod Trail climbed a 1,000-foot pass into the Nulato Hills. According to local villagers, the snow was deep on this side of the pass, but slippery thin on the other. A party of Kaltag trappers set out on snowmachines to break a trail for us. We had to get moving before the storm erased their work.

Tom Daily was in a lousy mood. He had squandered his nap time standing in line to make obligatory phone calls, but hadn't spoken with anyone—no one was home. Cooley, on the other hand, was strangely buoyant. Mixing a cup of hot Tang by the stove, Doc mocked our hardships with an impromptu recital of poems by Robert Service. The performance was then interrupted by Terhune's angry eruption.

"If your headlamp is missing, I'm sure it's an accident," Cooley said.

"Well, I'm sure it's not," replied Terhune. "I left it plugged in to the battery pack. That's got my name on it. If somebody had mistaken it, they would have taken the whole thing. But the battery pack is right here," he said, showing us the red case with his name clearly printed on the side.

"Whoever took my headlamp, knew what they were doing," he said, curling his lips in a feral challenge. "One of you is a thief."

Hard to accept, but Terhune's logic was sound. The missing headlamp was a freebie provided by Dodge Trucks. Each of us had started the race with an identical one, meaning that there was no telling who had pinched his. No one was sleepy now, and we eyed each other uneasily.

"I've got an extra one," Catherine Mormile announced, breaking the silence. She went out to her sled to get it for Terhune. She also loaned Daily a needle and thread to sew his torn sled bag.

"I could sure use a decent headlamp," I said, pointing to the toy I'd bought in McGrath.

"You need a headlamp?" said Herrman. "I've got an extra you can borrow."

The trappers were waiting at a rushing open creek a few miles out of Kaltag. Helping hands threw reluctant leaders into the frigid water. More hands were waiting on the other side to pluck our soggy fur balls and steer them onto the trail. The villagers' teamwork reminded me of crossing Sullivan Creek with Garth and Lee—both now gone.

Once again the Red Lantern belonged to Tom Daily, who followed me out of Kaltag. Crossing the creek, his team tangled. Daily got soaking wet straightening out the mess.

"Be careful," one of the trappers told him. "The storm coming is the worst I've ever seen in my whole life."

"Great, that's just wonderful," said Daily, who by now expected no less from the gods. Though his response was cavalier, Tom noticed that the trappers were geared to the teeth.

Daily generally traveled at night with his headlamp off. But he didn't want to lose me, and his team kept falling behind. Meanwhile, I kept overtaking the teams bunched ahead. So we worked out a system. Rather than creep in step with the convoy. I took a lot of breaks. Each time I rested with my back on the handlebar, shining my headlamp back toward Kaltag, watching for telltale blinks in the darkness—confirming that Moonshadow's musher remained on the march.

We were hit climbing a steep sidehill. Herrman's team shrugged off the frigid breeze rushing up the bare slope, and he made it through the pass. But several of the teams directly behind Sepp balked. The delay caused the dogs to start digging for shelter, shutting the rest of us down like toppling dominoes.

We struggled for maybe 30 minutes—through steadily increasing wind—trying to get the convoy moving. Mushers in the front switched their leaders. They tried dragging dogs forward by hand. Finally, half a dozen of us got together and attempted to walk those teams that were willing past those that wouldn't budge. It was slow difficult work. The trail's slippery groove, cut sideways into the slope, was impossibly narrow. The hill, terrifically steep. Heavy sleds kept tipping over and slipping, dragging drivers and wheel dogs downward; while other mushers grappled to arrest the slides.

Our attempt at hand-guiding teams up the sidehill was abandoned when we heard Catherine Mormile cry out.

"Don, help me. Help, help me please," she pleaded. "I'm cold."

Wind piercing Mormile's sweaty snowmachine suit had turned its clammy interior freezing cold. Shivering, she had fumbled for her sleeping bag, then panicked when she couldn't get it open.

Cooley took charge. "Has anybody got hand warmers?"

We clustered around Catherine Mormile's sled, blocking the wind with our backs. Kneeling within the ring of parkas, Cooley stripped off the stricken musher's boots and wet socks. He slipped on dry socks, loaded with fresh warmers. Then we guided Mormile into her sleeping bag. Daily stripped off his own gloves and fitted them on her hands. Through it all, Don Mormile stood by looking rather helpless.

Feeling the warm glow of the chemical heaters, Catherine

was stricken with another sort of fear. "Does this mean I'm disqualified because I can't take care of myself anymore?" she
asked, sobbing.

We laughed with relief. "Catherine," someone said, mock-
seriously, "We're going to have to confiscate your promotional
mail packet."

The crisis derailed our efforts to escape the hill.

Daily crawled inside his sled bag in full gear, spreading his
sleeping bag over the top as a blanket. He was warm, but spent a
miserable night racked by cramps.

Determined to feed my dogs a decent meal, I carved a hole
in the side of the hill and formed a windscreen over the cooker
with my body and the sled. It was only marginally successful. Although I burned twice the normal amount of alcohol, it only
produced a tepid pot of water. The dogs didn't seem too impressed by my hillside cuisine.

Frustration set in as I sought refuge in my sled bag for the
fifth time. Nibbling on a salmon belly cheered me a little, but
gloom invaded the cocoon. What a screwed up run. Fifteen
miles and we were shut down again. At this rate, Nome would
be another 20 days away. The novelty of the convoy action had
worn off, and Terhune's grumbling was making a lot of sense. I
might not have the fastest team, but the Coach and I had trained
our dogs better than to quit midway up a hill.

Atop the pass, Sepp Herrman mushed through a churning whiteout. The German woodsman had never seen anything like it: as
fast as his leaders might break a path, the surging drifts filled it
back in, pressing inward against the dogs and sleds following
behind.

That didn't stop his team. Sepp's dogs were accustomed to
breaking their own trails through untraveled back country. The

team dogs kept moving, carving their own footholds, and his sled crashed through the amassing barriers.

The trail here served more than occasional racers. This was the Kaltag Portage, an ancient transit route linking Yukon River villagers with residents of the Bering Sea coast. The route was marked by a line of tall wooden tripods, closely spaced for blinding conditions such as these. They made all the difference here, freeing Sepp to marvel at the sheer savagery of the passage.

It was cold. The trapper possessed such pride in his own handmade, richly lined gear that it was rare that he would make such an admission, even to himself. But Sepp Herrman was also a realist, a man who understood the bloodthirsty nature of wolves and the dangers of harboring illusions about Alaska's cruel environment. It was exceptionally cold tonight. That was the enormous thing.

Deviating from my usual routine, I left my bunny boots outside the sled overnight. It made my sled bag hotel a little more roomy.

It was calm in the morning, but the 30-below temperature carried a bite. My toes burned the instant I stepped into the stiff rubber boots. I launched into a series of frenzied jumping jacks, chanting "ouch, ouch, ouch" the whole time. From here on out, this traveler would be sleeping with his boots on.

When we were loaded and ready, the convoy resumed inching up the sidehill trail. The powder atop the pass proved too deep for Plettner's team, and Cooley's leaders were still soured. Word was relayed back: "Send up Daily."

Tom strapped on his snowshoes and placed Diamond in the lead. The musher stomped a path through the biggest drifts. His old lead dog tackled the rest. It was hard work, but Daily felt good about Diamond's performance. The old dog was cruising at speeds nearing two miles an hour. For Diamond, that was flying. Together they broke a new trail, following the weathered tripods across the windswept plateau.

As usual, my worst problem was getting Harley past old campsites. The big dog's concentration was destroyed by even a speck of discarded food. Mushers were supposed to pull their teams off the trail before stopping for a snack or rest. Obviously, our forced camp on the hillside was an unusual situation. I had fed my dogs on the trail there, same as everybody else. But it was evidently standard procedure for several of the teams ahead. I'd been stumbling over fresh dining stains ever since leaving Eagle Island. I dragged Harley by the collar up the hill, making frequent, aggravating pauses to right my sled.

There were two shelter cabins on the 90-mile trail to Unalakleet. Before we left Kaltag, some members of the group were talking about stopping at the first cabin, a trip of about 30 miles. Herrman made the stop after pushing through the storm. That made sense for him. I took it for granted that last night's hillside debacle had canceled such plans for the rest of us. My team certainly wasn't ready for another break midmorning Monday. We'd only driven 15 miles!

Outside the cabin nine dog teams were parked, end to end, blocking the trail for several hundred yards. The trail ahead was wide open, if I could get to it. In an absolute rage, I stomped to the cabin, threw open the door, and began screaming. Everyone looked at me like I was crazy. Herrman had coffee brewing. Most of the drivers were making a short breakfast stop. Only Urtha, Catherine Mormile, and a few others planned longer breaks. I remained incensed, demanding the immediate removal of those trail-blocking teams. And, from here on, I swore I'd file official complaints against anyone I caught snacking dogs on the trail in front of Harley.

A few mushers reparked their teams, off the trail, near the cabin. Most ended their break and cleared out. As the trail ahead of us cleared, Harley and Rainy threaded their way through the traffic jam. Watching the others depart, Catherine changed her mind about staying and hurried to get ready. Her team was still blocking the trail as mine approached.

"You go ahead," she said.

As I guided my leaders around her team, Mormile suddenly pulled her snow hook and tried to outrun us, nearly causing a tangle.

"My team is faster than yours. I'm supposed to be ahead of you," she snapped.

Both of us urged our teams forward, meanwhile cussing each other out. The argument was finally settled by the dogs—mine emerging in front.

So she was faster? Only in her dreams. Driving hard, I left her behind. Later, during a quick break, I described the scene to Terhune. He laughed for the first time in days. Mormile didn't catch up until we were camping that evening at Old Woman Cabin.

The plywood cabin was sparsely furnished with a pair of bunks and a fat stove. After tending dogs, mushers filtered inside. The tensions of the morning were gone, and everyone was in a sharing mood. Lenthar gave me a roll of film. I joined the mushers providing Herrman's dogs with extra food, giving the light-traveling trapper a big chunk of lamb.

My own acute shortage was in personal food. When I had shipped out supplies, I hadn't planned on two- and three-day treks between checkpoints. I hadn't sent out enough juice or snacks. My main-course menu was not only insufficient; it was sabotaged by flawed packaging. Two of my staples, Anna's meatloaf, as well as her potatoes, were sealed in plastic baggies which disintegrated in hot water. I had to chuck them, or nibble on icy half-thawed portions, another sorry testimony to the importance of prerace field-testing. I had more success with the precooked steaks and pork chops. Each was individually wrapped in tin foil. To heat one up, I merely set the wrapped foil on a hot wood stove. By Kaltag, I was developing a reputation as a carnivore.

My provisions had seemed extravagant when Mary Beth and Anna spread them all out in the newspaper's lunchroom. Yet I was running on empty at Old Woman Cabin. More was waiting in the supply sacks at Unalakleet, but here I was down to raiding the shelter's emergency stocks: peanut butter, stale crackers, and a pile of dried salmon scraps someone found in a corner of the room. Daily, likewise destitute, joined me in delving into the meager rations.

Trading stories by the stove late Monday night, I dug out the surviving bottle of Jack Daniel's. Plettner, Cooley, Herrman, and I toasted our impending arrival on the coast.

The Nome banquet had been delayed. Too many teams remained out in the storms pounding the coast. The postrace party was finally held Monday, March 18, day 17 of the race. While Daily and I gobbled stale crackers and scrutinized withered fish scraps, searching for edible chunks of salmon, 26 mushers and some 850 fans were moving through a buffet line at the Nome armory.

Accepting a $32,000 check for third place, Susan Butcher, her face puffy from windburn, graciously praised Swenson's unprecedented achievement—restaking his claim as Iditarod's all-time champ.

Martin Buser's three-year-old son, Nikolai, sang impromptu trail songs into the microphone as his heavily scabbing father collected a check for $39,500 for his second place finish. It wasn't the prize Martin had hoped to gain that final night. Hearing from a snowmachiner that Swenson was reported missing,

Buser had slipped on a white windbreaker, what he liked to call his "stealth shell," and sought to steal the lead. But Swenson, taking nothing for granted, had arranged to delay reports of his arrival at Safety, the final checkpoint before Nome.

As he presented Rick Swenson with a silver cup and the first-place prize of $50,000, Nome's perennial checker, Leo Rasmussen, recalled the musher's first appearance on stage as an Iditarod winner. The year was 1977, and the grand prize stood at $9,600, which, even then, hardly covered the expense of fielding a competitive team.

"He was so enamored with the race he couldn't stop talking. He must have talked for 24 hours to whoever would listen," Rasmussen said.

Swenson's Goose and Major were voted joint custody of the Golden Harness Award given to Iditarod's best lead dog.

Mere blocks from the finish-line arch, Nome musher Matt Desalarnos had the $14,000 check for seventh place in his grasp. Alas, his dogs veered toward an alley, and Dee Dee Jonrowe passed him. That last-minute move from seventh to eighth place cost him $1,000. Chief vet Morris also presented Dee Dee with the Humanitarian Award for displaying the best dog care among the competitive drivers.

Barve had regrouped after finding his lost dogs and finished seventeenth, winning $6,000. Garnie had also recovered his lost team and continued, but he missed out on the money, finishing twenty-third. The respect for their achievement, surviving storms on foot, was evident as the mushers in Nome awarded the pair jointly the Iditarod's "Most Inspirational Musher Award." The wind-scorched Eskimo had extra incentive pushing him toward the finish line; Garnie had to finish the race or forfeit the new pickup he had won in Skwentna.

The scars of the race were most evident on Adkins, whose windburned face was a swollen mass of scabs as he stepped forward to collect his $5,000, nineteenth-place check. The

Montanan was also presented with the Sportsmanship Award for rescuing Whittemore on the ice outside Koyuk. Several dogs had died during the storm, and both men had been hypothermic and frostbitten by the time they reached the village. The worst part of the experience, Adkins told the crowd at the banquet, was when village medics had stuck a rectal thermometer up his ass.

"That was probably the most embarrassed I've ever been on the Iditarod," he said.

Five more teams mushed into Nome before the banquet broke up. The last in was Redington. He checked in under the arch just before midnight, in thirty-first place. Cheers resounded through the armory hall at the announcement of Old Joe's arrival.

The custody of one more award remained unsettled as the main banquet ended. Its ownership floated among a select few of the 29 mushers left on the trail. It wasn't something anyone particularly wanted. Call it a booby prize. Such is the status of the Iditarod's Red Lantern.

A sudden cry shattered the peace within Old Woman Cabin. Asleep on the floor, I awakened to find Sepp Herrman standing in the center of the room. The disheveled German was hurriedly collecting his gear.

"I've got to sleep outside," the trapper mumbled, tightening the laces on his mukluks. "Where I live, I hardly hear nobody. I can't take a house of snoring men."

CHAPTER 10

Harley's Nose

Terhune awakened in excruciating pain. Another musher examined his eye with a headlamp to no avail. Jon assumed the pain came from a speck of dust or some other irritant caught under his damn contact lens. It would happen at a place like Old Woman, a cabin with no running water, when his lens fluid was outside frozen solid in the sled. Unalakleet was only 45 miles away. Looking at his filthy hands, Terhune decided to clean his contacts when he reached the village. A little pain wasn't going to kill him.

It was a glorious day. Daily stayed behind, taking his time. The rest of us leapfrogged past each other, trading positions, letting the dogs find their own gleeful pace. I traveled with Terhune for the most part. The last miles to the Bering Sea coast flew past in a blur of rolling hills, fat spruce trees, and winding river curves.

Several snowmachines buzzed past us as we neared the village. They swung around and waited on the flats. One of the machines was hauling a huge sled packed with gear. Rich Runyan had accomplished his lonely mission. The radio operator waved and fell in behind the dog teams for the final mile.

A jumble of structures, power lines, and smoke rose at the

end of the flats. It was Unalakleet, the largest village on the trail, and home to about 900 Inupiat Eskimo villagers, an airport served by Alaska Airlines, a satellite uplink station, and a medical clinic. And most significant to me, the gateway to Alaska's ice-locked coast. Nome, that almost mythical destination of ours, lay just 270 miles to the northwest.

The sun was setting as I approached the checkpoint, located by the village's school gym. I parked my team alongside a building across the street. Cooley and Williams already had their teams bedded in straw, and Daily soon joined us. A woman told Tom she'd drawn his name and had dinner waiting at her house, just down the street. I asked her if there was a restaurant in town. After two days of dining on crackers and raw Spam, I'd pay nearly any price for a fat cheeseburger. She gave me directions but told me to hurry. The place closed in half an hour. I sighed realizing that promised burger was out of reach. The place would be closed by the time I finished feeding the dogs.

"We have plenty of stew," she said. "Why don't you come over, too."

A reed-thin gray-haired villager struck up a conversation. His name was Mugsy, and he bragged about his feats as a champion sprint driver decades ago. The old musher smelled like booze, but he was entertaining. His stories were interrupted by the sudden appearance of the last person I ever expected to see.

"They told me I could find you guys back here," said Barry Lee. "Hey, Tom, your dogs looked really good coming into the village."

It was painful to see a musher, and a friend, who had traveled so many miles with me, but who was now out of the Great Race. If only he had come with Daily and me. If only we had waited in Grayling.

"Someday I'm going to write a book about this, Barry," I blurted out. "I'm going to dedicate it to you."

One of my dogs growled over a snack and I turned away. The distraction lasted a couple of seconds, but when I looked back Lee was gone.

"Am I going crazy," I asked Daily, "or was Barry just here talking to us?"

"I saw him too," he said, wonderingly. "He did sort of vanish."

But I wasn't having visions. Lee had flown into Unalakleet with his dogs and was waiting for a connecting flight to Anchorage. Earlier that day, Barry had got in an argument with local mushers, who thought we were "wussies" for traveling so slow.

"So you're Bobby Lee's brother," the man said. "Should I tell him you're a wussie, too."

"You don't know what they're going through," Lee said. "You have no idea."

Lee had spent the afternoon watching for us from a bank overlooking the trail. Lee had greeted Herrman, the first one to town. He had talked to the Mormiles, Johnson, and Lenthar. He had helped Terhune park his dogs and had discussed feeding schedules with Plettner. And he had assisted Cooley with his blood tests. This had enabled him to prolong his involvement in the Iditarod, if only for a few hours. Seeing us, he knew it was time to say good-bye. He took off because he was crying.

Daily didn't have time to dwell on Lee's disappearance. His fancy boots were wet again. Tom was changing them, with his back to Mugsy, when the old musher calmly stepped on the runners of Tom's sled and pulled the snow hook. In the excitement of the big village, Daily's dogs hadn't settled down. They were antsy and took off at the graying racer's command, loping down the center of the busy village street.

Throwing his boots aside, Tom Daily chased his Iditarod team down the street in his socks. Doc and I watched in astonishment as the villager dodged head-on traffic from cars and snowmachines and gradually pulled away. The guy could drive dogs, you had to give him that.

The infection in Terhune's eye warranted immediate attention from a specialist. The medic at the Unalakleet clinic advised the musher to consider flying to Anchorage for treatment at a real hospital.

"There's no way I'm going to scratch," declared Terhune.

Though his back also hurt and his hands were throbbing from a brush with frostbite, Terhune refused to accept any medication for the pain. He was worried that painkillers would make him sleepy. He settled for having his bad eye flushed out and treated with antibiotics. The musher left the clinic with a pocket full of pills and sulfa drops, shrugging off warnings that he could suffer long-term complications if the infection worsened.

Tom Daily found his dog team parked in a driveway a few blocks from the checkpoint. The sled bag was open, flapping in the wind. Dog pans and other small items were blowing across the yard. The woman who met him at the checkpoint greeted Tom at the door of the cabin. The old racer was her uncle.

The cabin was gloriously hot inside, spiced with the aroma of rich caribou stew. We passed a fine evening listening to Mugsy's stories. In the background, a child was watching *The Wizard of Oz* on a big color TV set.

Not long after dinner, Mugsy, the woman, and I cleared out, leaving Daily alone in the cabin.

"Whatever you do," the woman said as she departed. "Don't let my uncle in if he comes home drunk."

Daily didn't like the sound of that warning. The last thing he wanted was to become ensnared in a family dispute. He locked the cabin door and went to sleep. A few hours later, Daily's rest was disturbed by pounding. It was Mugsy. The villager was drunk, and he was furious at finding the door to his warm cabin locked. Daily explained his orders, which just made the old musher angrier.

"Let me in," the man cried, "or I'm going to kill your dogs."

This thrust Daily into a dilemma. If he opened the door, he sensed that Mugsy was going to come in swinging. Tom didn't want to fight the poor old guy. All he wanted was a few more hours of rest.

"Mugsy, if you're going to kill them, go do it, get it over with. I'm going back to sleep."

Leaving the sled dogs in peace, the old musher headed up the street.

After dinner I went to check on my dogs. They were sleeping peacefully, so I went over to the gym. I talked for a while with the checker, a local musher, and one of the race judges. Al Marple had flown in to Unalakleet that afternoon to "give us a pep talk" and make sure we backpack mushers didn't overstay our welcome.

"Don't lump me in with the guys who stayed three days at Eagle Island," I said, feeling defensive. "Doc, Daily, and I spent that time battling storms on the Yukon. We got into Eagle Island at night and pulled out in the morning, same as we're doing here."

Marple appreciated my attitude. "We want to see you guys make it," he said.

There was a shower in the gym bathroom. I let the burning steam wash away 900 miles of pain. The shower left me richly satisfied, but dizzy. I collapsed on the hardwood floor of the gym next to Cooley. I didn't bother with a sleeping bag, I just stretched out on top of my suit. A feather mattress couldn't have felt any finer.

Shouts awakened us a few hours later. I knew that voice.

Who was it? Oh yeah, it was that crazy old musher. I fell back asleep as a Unalakleet public safety officer, Alaska's village equivalent of a policeman, hauled the drunk away.

A cloud of smoke enveloped the streetlight. A pair of snow-machines throbbed in the street below. Doc, Williams, and I carefully lined up our dog teams facing the deserted intersection. It was 4 A.M. I was last in line.

The snowmachines took off around the corner. Doc and Williams charged after them. Chad got the call and seemed enthusiastic. He leapt in the air as I pulled the hook. Following his cue, my entire 13-dog team sprang forward with manic intensity.

I cut the turn too close. My sled climbed the berm and launched sideways into the air. I hung on, flying parallel with the ground. The sled finally crashed on its side, knocking the wind out of me, but I didn't let go. The snow-covered street was icy and hard-packed, a perfect surface for dragging. The dogs seized the opportunity to set a new kennel record, dragging me 500 yards.

I wouldn't have minded the dragging—I was used to that—but Chad and the wild bunch had so much fun that he lost track of the teams ahead. The snowmachines, Doc, and Williams—all had cleared out before I regrouped and righted the sled. Ahead of us the street was deserted. My bold leader didn't have a clue where to go next.

"Go ahead! Go ahead!" I shouted, sending Chad charging forward in hopes he would pick up the scent. There were side streets and snowmachine tracks leading everywhere, but no Iditarod markers. I would get lost in Unalakleet, the biggest labyrinth on the trail, where I hadn't talked to anyone about the route out of town—because we had arranged for guides.

I saw a light in the window of a nearby cabin. Could someone actually be awake at 4 A.M.? Probably not, I decided. But what did I have to lose. I threw the sled on its side again and jammed the snow hook in the ground. Then I climbed the icy berm by the side of the road and dropped into the yard of the cabin with the lighted window, thinking this was a great way to get myself shot.

An older woman opened the door. She stared at me, eyes widening, dubious. I realized that I filled her doorway in my bulky suit, which was smeared in snow from my dragging adventure. The headlamp shone crookedly from the side of my natural wool hat. A red face mask concealed all but my eyes and nose.

"Can I help you?" she said, in a perfectly reasonable voice.

"I was hoping you might be able to point me toward the Iditarod Trail," I said, gesturing toward my dog team, parked out in the street. "We're sort of lost."

"Oh my," the woman said. "I think it's by the river, but I really have no idea."

I thanked her and returned to my team. Nothing was going easy this morning. I was trying to decide what to do next when a snowmachine cruised up. It was a village cop. Chuckling at my story, he offered to lead the team out of town.

Jumping on the sled, I pulled the hook and—watched my leader lie down.

The officer zipped away. He returned before I finished placing Harley and Rainy in lead.

"Thought you were following me."

"So did I, but Wonder Dog had other ideas."

The officer lead me through a winding series of streets, past the last line of cabins, to a marker at the bottom of a small hill. "Here's your trail," he shouted over the wind and the whine of his engine. "Good luck."

I thanked the officer, delighted to be on my way. He gunned his snowmachine, fishtailing the rear in a tight circle, and buzzed away.

A sheet-metal sign rang in the wind, which had intensified now that I was beyond the sheltering streets of the village. In the distance, I could see the outline of hills against the stars. But a dark, churning haze gripped the flat landscape directly ahead. It looked mean out there. I walked up the line, petting most of the dogs, and retightening the booties on the Rat and Screech, who still had sore feet. Little Cricket watched me, shyly wagging her tail. "What a brave little girl," I said, stroking her chin.

Standing on the runners, I rezipped my suit, buttoning the top button. I adjusted my layered face masks, gloves, and mitts, and then—lacking any other good excuse for delay—pulled the hook.

"All right! Rainy, Harley. All right! Let's Go!"

Dodge Corporation was bankrolling a toll-free Iditarod information line. Jeff Greenwald, an old buddy, dialed the 800 number several times a day to track my progress from his home in San Francisco. Information was sketchy regarding teams like mine, traveling far behind the leaders. Making matters worse, the folks answering Dodge's phone knew next to nothing about mushing. They were merely reading statistics faxed from Iditarod headquarters.

One of the numbers readily available was the size of each musher's team. Jeff noticed early on that my dog team was steadily shrinking. Their numbers had dropped from 17 to 15 dogs when I had left Gnat and Daphne in Skwentna. He saw I was down to 14 after Grayling, where I had left Skidders to recuperate; and that I had just 13 dogs upon leaving Kaltag, where I had dumped Denali.

The statistics didn't explain that dropped dogs were placed in the care of checkers and veterinarians, or the effort devoted to evacuating them via Iditarod's volunteer air force. The numbers didn't hint at the attention dropped dogs received from prisoners at a state corrections facility near Anchorage, where the dogs were held for pickup by designated handlers.

Jeff had no way of knowing that most of my dropped dogs were already lounging in the woods at Cyndi's house in Wasilla, and that—except for Skidders, with his bandaged rear paw—there wasn't anything wrong with them. All Jeff knew was that my dog team, like most in the race, was getting smaller. He asked the people answering Iditarod's toll-free phone what was happening.

"Gee, I don't know," Jeff was told. "A lot of people ask about that. The dogs must be dying in those bad storms."

"Man," Jeff whispered, hanging up the phone, "it must be a bummer for Brian—having all those dogs die!"

Six dogs did die over the course of the race. Two dogs in Adkins's team died of exposure while he was saving Whittemore's life out on the ice. Mackey had a dog drop dead of heart failure outside McGrath. Suter had a poodle die of exposure in a storm near Unalakleet and had to drop the rest of his shivering poodle victims before continuing on, pulled by the team's true sled dogs. More violent were the deaths of two dogs and the injuries to two others in Rollin Westrum's team.

Westrum was nearing White Mountain, about 85 miles from the finish line, when his team was illuminated in the glaring headlight of a snowmachine.

"It came head-on," the musher told reporters later. "I thought it was all over. It hit the dogs and then glanced off to one side and went right by. It sounded like he had the throttle wide open. He didn't even slow down."

The collision left Westrum cradling a dog named Jeff, who was crippled, and weeping over the loss of four-year-old Ace and eight-year-old Bandit, his favorite lead dog.

The grim toll should be placed in perspective. Approximately 1,400 dogs chased mine out of Anchorage. The fallen six were magnificent athletes. They died giving all—too much, perhaps—pulling a sled with their teammates, as breeding and training inspired them to do.

We began descending into a ground blizzard less than a mile out from Unalakleet. So this was the haze I had noticed in the distance. It started with a flowing white carpet, which broke into streamers on contact with the paws of the dogs in front. The carpet steadily swelled to a foot deep, creating an illusion of a chain of disembodied heads floating on the gang line ahead. I could only guess what lay concealed in the approaching white tide. It kept rising until it swallowed the dogs, the sled and, finally, me.

We weren't in any immediate danger of charging off a cliff. Not crossing these flats. I knew it couldn't be more than a few miles to the clear area I spotted near the hills. It wasn't even that cold. But my headlamp was useless in this soup. And where were the markers?

The wind was kicking up all kinds of debris: snow, chunks of ice—I even tasted gravel on my lips. I had to content myself with glimpses of the leaders. But I noticed they were acting a little odd. Rainy's ears were up, but the bossy little lesbian looked unusually tentative. Damned if Harley wasn't leading her for once.

The team suddenly bunched in a mass tangle. Harley was to blame. The big dog had stopped, with his nose thrust into a half-buried plastic bag, ignoring the other dogs piling into him. As I ran up front, Harley wrenched the bag loose and furiously shook it in his teeth. The plastic tore as I snatched the bag away, spilling empty cans, used coffee grounds, and other trash.

Pig and several other dogs lunged for the scraps dancing on the gusts. I threw the bag away, but the wind caught it and slapped it back at the dogs. It skipped across the ground to Digger and Spook, which triggered a ruckus in the middle ranks.

More dogs grabbed loose scraps as I snatched the bag away again. This time, remembering my merchant marine days aboard S.S. *Sam Houston*, I heaved the damn thing with the wind. Most of the garbage had already spilled, and the feather-light bag took off like a punctured balloon, flapping and sailing on the currents. Bouncing up the side of a tall berm, it finally left us.

Dragging Harley forward by the collar, I sent him on down the trail. Where were those trail markers? The garbage bag should have been a clue. But I was too rattled to digest the surroundings. I was more in the mood to nurse my sufferings this morning. Give me a marker please!

I should have noticed that we weren't on a trail—it was a snow-covered road. The lesbian had been flashing me concerned looks. But Harley seemed so confident. His head was high. He had the team really rolling. So I ignored Rainy's silent protests. That was my big mistake. As if Harley ever gave a hoot about anything but his stomach. He was following his nose toward El Dorado.

Disaster struck quickly. Scar sunk his teeth into one of the mounds and yanked out a trash bag. Rat, Harley, Cyrus—in a matter of seconds they all joined in. Thirteen dogs each tearing into buried garbage bags, or wrestling over scraps. I yelled. I screamed. I picked dogs up and threw them as far as the lines would allow, tearing their greasy prizes away with my bare hands. But the dogs were beyond control. They were rioting before my eyes, intoxicated by the smells and gripped by instincts far more persuasive than my tenuous authority. As fast as I pried dogs loose, their companions burrowed deeper into the rotting treasure trove. There was nowhere to tie them down. On all sides and underfoot—I was surrounded by trash.

Evidence was literally piling up around me in snow-covered heaps, but I didn't grasp what was happening until Harley had followed his nose to the center of Unalakleet's village dump. I had to get the team out of this place. God knew what diseases were lurking here. But dragging my well-muscled Iditarod team out of the god-damned dump was just more than I could manage alone. I finally admitted defeat and gave up, barely holding back tears in my weary state. I'd never felt more enraged, or hopeless.

Realizing that I had to get help, I abandoned the team to its feeding frenzy and scrambled some 20 feet up the side of a trash pile. The wind was fading, and in the distance I saw snowmachine lights. I flashed my headlamp until they turned my way.

It was the guys who had led Doc out of town. The three of us wrestled my dogs out of the trash and over the side of the dump. The checker hopped on my sled and, displaying mastery far surpassing my own, rode it careening off garbage piles to the valley below. Firing up their snowmachines, the pair led me several miles into the hills. They wanted to make absolutely sure that this woeful excuse for a dog musher was headed someplace else.

The tunnel of trees gave way to a windy clearing in the hills. Day was breaking. Gunnar and several other mushers were parked parallel to each other, in what didn't seem like a social gathering.

"None of our teams can lead in this wind," Johnson yelled. "Think yours can do it?"

"Mine are pretty good in the wind," I said. "I'll give it a shot."

Harley and Rainy charged across the clearing, but my team tangled shortly after reentering the forest. I straightened the dogs out and was reaching for the hook when Gunnar called for the trail. He had some nerve.

"I can't believe you, Gunnar," I said, waving him by.

As I could have predicted, Johnson's team slowed immediately after the pass. We traveled bumper to bumper for several miles until Johnson's dogs found another team to chase.

Tom Daily had overslept. Instead of leaving Unalakleet with Cooley and me, he snoozed straight through the morning in his cozy cabin bunk. Like me, Tom had no idea where to find the trail out of the village. Seeking directions, he dropped by the village cop shop. After chatting with the local patrolmen about Mugsy's overnight escapades, Daily paid one of the officers $15 to guide the team into the hills.

It was bright and windy. Gusts raking the trail were so savage they knocked Daily's fully packed sled sideways and ripped the officer's goggles from his head. Tom speared them with one hand as they flew past. When the pair parted company in the hills, he surprised the officer by returning his goggles. Daily didn't need any extra souvenirs. He and his dogs were traveling alone, miles behind everybody, lugging the burden of the Red Lantern.

We climbed ever higher. The sheer beauty of these hills was staggering. Sunlight streamed through scattered clumps of trees. To the west, I caught glimpses of the frozen Bering Sea, a wasteland of glimmering blue-white shards extending to the horizon.

I ran as much as I could to lighten the dogs' load, borrowing occasional rides to catch my breath. The temperature was near zero, and the air was crisp. Hot and sweaty from the exertion, I steadily stripped off gear. The snowmachine suit went back inside the sled, as did the wind shell Nora had made me. I unzipped the sides of my bibs. What a day!

Terhune's team was directly behind mine. I couldn't mistake

him in that fluorescent orange musher's hat. Cresting the barren top of one of the hills, I stopped to get a picture of him passing a wooden tripod. Seeing me, he raised a pair of army mitts.

"Missing something?" he hollered.

Few items are more precious to a musher than his mitts. Mine were linked with a nylon rope that had a large hole to slip over my head. From the moment I stepped on the sled until I made camp, I almost never took them off. When I wasn't wearing them over my gloves, I let them dangle at my side. Sometimes it felt annoying having those mitts swinging free, but it kept them within reach.

Four years earlier, Peter Thomann, a thoughtful musher driving beautiful burly Siberians in these same hills, had gotten careless on what appeared to be a mild, delightful day. Figuring he could dispense with his heavy beaver mitts, Thomann stowed them inside his sled bag.

Later that day, Peter suddenly found himself in a wind so wicked his fingers stiffened at its touch. He stripped off his gloves, intending to place on dry liners for extra warmth. The wind sucked the life from his bare hands before the musher could get the liners over his fingers. Thomann's mitts would have come in handy then, but they remained out of reach, locked away by the frozen zipper on his sled bag.

He managed to get a glove over his right hand. The fingers on his left hand were "frozen stiff like pieces of ice," as Thomann put it later, in a hospital-bed interview with Medred.

Thrusting the frozen hand under his parka, the musher had raced for the village like Napoleon's army fleeing. "You panic for a minute. But once they are frozen, it is not a problem," he told the reporter. "They do not hurt anymore."

Thanks to an abundance of foolish climbers, mushers, and victims of unlucky outdoors accidents, Anchorage doctors possess great expertise in treating frostbite. Thomann didn't lose any digits. And rather than bow out of the sport, he developed new defenses to protect that damaged hand from further injury.

Out on the Quest Trail, one 40-below night, I quietly watched, prompted by usual reporter's curiosity, to see whether Thomann would skimp on dog care owing to his injury. I was surprised to find the musher working barehanded as he tended those paws with a diligence I've never seen surpassed. The trick was a small can of flaming Sterno, which he set down in the snow between his knees. Thomann worked a few seconds, then warmed the bad hand over the flickering blue fire, as he patiently nursed each of his furry friends.

Terhune smiled, something he didn't do often. I clutched at my sides, hoping to prove him wrong. No such luck. Changing out of my warmer clothes, I had carelessly rested the mitts on my handlebar or sled bag. Trailing us, he found them by the side of the trail.

"I figured you might want them back," Jon said, slinging the mitts over to me.

We both knew that the loss of those mitts could have proved disastrous in bad weather.

We continued through the hills for about 20 miles before the trail dropped into a frozen marsh. Looking down from the last ridge, the view reminded me of standing on top of a ski hill. The trail formed a winding white path through trees. Puffs of snow marked the progress of half a dozen mushers already descending. I was a little nervous as I launched my team over the edge, but the snow was deep, giving me fine control, and the ride was a joy.

I don't know if a frigid breeze suddenly picked up, or if it was there all along, waiting for me. But I hadn't gone 50 feet out into the marsh ice when the cold bit hard. Jamming the snow hook into a patch of crusty snow, I tore open my sled bag and grabbed the snow suit. With awkward, herky-jerky steps, I slipped my legs inside, thrust my arms into the chilly sleeves, and flipped the cowl over my head. Back to the wind, gasping, I leaned on the sled with my hands tucked under my armpits and collected my wits.

"That was close," I whispered.

I don't know how cold it was. It wasn't very windy, but the slight breeze sliced through living flesh like a laser. Perhaps it felt worse on the marsh because of the shocking transition from the warm hills. It was time for the arsenal anyway—that was definite.

Warming up a bit, I broke some fat sausages and threw each dog a piece. I had to keep them happy. Then I dug out my big parka and put it on over the suit for the first time since early in the Yukon trek. And I put hand warmers in the mitts. This was very likely the place where Thomann froze his hand. It was easy to see how it might happen, descending out of the warm hills.

My parka hood proved invaluable as we crossed the marsh. Zipped all the way to the ruff with the string drawn tight, the hood formed a narrow tube extending about ten inches in front of my face. Vision was a little limited, peering through the softball-sized gap in the fur, but I was amazingly warm inside.

The marsh was riddled with parallel snowmachine tracks, some were hard-packed and fast; others made for slow going. Johnson, I, and several other mushers traveling close together took different trails, and our dog teams soon fanned out across the icy flats. It felt as if we were an assault party of Arctic nomads, swooping down from the hills.

A narrow strip of ramshackle houses puffing smoke from oddly jutting pipes—that was Shaktoolik. The village had a harsh look to it. Not surprising for a community locked in snow drifts bordering Norton Sound, an immense frozen gulf, 125 miles long and 70 miles across. By the time we arrived, Wednesday, March 20, the annual excitement of the Iditarod had faded for the village's 160 residents. The local volunteers were burned out, and the streets were littered with windblown race trash.

I found the others camped outside the Shaktoolik armory building in the shelter provided by a line of rough drifts. Our supplies were stored at another house, several hundred yards away. I trudged over and dragged my sacks back to the team. It me took several trips, and I felt drained and dizzy by the time I finished.

It was a beautiful sunny afternoon, but we all knew that the calm was deceptive. Directly ahead lay one of the most infamous sections of the entire Iditarod Trail: the oft-stormy passage across sea ice to Koyuk.

In 1982 Nayokpuk and his Shishmaref dogs—conditioned in the polar-bear country surrounding his remote coastal village, 20 miles shy of the Arctic Circle—met their match on the trail that lay ahead. The bold Eskimo had attempted a solo breakout during a storm that had penned front-runners in Shaktoolik. No one else dared to follow him.

"It'd be like trying to go fishing in a ten-foot skiff in forty-foot seas," commented Dean Osmar, a fisherman destined to win the race two years later.

The Shishmaref Cannonball shot 22 miles out onto the exposed sea ice before the storm proved too intense for even his leaders. Humbled, with his dogs locked in tight balls, the musher spent a long, sleepless night shivering in his sled bag. In the morning, Herbie Nayokpuk turned his team around and returned to Shaktoolik.

"I've been out many years in the cold," Nayokpuk told a reporter. "But that was the coldest night I ever spent."

Swenson had won the 1982 race, with Butcher trailing 3.5 miles behind. It was the pair's first one-two finish and foreshadowed the rivalry that dominated the sport in the next decade. Nayokpuk spent a day regrouping and then mushed into Nome in twelfth place, slipping from Iditarod's top ten for the first time.

Three years later, in 1985, Libby Riddles clinched her victory in a similar situation. Arriving in Shaktoolik on a stormy afternoon, a few hours ahead of Barve and Swenson, Riddles fed her team and then agonized over whether to set out along the 58-mile trail to Koyuk. She was packing, yet struggling with her decision, when Barve mushed into the checkpoint. The blocky printer couldn't believe the woman was even considering going out.

"If it's anything like what I just came through, it's impossible," Lavon declared.

"That set me," Riddles later wrote. "Impossible? This was the whole point of all the work and energy I'd put into the last five years." Infuriated by Barve's macho certainty, Libby climbed on the runners of her sled and pulled the snow hook.

"Okay, gang," she said. "Let's go."

It was zero out, but the wind chill amounted to 56 degrees below as Riddles mushed out of Shaktoolik that afternoon. She didn't get as far as Nayokpuk. She hadn't passed Lonely Hill, hadn't yet reached the beginning of the 30-mile run across the sea ice, when the storm halted her team for the night. Though morning brought no relief, Riddles stayed on course, struggling through another day of storms before she mushed into Koyuk after 24 hours on the trail. The other mushers weren't far behind, but Riddles rode her hard-won advantage to Nome, finishing 2 hours 45 minutes ahead of Dewey Halverson.

Everyone in our group knew Libby's story. And nobody, least of all me, wanted to duplicate her heroics. Riddles had been reaching for the crown, $50,000, and lasting glory as the first woman ever to win the Iditarod. Our motivations were far less grand. We had, at best, a belt buckle and a finisher's patch waiting if we made it. There were other, less tangible, rewards—such as the right to raise a beer with Hobo Jim and sing, "I did, I did, I did the Iditarod Trail." We also faced, perhaps, a lifetime of regret if we flamed out in the remaining miles.

Today's sky was clear over Shaktoolik, signaling a tiny window ahead. We meant to push through before Nature slammed it shut. By 4 P.M. everyone was packing to leave. Daily hadn't yet arrived. Doc and the others weren't going to wait—and neither was I.

Just the other night in Unalakleet we were talking about the Red Lantern. I protested when Daily said he wouldn't mind getting it.

"Better watch it," I said. "I heard Barry say that same thing. Garth too. Start thinking the Red Lantern wouldn't be so bad, and the next thing you know—you're history."

The Red Lantern was becoming a curse. And Daily appeared to be another victim.

There was an undercurrent of panic as we broke camp. Vague rumors were circulating about more storms on the way. I nearly lost it on Rainy when I saw her bite through another harness seconds after I had slipped it on. I smacked her on the nose with my mitt and yelled. The lesbian seemed not to hear me. Her lips were tight. Her attention was completely absorbed by the exodus taking place around us.

My spares were shredded. I decided to let Rainy wear a crooked harness for a while and see if that made an impression. I mushed from the village at 4:45 P.M., led by a unrepentant bitch trailing webbing in the snow.

The trail again rose into rolling hills. Gunnar Johnson repeatedly passed Terhune and me. Each time, his team bogged down as soon as he was in front, forcing us to pass again. Terhune finally exploded.

"If you pass me again," he yelled at Johnson, "I'm going to knock you right off that goddamn sled."

"My team's faster . . . "

"Your dogs are as fast as the team in front," Terhune snorted. "They won't go nowhere without somebody to follow."

His point was demonstrated as Herrman's team overtook us. Latching on to the superior team, Johnson left us behind.

"Good riddance," Terhune shouted at the vanishing hitchhiker.

CHAPTER 11

Off to See the Wizard

Lonely Hill rose from a flat frozen marsh, a solitary sentinel guarding the Iditarod Trail's entrance to Norton Bay. At the foot of that towering rock stood what, on clear days, you'd have to call a crude plywood shack. On bad days, when searing winds whipped the barren coast, grateful travelers found those worn boards a priceless sanctuary.

The shelter looked bleak and unappealing when I caught the others there. A quick visit inside did nothing to change my opinion. Then again, it was a hospitable night. No wind to speak of, it was relatively mild, with darkness just slipping over the gray horizon. And there was comfort in the company gathered at Lonely Hill. Only Daily was missing from the convoy.

A faint breeze was rising. Cooley wanted everyone to agree to stick together crossing the ice. Plettner protested. She didn't want to play nursemaid, as she had out on the Yukon. Her dogs were faster, she pointed out, so she had to keep stopping and waiting for the slower teams. Stopping at some arbitrary exposed place, midway across the ice, sounded awful cold to her.

I didn't like the idea any better. I may have needed help with the deep Yukon snow, but this was entirely different. I was confident that Rainy and Harley, even Chad, Raven, and Rat, could handle the ice. My team was slower, not slower than everybody else's, but definitely slower than Plettner's, Herrman's, Cooley's and, perhaps, Williams's. Traveling with the convoy compounded the speed differential. Speedsters shot ahead, then rested awaiting us slow pokes. As soon as teams like mine closed the gap, the fast drivers took off again. The net result was that the teams in the rear of the convoy were getting progressively less and less rest, resulting in our slowing down even more.

Scar was curling so tightly at every pause that he looked like a pretzel. Digger still leaped like a pogo stick when the team paused, but that bouncing exuberance seemed reflexive, almost zombielike. Even Harley seemed a bit shell-shocked, but his trembling had always been disconcerting. I argued that my dogs would be better off setting their own pace.

Cooley hung tough. "Every team in this group is going to get to Nome" he declared. "And that means we're going to stick together tonight." He suggested that we all go inside the shelter to discuss it.

Plettner was sick of discussions. The group was making her crazy. She pictured herself holding a machine gun and laughing as she shot us down. Rather than waste more time, she agreed to Cooley's plan. I went along, albeit reluctantly. Each musher pledged to watch out for the team directly behind. We came up with a code for the headlamps. One blink meant "everything is all right." Two blinks: "I'm in trouble."

Based on the order of our arrival at Lonely Hill, Don Mormile owned the last spot in line crossing the ice. He approached me before we broke camp.

"I'm having some trouble with my leaders . . . "

Mormile was a ceaseless complainer. He whined about checkpoints, about race officials, and about his dogs, which were leased from Redington. I didn't like Don Mormile. I didn't trust him. But my personal distaste faded when I saw the fear in his eyes.

"Why don't you go in front," I said. The parade order made no difference to me. Not with Nome still 200 miles away. "But you better be watching for me, Mormile. You better be watching."

Tom Daily enjoyed the climb out of Unalakleet. He hadn't expected to see so much timber this far north. The sun was so inviting he lay on his sled and napped atop one of the hills. He awakened feeling refreshed.

Reality was waiting in the marsh below. Clouds rolled in, hurling a bitter wind at the Red Lantern musher and his dogs. The only encouraging sign came from Bogus. From the moment he hit the coast, the dog had undergone a personality change. His tug line was taut, and he trotted with the enthusiasm of a pup.

Daily assumed he would catch us in Shaktoolik. But all he found waiting behind the armory were empty beds of straw and a loose pile of race-related trash.

"Oh, you Iditarod mushers. Thank God you're the last one." As if it weren't depressing enough to find us gone, the village checker's sour greeting stung.

"Let me use a bathroom, and I'm out of here," Daily said.

The armory's compost toilet was overflowing owing to heavy use from earlier racers. Tom was directed to a nearby house. The family was very friendly. They ushered him into a room with a toilet in a corner. He was taking off his gear, layer by layer, when he noticed a little Eskimo girl watching. He tried to shoo her from the room, but the little girl kept sneaking back inside, delighted by this new game with the oddly costumed stranger.

"Nothing comes easy on this Iditarod," the musher mumbled.

Conditions became hellish after Daily left Shaktoolik about eight that night. Loose snow shot across the hard drifts making it tough to see. And while Bogus set a good pace, he kept veering from the marked trail. "Gee! Gee! Gee!" Daily felt as if he had shouted the command a thousand times.

Daily sensed his dogs were nearing their emotional limit. He was being sandblasted by the wind and was starting to doubt his own judgment. The trail ahead looked awful, but Tom wasn't at all sure he could find the way back to the village. Less than 15 miles out from Shaktoolik, Daily's sled abruptly stopped. Curling into balls, his dogs lay down in the storm.

Begging my way onto the Associated Press plane one year, I got a look at what mushers faced crossing Norton Sound. The pilot, Larry, swooped low over several teams so Rob Stapleton and I could get pictures. The light was magnificent. The sun, already low on the horizon, threw long shadows off the dog teams, which were cutting a straight line through patches of white snow and dark blue sea ice. As Larry circled and banked, Stapleton and I leaned out the windows, chewing up film in our motor drives.

Mushing across the ice wasn't bad, not at first. The dogs were rolling. My runners neatly sliced the crusty mounds. In the areas free of snow, numerous white cracks showed through the dark ice, but the visible depth of the fractures was actually a comfort. I caught Mormile whenever I pleased. He was conscientious about checking on me. Every five minutes or so he turned back and flashed his headlamp, awaiting my response. The bouncing lights of the full convoy stretched out half a mile or more into the darkness. Odd shouts floated back across the ice, mixing with the wind and the steady crunch of sleds on the move.

It was the perfect moment for listening to my much-traveled Miles Davis tape. I was still amazed at the journey the tape had made. A race volunteer had found it on the trail leaving Rohn, where the tape had fallen out of my overturned sled. It had then been sent ahead to Unalakleet, via Iditarod's air force, and the checker there surprised me with it. I had the tape with me, but it was purely a good-luck charm. My Walkman had quit. Too bad, the trumpeter's wail would have suited this forlorn place.

Another annoyance: my thermos was empty. I had meant to refill it when I melted snow for cooking in Shaktoolik. But I had forgotten and used all the hot water for mixing dog food. I was thirsty.

As the temperature dropped, I reached inside the sled bag and pulled out my parka. Wearing the coat loosely over my shoulders helped, until it got colder. The parka zipper was icy, and I had trouble sealing it. I needed that full hood—the breeze was turning vicious. Balancing on the runners as the sled continued to bump and slide across the ice, I gripped the zipper tab with Channellock pliers. I had worked the zipper to just below my neck when the goddamn tab tore loose. Lurching backward, I almost fell off the sled. I swung my arms until I regained my balance on the runners.

The hood on my parka now became a wind scoop, funneling the subzero breeze into my chest. I held the neck of my parka shut with one hand, while I gripped the sled with the other. Hunched over the handlebar, I concentrated on keeping Mormile in sight. Northern lights were rippling overhead, neon green, soft white, and hints of red, but I was in no mood to appreciate them. I was cold, damn cold. Too cold to care.

Later, I don't know how much later—time having become secondary to the absolute necessity of clinging to the sled and staring at Cyrus's and Rat's steps as they ran in wheel—I came upon the others. They were stopped for some reason, talking and snacking their dogs. I watched them, making no move to get off my sled.

"You OK?" Terhune asked.

I had trouble even processing the question. And when I

sorted "yes" from "no," my mouth just wouldn't work. I shook my head. By then, I was surrounded by headlamps.

"Drink this," someone said, handing me a cup of warm juice.

The liquid was startling, rolling down my throat like fire. I drank several cups and felt the energy spreading through my body. Snapping out of my delirium, I babbled about the zipper. "You need a shell, something to block that wind."

I dug out Nora's shell. It was too small to fit over my big parka, but it might fit between the parka and the snowmachine suit. The zipper was still locked under my neck. The others helped me duck out of the stiff parka and slip on the lightweight shell, which was really too tight for this purpose. I felt like a mummy as they lowered the parka back over my head, but the deadly chink in my armor was closed.

Gripped by the cold, I'd stopped eating, a telltale sign that I wasn't thinking clearly. As I revived, I felt ravenous. But I was careful. I hadn't forgotten the story of the musher who had knocked himself out of the Quest with a handful of M&Ms. Popping them in his mouth on a 40-below night, he gagged as they froze to his mouth and throat.

I settled for gnawing on a rock-hard brownie. Then I took care of the dogs. Their ears perked as they heard the rustle of the stiff plastic snack bag. They were tired, I could see that in Rainy's brown eyes, and in the way Cricket, Screech, and Scar sprawled, wagging their tails lightly as I approached with the goodies. Harley stood stiffly, trembling with anticipation. Only Pig and Cyrus showed no signs of fatigue and leaped for the chunks of sausage fat and frozen whitefish.

The rest stop abruptly ended when Tom Cooley called our attention to a low black fog swallowing stars on the horizon.

"A ground blizzard is coming," he said. "We better run straight through."

Low-blowing powder was streaming across the ice, parting

on contact with the dogs like water around boulders. Eye-level, visibility wasn't bad, but the wind penetrated my face mask, making my cheeks ache.

Crossing a dip, Spook caught a foot in the lines. I let him hop for a few seconds, hoping he would clear it on his own. No such luck. Mormile pulled away as I stopped to clear the tangle. Nothing to worry about.

I ran back to the sled. Yanked the hook and . . .

Harley had doubled back and was humping Raven.

"Harley, no!" I ran up front and tried to separate them. Too late. They were locked together in the unstoppable romance dance, indifferent to the blizzard gathering force around us.

"Why now. Why now," I groaned.

Mormile's light steadily sailed away. I looked at my watch, marking off 20 minutes, wondering how far ahead the others could get in that span of the dial. Would I still be able to see their lights? Two, three minutes passed, Mormile hadn't turned around. I cursed him, calling on the stars to witness his perfidy. Finally, he turned.

One blink. Was I OK?

How to explain? Hell. I returned one blink. "A-OK here," sure. So I was trapped on the ice with a storm bearing down, waiting for Harley to get his rocks off. Up front, the lesbian was trying to mount Screech. The other dogs were watching me. Scar and Pig looked envious. Cricket was shyly wagging her tail. I started laughing and petted them. I wasn't scared, and I wasn't alone. These 13 friends of mine provided plenty of company.

Mormile, much farther away now, turned his light back toward me again.

I blinked once, sending the "A-OK" message. I was delayed, but there was no serious trouble to report from the Norton Bay Sex Club.

Mormile slowed down and waited for me. The musher directly ahead of him, Terhune, stopped when he lost sight of

Mormile's headlamp. In theory, this should have put the brakes on the entire convoy. But Gunnar Johnson, traveling in front of Terhune, never looked back. The chain was broken.

Daily couldn't let the dogs quit on him. Not here, crossing an exposed, windy marsh. He grabbed Bogus by the collar and dragged the team forward. It was a struggle, but he got the dogs moving. Tom didn't know anything about the shelter cabin at Lonely Hill. Somewhat miraculously, he found it anyway. Being inside the rickety structure was better than being outside. Daily was tempted to bring in his dogs. That was against the rules, but who was going to know? He sighed. He would know. Daily wasn't comfortable with that, and he hadn't come this far to be disqualified by a stupid mistake.

Daily started a fire with the alcohol left by Plettner. After feeding his team, the musher became depressed. Partly, it was the storm, which was really howling now. The surroundings didn't help. The cabin was filled with trash. He could tell it was mostly from other mushers. Iditarod mushers trapped here, like he was now. While the storm rattled the shelter's exterior walls, Tom Daily busied himself, cleaning house.

Harley and Raven didn't get to savor their rendezvous. The second they separated, I put the lovers to work chasing Mormile, who had slowed to wait for me.

When Don and I caught up with Terhune, he took point for our trio, driving his dogs with a verbal whip. The storm blew over, and the stars soon returned. When we caught up with the group, Terhune quit yelling at his dogs and yelled at Johnson instead. The young musher swallowed the abuse; there wasn't much he could say.

My night of torment continued. The sled was pounding, pounding, pounding over rock-hard drifts. I lost my footing several times and was dragged on my knees or chest. The lights of Koyuk beckoned, but the village didn't seem to be getting any closer. Checkpoints were never more than an hour beyond the first hint of lights. Yet these lights stayed out of reach. I found it harder and harder to stay awake. The temptation was growing to park and curl up inside my sled.

Harley was giving me fits. Those lights and the other dog teams were dead ahead, yet he kept veering to the right. Always to the right. I kept having to drag him back to the tripods and the scratches in the hard drifts that defined the trail.

Convinced, at last, that Harley was dragging us toward another village dump, I lost my temper and ran up front. The big dog was cowering as I caught myself on the verge of making an unpleasant scene. He didn't deserve blame for seizing the opportunity to get laid. It had happened during my watch. I put Chad and Rat in lead, figuring they wouldn't lose sight of a checkpoint. But they too kept turning right. What was going on?

Man, was it hard to stay awake. We had to be close. So close. I kept driving, screaming at Chad and reaching for the pretty lights. We were mushing toward the Emerald City. In the distance, I could see the headlamps of my companions. They were driving their dogs up a spiral staircase, climbing twin towers rising on either side of a huge gate in front of the village. I calmly wondered what it was going to be like, climbing that Emerald City tower. Nothing seemed unusual about the scene. Reality was blending with fantasy, and the Yellow Brick Road wasn't all that strange compared with mushing dogs toward these unearthly lights.

My trip to Oz was rudely interrupted when the dogs plunged over a ten-foot cliff, the result of a pressure ridge formed by past movements in the ice. I hadn't noticed that we were climbing a big fold. The sudden drop flipped the sled and sent me crashing hard. I hung on, landing chestdown on the ice and smacking both knees. That one hurt. I wondered if my legs were broken. The dogs sensed my distress. For once, they passed up a chance to drag me.

Nothing was broken. I pulled myself together and resumed the march. Herrman was the first to arrive in Koyuk, checking in at 5:25 A.M. Traveling about 45 minutes behind, I watched the other teams entering the village. Drawing closer, I could see headlamps moving near a brightly lit building. Had to be the checkpoint.

The trail swung left, looping into the village. Observing the activity by the checkpoint, Chad made a beeline for it. Too drained to protest, I concentrated on hanging on as the team crashed through several backyards, dodging parked cars and snowmachines, before finally emerging on the street below the checkpoint.

"Why didn't you follow the trail?" the checker asked sternly.

"These guys had other ideas," I mumbled, terrified he might make me reenter Koyuk using the marked trail. I was at my limit, ready to beg. Please. Please don't make me do that. But the villager was just curious.

A mushing angel appeared at my side.

"There's a good place for the team over there," said Catherine Mormile, aiming her headlamp at an open spot between two houses. "Need help?"

"Please," I said.

After parking the team, I unhitched Raven and tied her to the sled, separated from potential lovers. I heated water for the dogs, petting and scratching them while I waited for it to boil. I served them a meal. Then I grabbed my sleeping bag and trudged inside the checkpoint on leaden feet. The long room echoed with snores. Finding a clear spot near a video machine, I carefully spread my sleeping bag on the floor and flopped on top of it. Still dressed in my snowmachine suit, bunny boots, and three layers of facial masks, I fell asleep instantly.

I was falling off the sled. Reaching for the handlebar, I awakened inside the Koyuk checkpoint. I wasn't capable of sleeping more than a few hours anymore. None of us were. Trail rhythms were too ingrained.

Feeling groggy, and a little foolish about awakening with a lamp still strapped on my head, I went outside to check on the dogs. They were fine, luxuriating in piles of fresh straw, which I didn't even remember spreading. I threw each of them chunks of frozen beef and liver.

It was gray and blustery. Gusts of wind picked at a mound of Iditarod trash outside the checkpoint and sent scraps dancing in the street. Inside the checkpoint, the others were talking about staying awhile. A monster of a storm was on the way.

Sticking around sounded fine to me. The dogs and I were running on reserves. I walked over to the Koyuk general store. Strolling down the aisle, I found myself staring at a packet of spaghetti. Practically drooling, I scooped up the noodles, a fat brick of hamburger, and sauce.

There was a long line at the cash register. Waiting my turn, I realized that I had other needs besides food. I crossed my legs. I shuffled from foot to foot. There was a white outhouse across the street. I could see it in my mind. It wasn't far. I was close to making a run for it when my turn came at the cash register. I collected my change, and bolted for that outhouse.

I threw down my shopping bag. I yanked the suit zipper, the vest zipper, pulled up my fleece shirt, fumbled with the drawstring on my pants . . . and . . . sighed as the burning stream ran down my right leg and pooled inside the rubber boot.

The wind was blowing even harder, if that was possible, when Daily left the shelter cabin at Lonely Hill. But it was daylight. He could see a marker, maybe two. And, if he waited any longer, dog food was going to become a problem.

The team hadn't gone more than a few miles when Bogus quit again. Daily tried each of his leaders. Each refused to go. On a hunch, he placed Diamond—the slow leader he had bought from Barve—in front. The dog balked. So Daily bit him in the ear. That got Diamond's attention. Moving at one mile per hour, the old dog led the team across the ice, traveling marker by marker.

In Koyuk, like many Alaska villages, most homes lacked running water. People made do with a public shower and laundromat. I made an emergency visit, toting an armload of dirty gear and chewed dog harnesses. After loading the washer, I climbed in the shower and soaked for the second time since leaving Anchorage. While I waited for the laundry to dry, I patched the dog harnesses. Part of me was embarrassed at squandering racing time in a laundromat. But, even barring my outhouse mishap, having clean clothes was beneficial. Sweat reduces thermal protection in cold-weather gear. The final miles would be warmer thanks to this village pit stop.

Later, I walked over to the village school to see if I could borrow a Coleman stove to cook my spaghetti.

"The kids in the village really enjoy seeing you guys," one teacher said. "Most of the mushers pass through the village in such a rush they don't often get a chance."

I've always enjoyed talking to school groups about my profession. I offered to return in the morning and speak to an English class about careers in journalism, or just talk about the race, if that's what the kids wanted. My presentation was scheduled for 9:30.

Owing to the approaching storm, a scheduled basketball game with another village had been canceled. Concern was also growing about Daily, who had left Shaktoolik the night before. Villagers were talking about sending out a rescue party when Tom was finally sighted in the distance, late Thursday afternoon.

I was talking to an AP reporter on the pay phone when Tom walked in. I collared him, Herrman, and a few other mushers who happened past and put them on the phone for interviews. It was part of my campaign to make sure the Iditarod headquarters didn't forget us.

"You should see O'Donoghue," Daily told the reporter. "Skin's falling off his face. He looks hideous."

I was a little nicked, that's all. Coming across the ice, wind had leaked between my goggles and the face masks and burned a line across my cheeks and nose. The shower had left the branding raw and bloody. It looked worse than it felt, but I was embarrassed by the way people kept gasping.

Later, Daily trudged up to the laundromat with a load of his own. Cooley was already there and had beat him to the bathroom. Tom shrugged and put his clothes in the washer. Long minutes passed. Cooley remained busy in the bathroom stall. Finally, Daily couldn't wait any longer. He knocked. There was no response. Yanking open the door, he found Doc sitting on the toilet, sound asleep.

Back in the checkpoint, I cooked my spaghetti feast in a dog pan. Other mushers laughed as they saw what I was doing.

"You're not going to eat all that yourself, are you?"

"Watch me."

We were shell-shocked. Twenty days on the trail, and Nome was another 170 miles yet. But no one was complaining tonight. Half a dozen mushers agreed to accompany me to the school in the morning. Don Mormile was in rare form, mumbling songs and waltzing across the floor with a broom.

"We're going to be here until spring," someone cried.

"You already are," another musher shot back.

It was indeed March 21, the spring equinox. The concept seemed ludicrous.

A television, tuned to the state's rural satellite network, was blaring in the kitchen area. A news program was on. No one paid much mind until the Iditarod update started. "Snowmachiners are out searching for musher Tom Daily," the announcer said, looking grave. "The rookie, traveling in last place, has been missing since Wednesday and is feared lost in a storm. . . ."

Inside the checkpoint, all eyes turned to Daily, who was also watching the broadcast, munching a handful of caramel-coated Screaming Yellow Zonkers.

"Gee. And I didn't even know I was lost," Tom said, beaming. "Should I be worried?"

By morning, the sky had cleared. Below the village, the next section of trail stretched before us, flagged by tiny markers streaming bright orange tape. Other mushers scrambled to depart. I had an appointment to keep at the school. Let them go. I figured I could catch the slower teams without difficulty.

Looking at the bright faces of the school's older students, I was glad I had kept my promise. Life is so cloistered for kids in Alaska's small villages. Personal contact with outsiders can have a big impact. I'd learned that traveling to small villages as a reporter. It was even more true for a visiting Iditarod musher, a role that bridged our two worlds.

Sepp Herrman was the only musher left when I returned to the checkpoint. He was sweeping it out. The small contribution made him feel a little less ashamed of the Iditarod trash blowing through the streets outside. It may have been piled neatly when the front teams passed through Koyuk, but ten days of wind had spread the mess the length of the street.

Leaving Sepp working the broom, I crossed the street to my team. The males, now rested, were enraptured by Raven's alluring scent. Cyrus was a hopeless case. The young male was on his feet, straining toward Raven rigid as a pointer, barking and barking. The other dogs stretched and sniffed each other as I moved through the team checking their feet. Their paws looked remarkably good, even those that had been sporting cuts a few days before. Coastal snow was kinder to sled-dog feet.

A sudden snarl spun me around. Harley had Chad on the ground, with his big jaws clamped around Golden Dog's neck. You could hardly call it a fight. Chad, limp, was on his back in complete submission.

Herrman had come over to look at my team. He understood the situation instantly. "You have a bitch in heat. Yes?" the German said. "The males fight for the lady's love."

No blood was spilled. I shifted Harley to the rear of the team and tried to shelter Raven among the females up front. The lesbian promptly spun around and tried to mount her.

Herrman remained behind in Koyuk, but caught me within the hour. We shared a snack in another crude shelter cabin, then he left me behind.

Out of habit, I grabbed teetering markers whenever I could, firmly replanting them for the teams following behind. Did that for an hour or two, before a startling thought stopped me in midmotion. I was again mushing the last team on the Iditarod Trail. Chuckling, I slipped the marker into my sled bag. With Nome a mere 100 miles away, I had room for a souvenir alongside that damn Lantern.

If it weren't for the rooftop-high drifts and the spider web of snowmachine tracks, Elim, population 220, could have been a small suburban community anywhere in the United States. The streets were laid out in a grid with matching modular houses arranged in neat rows, the legacy of a federal housing project.

Within those homes, however, resided a traditional Eskimo community, which had taken root here around the turn of the century, tending the local reindeer herd.

Daily was staying with a family that had only recently moved into their new government house. There was no curtain on the new shower, but the musher wasn't going to pass up the opportunity for a soak. He cranked the hot water valve and nearly leaped out, scalded by the first truly hot water to touch his skin in weeks.

A feast was waiting at the family's dinner table: moose, caribou, and fresh buttery cinnamon rolls. Afterward, Daily's hosts sat down around their television to watch an hourlong Iditarod special.

"If you folks don't mind, I think I'll take a nap," Tom said.

He'd been asleep for about an hour when a conversation on the family's CB radio roused him. In a voice that creaked with age, a village elder delivered a warning.

"Don't let those mushers leave," the man said. "They'll be lost on McKinley."

The argument continued over the CB, with what seemed like half the village chiming in. A young-sounding local musher declared that he would personally lead the Iditarod teams across Little McKinley, a treacherous hill overlooking Golovin Bay. Listening from his bunk, Daily thought that we probably ought to do what the old guy said.

My host was a young teacher. Sue and her boyfriend, Marty, shared a house in the center of the village. Outside, children, sporting furry parkas, flocked around, spreading out straw for my dogs.

As I requested, Sue awakened me after a two-hour nap. "Is there anything I can get you?" she asked.

Three more checkpoints lay between me and Nome. White Mountain was the only place I planned to stop. My thermos was already filled with hot Gatorade. I had the teacher place a few spoonfuls of instant coffee in a sandwich baggie. It was a secret weapon for the final push. I was ready to start racing again.

Sue's boyfriend Marty led me out of Elim on his snowmachine at about 11:30 P.M. It was dead calm and dark. Snow was falling in wet, feathery clumps. About a mile out of town, I saw a headlamp behind me. The team closed in on us depressingly fast. It was Plettner. Exchanging a few words, she took off like a rocket.

Snow was coming down hard as my team climbed Little McKinley. Rainy and Harley weren't the least bit bothered. I was running blind myself. There were hardly any markers. I was thankful for the tracks of the other teams. It was hard to miss the groove, six to eight inches deep, which they had kindly left behind.

Descending the formidable hill was more of an adventure. It was a steep sidehill slope. The teams ahead had cut an erratic weave of traversing paths. I tipped my sled, riding on one runner, fighting to hold the team in a straight line. But it was hopeless, too many of the teams had already slipped sideways, carving cutaways that repeatedly slammed my sled into downhill bushes and trees. Roughly halfway to the bottom, I caught Plettner and the others. The convoy was stalled. Our lone Iditarod veteran was furious.

"None of them knows how to find a trail," Plettner said. With a sigh, she slouched down against her sled.

After a lengthy pause, word was relayed back up the line that Sepp Herrman was in trouble. That was a jolt. I hated to imagine a situation Sepp couldn't handle.

More shouting back and forth yielded word that Herrman's team had charged off a mountain cliff, or something to that effect. Cooley and a few others had heard the trapper shout "help" from below. Doc was leading a party to investigate. Naturally I was curious. But our parking spot was precarious. It wouldn't take much for the team to bolt and crash into the others directly below us.

"Send a gun!" Cooley's message was relayed by Urtha Lenthar, who was positioned midway down the hill.

"What?"

"Cooley says to send down a pistol," Lenthar repeated.

Terhune figured the comment was directed at him. Cooley knew Terhune was packing a large-caliber pistol. Well, the vet was asking the wrong guy for help. Terhune had no intention of lifting a finger to assist Super Trapper. "Fuck Sepp," he snarled.

I turned to Plettner.

"What could be going on?"

"Maybe he injured some dogs, and Cooley wants to put them out of their agony," she suggested, shaking her head at the thought.

Throwing my sled on its side, I stuck my borrowed .357 in my pocket and set forth down the slope. The snow on the hillside was waist-deep. Half-walking, half-sliding past scrubby bushes, I made my way to Urtha.

"Give it to me," he said, demanding the gun.

"No way," I said. "It's my gun, I intend to see how it's used."

Joined by Daily, I continued slogging down the hillside. It was a long hike to where Cooley was waiting. Using snowshoes might have been a good idea. It also occurred to me that it was going to be a lot tougher climbing back up.

We found Cooley bent toward the ground, studying tracks left by Herrman and the local musher.

"You brought the gun?" he said.

I handed it to him.

"Good. They must have been attacked by a moose," Cooley

said, aiming his headlamp several feet ahead. "Look at those tracks."

A line of moose holes stretched across the tracks of both dog teams. The intersection was marked by a large patch of churned snow. "I didn't want to go any further without a gun," Doc explained. "Be careful, we might have an angry moose on our hands."

Shouting Sepp's name, we trailed the sled tracks into the thickets. It was hard work. Every third step the crust would give way beneath our boots. The effort was wasted. We never found Herrman, or any sign that either musher had so much as paused.

"I just can't understand it," said Cooley, who thought very highly of Herrman. "Where I come from, you don't yell 'Help!' and take off. And I heard him. I know I heard him."

Later, listening to the story, Terhune decided that Herrman probably did cry for help, and that it was probably a deliberate trick. Now that Herrman was close enough to make it to Nome without bumming dog food, Terhune figured the so-called cry for help was a trick to slow everyone else down. Terhune chuckled at the way Super Trapper had the rest of us fooled.

Cooley and the other mushers at the front of the pack were reluctant to try Herrman's kamikaze route. But no one could find any markers.

"More of the void," mused Daily.

By the time I climbed the hill to my team, I was drenched in sweat. Before long, chills were invading my clammy gear. I needed to change clothes before continuing. But everything I had with me was wet. Everything, that is, except my green wool, military-style sweater. As cold as I had been so far, it gave me confidence knowing that I had the sweater in reserve, one more layer in case it got really bad. But I was reluctant to dig it out. If I put the sweater on and still felt cold—then what would I do?

My dilemma was resolved when the mushers at the head of

the line decided to camp. Stripping to my wet skivvies, I dove inside the sled bag. Would have been warmer if I took off the damp underwear first. But I was hoping my sleeping bag would absorb some of the moisture before I had to face another day in those wet clothes.

Shivering inside the sleeping bag, I had doubts about the plan. The blotter effect was an untested theory and might dampen the sleeping bag for no useful purpose. I forced myself to eat and drink, and tried to stay positive.

The musher from Elim had said something about a "short cut." The comment was made in passing. Herrman forgot about it, working his sled on that tricky sidehill trail. Out of the blue, the villager suddenly ordered his dogs over the hillside. He was showing off, sure. But the local musher knew the trail, and two could play this game. Sepp gave the word, sending his team over the edge. Herrman stuck to the local musher like glue down the steep incline. What a ride. What a ride!

Later, resting in Golovin, Sepp concluded that Cooley and the others must be stuck on that hill. Just as well, he thought. That ride was more than most of them could handle. There was no reason for Herrman to stick around, not with White Mountain a mere 18 miles away. He checked in there at 8:30 A.M., Saturday, March 23, starting the clock on his mandatory six-hour layover.

Herrman later denied yelling anything. It was puzzling to him. Everyone sounded so certain. Even Cooley, whose word Sepp respected. Some of them were actually mad at him, as if HE was responsible for their extra night on the little hill. It was ridiculous. Utterly ridiculous. Sepp's conviction weakened in the face of the group's certainty. Maybe, just maybe, he had said something. He might have blurted "Aieee!" Something like that. Sepp wasn't at all sure that it had happened—involuntarily, of course—but he couldn't rule out the possibility. Funny things occur when one is mushing off the side of a mountain. That was the truth. But he never yelled "Help." No matter what people thought they heard. He, Sepp Herrman, never called for help. He would have remembered that.

CHAPTER 12

Last Hurrahs

In the morning I was damp, but warm. My polypropylene underwear actually felt dry to the touch. Maybe there was something to those moisture-wicking fiber advertisements, though I'd never experienced much benefit wearing soggy polypropylene socks.

Daylight revealed plenty of markers on the trees ahead. Convoy leaders had missed them in the dark because the reflectors were dusted with snow. Had I been in front, I think I would have spotted them. But it didn't matter now.

Local villagers were sipping their Friday morning coffee as our group streamed into Golovin. Terhune and I were the last to reach the cluster of dog teams parked by the village hall. A sly smile shone through Terhune's scruffy beard.

"I'm not staying," he said. "I'm leaving as soon as they're all inside."

Not only were our dogs fresh from last night's forced camp; White Mountain lay only 18 miles away.

"It's time to remind these people it's a race," I agreed. "But I've got to find a bathroom before I go anywhere."

I was swimming in gas. My bubbling gut felt ready to explode, and I didn't want a repeat of Koyuk. Terhune wanted to get a cup of coffee. Playing it cool, we packed our sleds for departure, then sauntered inside the checkpoint.

Cooley was interrogating the checkers about Herrman. Most of our companions looked as if they were ready to relax for a good spell. I grabbed a cup of instant coffee and headed for the bathroom.

Terhune and I soon strolled back to our dogs.

"Let's go," he shouted, reaching for his hook.

"Daisy, Daisy on by!" he said, directing his lead dog past the teams crowding the checkpoint. It was a perfect place for a breakout. The snow was hard packed across a wide area from local traffic, and the trail exiting the village began 100 yards ahead.

The movement of Terhune's dogs sent other teams into a howling frenzy. Mushers spilled out of the checkpoint. Bedlam ensued. Shouts mixed with barking, while local villagers clapped and cheered, applauding Terhune's getaway.

I was right behind Jon approaching Gunnar Johnson's team. But then my dogs bunched up. Bo seized the chance to hump Raven. I leaped off the sled and separated the lovers.

"All right! All right," I shouted, still intent on following Terhune.

Other mushers were madly pitching gear at their sleds. As we were passing Johnson's parked sled, a tussle erupted in the middle ranks of my team. Pig, Digger, and Spook all had their teeth locked on a big chunk of meat. Wading into the center of the melee, I ripped the meat free and threw it at Johnson.

"What kind of bullshit is this Gunnar! Leaving meat on the ground next to your sled?"

"It wasn't on the ground," he protested. "Your dogs dived inside my sled bag and pulled that meat out."

"Oh, sorry about that."

Looking over his shoulder, Terhune watched my dogs seize the meat. He nearly fell off his sled laughing at the resulting mess. So be it, he thought, watching me fall behind.

Daily welcomed the sudden excitement. Lounging in the checkpoint, he had overheard Lenthar talking about staying to do a load of laundry. That was too much. He felt like grabbing the other musher and screaming "LET'S GET OUTTA HERE!" This absurd maneuver of Terhune's was just the jolt everyone needed.

While I fought for custody of the meat, Chad decided it was his turn to mount Raven. I broke up that love affair before it got started, and quickly got the team rolling. It was too late to gain any advantage. Everybody but Gunnar was already moving out, chasing Terhune. So much for my great escape.

Gunnar and I joined the tail end of the chain leaving Golovin. He was carrying the Red Lantern for once, but that didn't last. Another tangle halted us dead. This time Digger had pounced on Raven, my disruptive princess of love.

"Go ahead, Gunnar," I said, leaping off the sled to pull the dogs apart.

"Are you sure?" he said.

"Yeah, go for it."

I had the team lined out in about ten seconds flat. That much I was getting good at.

Terhune couldn't hold his lead. Never had a chance. Daisy's trotting speed had dropped to five, maybe six, miles per hour. The others closed in on him less than a mile out from the checkpoint. Terhune cursed to himself. He hated to see this. But there was nothing to be done. Dogs can only do what they can do. Terhune pulled aside and let the faster teams by, watching the smug looks on the faces of every racer who passed him.

"What happened?" I said, shocked to see him parked there. Terhune shrugged.

I'd been angry with myself for blowing that escape. Yet here we were together in the back of the train again.

"Well, we sure showed them."

"Yeah," Terhune growled. "Next time FEED your dogs first."

The sun was out and it was warm, 20 or 30 degrees above zero.

"At least it's a nice day," I yelled back. "I don't even need . . . my parka."

Sharp as an eight-by-ten photo, I recalled my big coat draped over a chair in the checkpoint bathroom. "Son of a bitch," I gasped, staggered by the magnitude of my screwup. I considered continuing on without it. It was so warm. Nome was so close. One word restored reality: "Topkok."

The area surrounding the Topkok Hills was one of the most dangerous on the trail. Mushers were sometimes trapped for days on the hillsides, or in the windy valley below. Continuing without that parka put my entire race in jeopardy. I stopped the team and dragged my dogs off the trail, waving Terhune ahead.

"What're you doing?"

"Left something behind," I said grimly.

Grabbing the lesbian's collar, I pulled the team back around and mushed toward Golovin.

What a pisser, thought Daily, watching me turn back. His own dogs were flying, soaring at a previously unimaginable pace behind Bogus. The lead dog appeared to actually smell Nome; Tom didn't know how else to explain it.

My dogs broke into a joyous lope. Returning to Golovin, an easy three miles back, was obviously a popular idea with the team. I hadn't even parked when one of the ladies staffing the check-point burst through the door with my parka under her arm.

"We found it as soon as you left," she said. "You didn't need to come back for it. We would have sent it to White Mountain on a snowmachine."

I sighed. "Came too far to take that chance."

Facing the exit trail, I snacked the dogs and petted them, trying to make a game of this latest pilot error. The crew responded as I hoped, wagging their tails, acting perky. But their spirits crumbled when I ordered Harley and Rainy to move out again. The lesbian didn't want to go at all. Raven's crotch was suddenly more interesting than anything waiting ahead. Harley froze, torn between my demands and the lure of Raven.

"Go ahead! Go ahead, Harley!" I insisted.

The big dog looked at me, a forlorn expression written on his face, then he lurched ahead, dragging Rainy to work. My dogs stumbled out of Golovin like POWs. Their ears were down. Pauses were frequent. All thirteen dogs had to relieve their bladders, or take smelly dumps, or both. I was the Bad Guy riding the heavy sled.

The accusatory looks didn't impress me. We were only going eighteen miles. Not a damn one of them was really tired. Hungry, yes. They hadn't had a hot meal since Elim. But my fine athletes couldn't be tired, not after that extra break on Little McKinley. They were just disappointed. And I couldn't blame them for that. I had broken the all-important Deal.

The dogs pulled and I fed them at each checkpoint: that was our unspoken compact, which had been reaffirmed at every stage of the last 1,000 miles. Every stage, that is, until Golovin, where I had broken that trust—twice in a single morning.

My assumption was vindicated as the dogs broke into a lope scenting White Mountain. The morning's betrayal was forgotten. Happy days were here. Ears perked, shoulders pitched forward with effort, Deadline Dog Farm's finest pulled with abandon. A checkpoint was ahead. Dinner was about to be served, thus reestablishing justice throughout dogdom as they knew it.

"HEP, HEP, HEP." That simple phrase was all it took. Bogus kicked the team into overdrive, and Tom Daily easily beat everybody else into White Mountain.

Jacked by his team's performance, Tom spent the next 45 minutes proudly greeting incoming teams. He wasn't paying attention as the checker, who was late coming down from the lodge, made his rounds.

Daily was bummed when he saw the time sheet later. It had Lenthar arriving first at 11 A.M., March 23. Daily was listed as fourth, adding an unwarranted 36 minutes to his mandatory 6-hour stop.

"Jesus" he said, "you can't win in this thing."

I shared Tom's disappointment in the White Mountain standings. Thanks to my parka snafu, I had arrived 70 minutes behind the closest musher ahead of me, and some two hours behind the Mormiles, Terhune, Daily, and Lenthar. Those were teams I expected to beat; 55 miles didn't offer much opportunity for a rebound. But a lot could happen. Look at Swenson.

After serving the dogs a meal, I unhooked little Raven and escorted her to the picket line for dropped dogs. I hated myself. Wasn't I the guy who had planned on mushing every dog to Nome?

Now I was abandoning a hard-working girl merely for being in heat, a situation I should have been able to deal with. But I couldn't, and that was the truth. That mating on the ice was nearly disastrous. The fight and the subsequent delay leaving Koyuk offered further proof that Raven's presence threatened the entire team.

The little black dog whimpered as I walked away. I

hesitated, and Raven flopped on her back, legs spread, inviting me to stroke her. My princess deserved no less for hauling me 1,100 miles.

"You did a good job, little girl," I said, rubbing her tight belly. "Too bad the boys won't leave you alone."

I was tired as I trudged up the hill to White Mountain Lodge. If there hadn't been a free meal waiting, I would have gladly slept with the dogs on the frozen river below.

Inside the clean lodge I felt decidedly out of place. The thick steak, rolled napkins, and polished forks—all seemed unreal after three weeks on the trail. And the lodge's interior was so hot I felt light headed.

My nap was interrupted. Mowry was on the line. The Coach berated me for not dropping Raven sooner. But that was just in passing. The Mowth wasn't calling to criticize. He sought to motivate me with a new shining goal.

Though I had already been defeated by the Poodle Man, the Russians, Madman, and over 40 others, Mowry said, a means yet remained to salvage Deadline Dog Farm's reputation. His old dogs—the team Old Joe had repossessed last spring—were pulling Don Mormile's sled. Catherine was also mushing a Redington team. The way Mowth saw it, if I beat those two teams to Nome, the feat would command respect throughout Knik. That wasn't just his own opinion, Mowry stressed. No less an authority than Marcie had agreed.

"Bri," he said. "Beat the Mormiles at all costs. Got that? BEAT THE MORMILES AT ALL COSTS!"

"Hey, those dogs look sort of skinny," said Plettner, offhandedly. She was picking up the pans from her team's second full meal at White Mountain.

My dogs did look kind of bony. I cooked them a second

meal. Plettner watched approvingly as my dogs sucked up the steaming pans of food. She was putting the last touches on packing, her own six-hour layover nearly complete. Shortly before six in the evening, Sunday, March 23, Plettner mushed out on the frozen river below White Mountain. Don Mormile followed close behind.

Watching the teams quietly slip away, I knew I'd never catch Plettner. The Mormiles? That game was still afoot. We'd find out soon enough.

I looked the team over. Even with bellies full the dogs' ribs—rising and falling with each breath—looked more defined, all right. Bo, Digger, and Harley, in particular, appeared strikingly gaunt. It was their attitudes, however, that showed the most change. Three weeks ago Cyrus would have been pacing and whining. Like soldiers or laborers everywhere, he and the others had learned to snatch a meal or rest whenever it was offered.

Even our maniacs now exhibited workmanlike calm. In leaving Raven behind, I was losing the one dog left in the team who barked at the first hints of departure. The changes were subtle, but profound. Pig no longer squirmed. Spook even welcomed my touch as I placed on booties.

In terms of pulling, the dogs had become a fine-tuned engine. When I let off the brake, tug lines snapped taut, and the team pulled in unison. Whisper "Whoa," and the dogs halted on a dime. The had become a single unit, possessing ability beyond the sum of the individual members. Though I didn't know it, I hadn't entered the race with a dog team. But I had one now.

Mushing from White Mountain, I was an hour behind the nearest sled. The trail and sky merged in a seamless gray landscape. I switched on my headlamp although it wasn't yet dark. There was comfort in the line of reflectors glowing in my beam. With Raven gone, I had 12 dogs left. Rainy and Harley were in lead. The odd couple had brought us most of the way. No reason to change now.

I had, incredibly, forgotten to get a weather report. The failure nagged at me as light snow began falling an hour out of White Mountain. "Here it comes," I whispered. "Three feet of snow in two hours. The biggest blizzard Nome's ever seen."

Daily had reentered the void. Judging from the slope, the team was probably climbing Topkok Hill. But it was just a guess. Tom couldn't see anything except the dogs and his sled. The world beyond was utterly white. This whole Iditarod was like wandering through heaven, the musher thought, a white misty place, with no beginning or end and nothing but dogs for company.

Topkok's bare crown was serene. The fog lifted as Daily and several other mushers descended toward the valley below. The Nome Kennel Club's shelter cabin waited at the bottom. Plettner, the veteran, knew better than to dally in this stretch. Wind seldom rested in the so-called "Solomon Blowhole." When it did blow, a layover in that cabin could mean the difference between life and death. On rare moments when it didn't, only fools stopped to visit.

Sepp Herrman was already closing in on Nome. Plettner's final drive was also underway. Cooley urged the others to assemble at the shelter cabin, and then mush together into Safety. Doc figured he'd brought his rookies too far to let one stray into the Bering Sea.

Don Mormile was outside the cabin working with his team when Terhune's dogs popped out of the darkness. That meant I was the only driver still on the way.

"You've got to stop," Mormile began. "Cooley says—"

Terhune cut him off. "I told you people, if you stop again—I don't care what the goddamn reason is—I'm going around. I don't want nothing to do with this group!" Ordering Daisy past the parked teams, Terhune rounded the cabin, followed the markers into the brush, and vanished.

Mormile went inside. The group got a chuckle out of this latest declaration from Terhune. No one felt threatened. This was, what, the third time the sourpuss had tried to get away? Those Kenai dogs were slower than dirt. When would he give it up?

As far as Daily could tell, Terhune couldn't get ten feet without screaming bloody murder at his poor lead dog. Daily saw nothing noble in it, not when the price was being paid by those poor tired dogs.

It mattered to Terhune. Every inch between him and those other people mattered. Rounding the shelter cabin, the musher switched off his headlamp. His dogs were slow, but they were tough, like him. Jon Terhune and Daisy meant to show them all.

I was startled by an approaching light. It came so fast I knew it had to be a snowmachine. The driver, a burly Alaska Native, stopped alongside the trail and beckoned to me. As I drew closer, the man smiled and reached inside his suit. He pulled out a tall bottle of Bacardi 151.

"Here, take a swig," he said, handing me the rum.

"Wind blew down the markers through here," the snowmachiner said, as I handed back his bottle. "Don't worry. I put in new ones for you guys. You won't have no trouble."

For the last hour, I'd been climbing featureless, snow-covered hills. The trail was barely discernible on the hard windswept surface. I hated to imagine this place in a whiteout. The trail rose steadily higher and higher over bare rounded steps. Several times I thought I was cresting the summit only to discover another steep hill waiting ahead.

The moon, near full, shone brightly through the misty night sky. After I switched off my headlamp, the snow seemed radiant with reflected light. The dogs and I were cast into a realm of living negatives. I rubbed my eyes and pressed on. The top—it had to be the top—was getting closer.

Cresting Topkok, the trail crossed a short flat plateau. I stopped the team and studied the valley below. The view was surprisingly clear. I could trace the trail, winding through bushes and shrubs to a shelter on the valley floor. It looked dark and deserted. Way, way off in the distance, I saw a string of moving lights.

"Gotcha!" I said. Releasing the brake, I sent my dogs charging downward.

I'd come straight through from White Mountain. The dogs were due for a break, so I paused to check out the shelter cabin. Leaving the crew gnawing on chunks of whitefish, I headed inside. The cabin interior was hot. Coals were still glowing in the stove. Obviously, the others had spent a fair amount of time at the cabin.

I found some crackers and munched on them as I read the graffiti on the walls of the cabin. Recently refurbished, the shelter cabin beneath Topkok was in the best shape of any I'd seen on the trail. Most of the graffiti must have been left by mushers in this year's race. I saw comments from quite a few people I recognized, including Swenson, who was already gloating about win number five.

I scrawled a ditty about slipping from first to worst. "Let historians ponder that," I muttered, signing and dating it. Then I headed back outside and roused the dogs. It wasn't over yet.

Terhune kept Daisy on the march. He watched over his shoulder for headlamps, but none appeared. He traveled as much as possible with his own headlamp off. No reason to give those bastards a target to shoot at. Finally, Terhune saw a red-neon bar sign. Safety. He'd made it. Goddamn.

Terhune snacked his dogs and then studied the exit trail. Inside the bar he grabbed a plate of food and took a seat at a window overlooking the incoming trail. He wanted to give his dogs as much rest as possible. Exactly how long that might be, Jon didn't know. It depended on what he saw through the window.

Herrman had mushed into Nome early that morning, finishing in fifty-first place. Plettner had pulled across the finish line at 6 A.M. It galled him, but nothing Terhune could do would ever change that. But he could still stick it to those guys behind him. Thirty minutes passed, then 45.

"Good," the musher said, studying his watch. His dogs were getting a decent break. His stay was approaching an hour, when Terhune spied a distant bobbing light. He dashed for the bar door.

"Daisy!" the musher called the lead dog's name as he rushed toward the team. He grabbed several dogs and jerked them to their feet. Jumping on the runners, he reached for his snow hook. The finish line was 20 miles away. The others might be faster, but he had the jump.

Mushing away with his own headlamp switched off, Terhune watched over his shoulder. The single light had swelled to a moving cluster. Near the bar, the lights stopped. He had expected that. They had to stop to sign in. OK. OK. What would they do now? The lights remained stationary, and he slowly pulled away. Jon Terhune smiled. The fools were letting him get away.

"I can't believe Terhune is going to beat us," Mark Williams repeated. "He had the slowest dogs in the race."

Sitting at the bar, Daily shrugged. He wasn't impressed with Terhune. Daily's dogs would arrive in Nome in better shape. He was sure of that. And he wasn't impressed with Gunnar Johnson's deceitful little maneuver. The way he had snuck off, deserting everybody here at Safety, minutes after pretending he agreed with Cooley's plan to wait for O'Donoghue and mush into Nome together. It rubbed Daily the wrong way.

What was the rush? Next year he would come back and really race.

Daily ceremoniously bought himself a beer, the first he'd had in 21 days. He bought Cooley one, too.

The veterinarian was embarrassed. "Can I borrow money for a burger, Tom?" he whispered, confessing that he was flat broke.

If it wasn't the worst night of my life, it was close. Taking that short break at the cabin had been a major mistake. It had destroyed the team's rhythm. Leaving the cabin, Rainy and Harley slowed to a crawl. It was a repeat of the Golovin turnaround.

I was in trouble myself. Couldn't keep my eyes open. Looking for a caffeine jolt, I started dipping my fingers in the baggy of instant coffee and licking the powder off my fingertips. The secret weapon was a dud. All I got from chewing that lousy powder was cramps.

The mist returned, and world closed in around me. The whiteness just went on and on. At one point, I saw a light coming up from behind. It looked like a musher's headlamp, but it couldn't be; the light was coming too fast. Yet it was a dog team, closing so fast that my dogs seemed to be standing still.

"It's got to be Plettner," I decided by process of elimination. No one else had that kind of speed. The musher waved as the team caught and passed us. It was a man. That didn't make any sense. I couldn't figure it out, and then I realized the team and the sled looked all wrong. It wasn't an Iditarod musher. The sled was empty. It must have been some local speed demon.

The trail joined an unplowed road. Misery incarnate. Clocking the accompanying mile markers, I calculated that the team had slowed to under three miles an hour. No wonder it felt like we were crawling tonight. Rainy kept stopping to stare at . . . nothing.

Tonight my space cadet was in total orbit. Her pauses hobbled us. Watching the lesbian blast off for the third time in a mile, I stopped the team and switched Chad into lead with Harley. The team's pace improved. But it felt like we were just plowing faster into the void. A light snow caused spots to dance in the beam of my headlamp. I had a terrible time holding on. The road was so smooth. So endless.

With absolutely no warning, I drew alongside another parked Iditarod team. I didn't recognize the sled, but it was fully packed. The musher was nowhere to be seen. Dusted with snow and curled in tight balls, the musher's dogs were sleeping in front of the sled in a straight line.

Dazed, wondering who I'd caught, I stomped my snow hook into the ground. When I looked up, the other team was gone. A line of driftwood rested in its place.

I didn't need my headlamp anymore. The slow-falling snowflakes taunted me, jittering unpredictably, straining my eyes in the blue predawn light. It was approaching eight A.M. We'd been mushing down the lousy road for what seemed like days. The coffee baggie was half gone, and I was feeling queasy.

At last, a light gleamed in the distance. A red and white bar light. A checkpoint called Safety. "Let's go home!" I whispered. Chad raised his head. Ears shot up along the line. The dogs shifted gears, recharged with purpose.

I clung to the hope that others might be having similar

problems. Surely I'd catch a few other teams lingering in Safety. I knew Terhune wouldn't wait. But Cooley had talked about it. And the Mormiles couldn't be too far ahead, could they?

All I found waiting was a tattered Iditarod banner, flapping in the wind. And a beer Daily had bought me on his way out the door.

"How long ago did the last team leave?" I asked the weary checker, hope flickering an instant longer.

"No more than twenty minutes," he said.

Calculations raced through my mind. It was 20 miles to Nome. Except for Cooley's dogs, the teams ahead weren't anything special. They'd be lucky to do six miles an hour. That gave me . . .

"They rested here two, maybe three hours," the checker added.

Hope died. Dead last. I was going to finish dead last.

A musher was sighted on the outskirts of Nome. The news was broadcast on KNOM radio at 9 A.M. Sunday, March 24, day 22 of Iditarod 1991. The banners and other decorations that greeted Swenson were no longer present, long since torn down or damaged in the numerous storms of the last 10 days. But the Burl Arch marking the Iditarod's finish line remained standing downtown. That was all that mattered.

No other dog teams were in sight as Terhune climbed off the frozen beach and turned his dogs down Front Street. At long last the old paratrooper relaxed. The fifty-third musher into Nome was a satisfied man.

He found Dawn and his two grown daughters waiting near the arch. They were holding a long handmade banner. "Welcome Jon," it read.

Gunnar Johnson mushed into town 45 minutes later.

The others weren't far behind. Johnson's desertion had

sparked a general exodus from Safety. To hell with waiting for me. The race was on again. A wild contest developed in the final miles. Charging across the icy drifts outside Nome, Daily thought he had the edge. Bogus, looking inspired, loped like a frisky pup. He dusted the Mormiles and surged ahead of Mark Williams. But Tom Daily's eight dogs were simply outpowered by the fourteen dogs pulling Urtha Lenthar's sled.

Lenthar, Daily, and Williams finished within one minute of each other, notching the fifty-fifth, fifty-sixth, and fifty-seventh positions in the record book. Not long afterward, Catherine Mormile won the race that mattered most to her—beating her husband, Don, and the Mowth's old dogs to the arch by almost 20 minutes. Cooley, our unofficial participant, let the others go ahead and followed Mormile into town, finishing at 10:43 A.M.

Bellies warmed by a hot meaty broth, my dogs slept on the lee side of Safety while the other teams raced for Nome. I lingered at the bar, sipping the beer Daily had bought me, sinking ever deeper into depression as I listened to the live radio coverage. The voice of Nome's checker, Leo Rasmussen, pierced my funk.

"If Brian O'Donoghue would ever leave Safety," I heard Leo say on the radio, "maybe we could get this over with."

I briefly wondered if there was any way to sneak into Nome, hide the dogs, and keep Rasmussen waiting forever. That would show him.

The one thing I had in my power to do was scratch. Let Mormile keep the damn Red Lantern. That was tempting. For the first time in the entire race, I seriously considered scratching.

Pondering the ramifications, I ordered another beer.

Two and a half hours later, I'd run out of reasons not to go. The wind kicked up as I prepared to leave. Drifts had erased every trace of the trail.

"Perfect," I said, dragging Chad to the closest marker, the first in a line of flapping streamers, which stretched toward a cluster of subdivision homes.

Golden Dog was in a contrary mood. He ignored my commands and repeatedly dragged Harley and the team away from the markers. I wanted to win this last battle of wills, but Chad was equally determined to follow snowmachine tracks leading to nearby homes. Forty-five minutes after leaving Safety, the bar remained in view behind us. The checker came outside and stared. This wasn't going to work. Demoting Chad, I placed Rainy up with Harley. The lesbian quickly sniffed out the trail, and Safety finally faded behind us.

Wind, fog, mist, and blinding snow—we encountered the whole gamut on the Iditarod's final 20 miles. The dogs paid no mind. They were too hardened to flinch.

Passing through a cluster of homes near the beach, I saw a couple sitting on chairs next to a marker. It was an older man and woman. They flagged me down.

"We were waiting for you," the woman said, petting Rainy and Harley. "Could we offer you a cup of coffee or a bite to eat?"

"Thanks," I said, "but I guess there's some folks waiting for me."

I was flattered that strangers would take the time to welcome me. The wind was dying down, and the day appeared brighter.

Rounding a bend, I confronted several dog teams, headed right at us. I realized we must have crossed the trail of another race as three teams passed, head-on, going full bore. I was startled by a face I knew, Iditarod musher Peryll Kyzer. She'd not only finished an impressive eighteenth; she was already running another race.

"Hi, Peryll," I shouted as she flew past on my left.

"Brian!" she said. "Welcome to Nome."

A few miles ahead the trail neared a plowed road leading to

Nome. I knew the area well. It was the place where I had once had a pair of cameras freeze up while I was shooting Nayokpuk leading another musher through a storm, which subsequently halted the race for days. I had also been waiting here as Butcher charged into view, en route to her third straight victory. And it was at this same spot, 40 hours later, that I had witnessed Redington cap his bold run as Smokin' Joe.

With the race lost to Susan and the other young hounds, Redington had waited at Safety for Nayokpuk. The two veterans traded stories over coffee, then Old Joe issued a challenge.

"Now we're going to race," he said.

The lead switched several times during the furious 22-mile sprint that followed. Redington emerged victorious, crossing the finish line 1 minute, 16 seconds, ahead of Nayokpuk.

"This is fantastic," Butcher said, greeting the pair under the arch. "This is the best race within the race."

Iditarod's 70-year-old founder had failed to take the big prize, but Smokin' Joe's style couldn't be beat. He earned $9,000 for the fifth-place finish, which equaled his all-time best.

In the morning, Nayokpuk awoke with a tingling in his left arm.

"I just hate to think our race had anything to do with it," said Redington, pacing the floor of the Nome checkpoint as his friend was being flown to a hospital in Anchorage. "But Herbie, he was pushing pretty hard."

Nayokpuk was hospitalized with a mild stroke. He recovered, but his Iditarod days were over. Thus ended the racing career of the Shishmaref Cannonball.

As for Redington, he never topped that 1988 run.

"In my mind," Swenson said, years later. "There's no question Joe would have won that race if he had a trail out of Cripple. It's a damn shame."

As I pulled within sight of the road, I heard honking and whistling. People were cheering. The reception awaiting us grew wilder by the mile. A procession of snowmachines fell in on either side of us. Cars and trucks paced the team on the nearby road. People were clapping and waving from every drift.

A man leapt out of the back of a pickup truck. Clambering down a snow berm, he tossed me a can of beer. "This Bud's for you," he shouted. "We knew you were going to make it."

"Never any doubt," I said.

The dogs responded to the attention like pros. With nary a flinch or misstep, Rainy and Harley kept the team rolling across the frozen beach and through the crowds perched on the hard drifts at the edge of town. I was proud watching the team climbing the last berm onto Front Street. Once on the road, Rainy and Harley eagerly chased a police car, which lead us to the arch, lights flashing all the way.

A crowd of a hundred people, maybe more, was waiting at the finish line. The bodies parted before Rainy and Harley, who led the team right up the middle. Leo Rasmussen stood at the end of the tunnel, a microphone in one hand and a clipboard in the other. The lesbian passed by him and ran straight under the twin burls. Jamming the hook down, I ran up and slapped the overhead arch.

The time was 2:55. My name boomed through the loudspeakers. Rasmussen was saying something about my setting a new record: first musher to ever start first and finish last. Flashes popped. Familiar faces shouted things I couldn't quite make out. Rasmussen inspected the sled, checking off one sleeping bag, hand axe, and a pair of snowshoes. He collected the packet containing our commemorative mail delivery, via dog team, from Anchorage. Then Leo presented the clipboard. I scrawled my name in the line reserved for the sixtieth musher to Nome. Next to the signature was my team's total elapsed time on the trail: 22 days, 5 hours, 55 minutes, 55 seconds.

Leo was holding an old kerosene lamp, which had been burning since the race started March 2. "Go ahead," he said, "blow it out."

Nome's checker then handed me a shiny red lantern topped with a brass dog. Cheers resounded on Front Street as I hoisted it above my head.

It was official: the Iditarod was over.

Epilogue

It was payback time. From the instant I touched the arch, I began falling apart. The sun's glint on the snowy street seemed overly bright. Surrounding voices merged into a locker-room din. I felt that hot glow of staying awake all night, utterly drained, yet too excited to slow down.

On cruise control, I used the Nome Nugget's phone to file a story with Joling. We were wrapping it up when a woman from the Nome Kennel Club barged into the office and passed me a note.

"Brian," it read, "your dogs are at the lot. They were unharnessed, tied, bedded down—and your food is on your sled—at the end of your chain line. You need to go feed them and check them. Welcome to Nome."

From her look, I could tell she took me for an uncaring bastard, a person who'd drive poor dogs 1,000 miles and cast them aside.

"The dogs just had a hot meal in Safety," I said cupping the phone. "I doubt they're even hungry."

The woman's face softened. Maybe I wasn't quite the monster.

"I've seen the club's operation here in Nome," I added. "I

trust you folks put the team in a good spot. Give me a minute, and I'll be down to check them out."

The dogs were lounging on straw in a cargo yard on the edge of town. My team's picket line was flanked by dozens more. The chains were strung between tall containers, which provided shelter from the wind. On rubbery legs, I took my cooker pan and fetched hot water from the checkpoint. As the food soaked, I gave each dog a special rubdown.

"We made it, guys," I said, gathering the pans after feeding. "Take tomorrow off."

Listening to the banquet speeches, I felt feverish—the product of windburn and cold beer. Bill Jack, seated across from me, eagerly rehashed his own dramatic finish. The Nome rookie had placed a respectable twentieth, after leapfrogging past 30 teams in the coastal storms.

"Admit it," Jack said, "you planned to finish last and win that Red Lantern."

"No. No. No," I said, wearily. "You've got it all wrong. I did everything I could to dodge that bullet for seven hundred miles."

With great solemnity, Leo, the old Nome checker, presented each of us with an Iditarod patch, an official finisher's belt buckle, and a check for $1,000, which was given to every musher to complete the race that year. I'd counted on that money to get us home.

After formally accepting the Red Lantern from Leo, I briefly talked about the setbacks that had sealed my fate. Daily caught the frustration in my voice as I described the mutiny at the dump, but even he, our convoy's sensitive soul, laughed so hard tears dripped from his chin.

Decked out like a banker in suit, vest, and tie, Swennie took a front-row House gallery seat in Alaska's state capitol. An excited buzz spread through the chamber. Lawmakers swiveled in their chairs to get a look at the master musher in the flesh.

At last, the anticipated moment arrived. The representative whose district included Two Rivers rose and read into the record a citation celebrating my neighbor's come-from-behind victory and his reaffirmed status as Iditarod's all-time champion.

After the hurrahs subsided, Swenson said a few polite words. The champ was in good form on this, Rick Swenson Day.

I was seated at the press bench immediately in front of the gallery. Swennie stuck around after the citation, wearing a thoughtful expression as he watched his government at work. After a while he leaned forward and tapped me on the shoulder.

"You sit through this bullshit all day long?" whispered the champ.

Later a reception was held for Swenson at the governor's mansion. With Gov. Wally Hickel out of town, it seemed natural to find Iditarod's all-time champion playing lord of the big white house. Amused by our first and last combo, others in attendance put Swenson and me together for a picture. I gave someone my camera to get a shot, but my flash batteries were dead. The misfire summed up my life.

The champ was being chummy. "I wouldn't know myself—because I've never been there," he said, "but I've always heard it's tough on you guys in the back. How long did it take you?"

"Over twenty-two days, nearly twice as long as you."

"Well then, you'll have twice as much to write about, won't you?"

The snow had melted, even in Fairbanks, by the time the law-makers and I headed home. Howls sounded as soon as I pulled into the Deadline Dog Farm's driveway. Out in the lot, the dogs greeted me like a lost brother. Licks all around.

The reception demonstrated, once and for all, that I hadn't lost anything important. I wanted to mush the Iditarod Trail, and I had. I dreamed of starting first, and that had come true. The rest? Well . . .

In the kitchen that night, I unveiled my new plan to Mowry.

"I want to put up a sign by the end of the driveway," I said, nodding toward the glittering memento on our bookshelf. "A sign saying 'Home of the Red Lantern.'"

"Over my dead body, O'Donoghue."

Someone shakes my shoulder. "Get up! Get up!" the man says, an Inupiat accent coloring his voice. "You told me to wake you."

Wind howls outside the steamy-warm cabin. My body is stiff, wooden. I'm so tired I could cry. Where the hell am I?

"It's time to go," the man insists. "The next checkpoint isn't far."

Another checkpoint? What? That makes no sense. "The race is over," I cry.

Searching my clothes for proof, I find the buckle and the patch. "See," I say, showing them to the man. "I already made it to Nome."

The checker, faceless, shakes his head. "Your dogs are waiting," he says.

Wind rattles the cabin walls. A strong aroma of coffee tickles my nose. I sigh, not understanding, but accepting. Time to go.

That's when I awake, drenched in sweat.

For months after the race, the nightmare replays almost nightly. Each time I'm victimized by my own conditioned response: Rainy and the team need me. I can't let the dogs down.

1991 IDITAROD ORDER OF FINISH

1. Rick Swenson: 12 days, 16 hours, 34 minutes, 39 seconds
2. Martin Buser   12:18:41:49
3. Susan Butcher   12:21:59:03
4. Tim Osmar   12:22:33:33
5. Joe Runyan   12:22:36:30
6. Frank Teasley   13:12:27:57
7. Dee Dee Jonrowe   13:13:44:10
8. Matt Desalarnos   13:13:44:35
9. Rick Mackey   13:13:54:39
10. Bill Cotter   13:13:57:28
11. Kate Persons   13:14:20:59
12. Jeff King   13:14:24:40
13. Jacques Philip   13:15:07:39
14. Jerry Austin   13:17:10:51
15. Michael Madden   13:20:06:26
16. Ketil Reitan   13:21:54:12
17. Lavon Barve   13:22:20:14
18. Peryll Kyzer   14:16:26:26
19. Terry Adkins   14:16:46:51
20. Bill Jack   14:19:38:14
21. Beverly Masek   15:09:03:51
22. Laird Barron   15:10:07:15
23. Joe Garnie   15:11:53:33
24. Rick Armstrong   15:12:24:07
25. Linwood Fielder   15:23:45:15
26. Burt Bomhoff   16:08:48:36
27. Dan MacEachen   16:09:08:46
28. Dave Olesen   16:10:01:52
29. Raymie Redington   16:10:02:23
30. Dave Allen   16:10:25:26
31. Joe Redington Sr.   16:11:56:56
32. Jerry Raychel   16:17:51:17
33. Mark Nordman   16:17:55:38
34. Malcolm Vance   17:09:30:00
35. MacGill Adams   17:10:10:13
36. Nikolai Ettyne   17:10:53:00
37. Alexander Reznyuk   17:11:54:12
38. Tony Shoogukwruk   17:12:34:11
39. Rollin Westrum   17:13:44:00
40. Brian Stafford   17:15:35:48

41.	John Suter	17:18:23:31
42.	Roger Roberts	17:22:08:00
43.	Larry Munoz	17:22:59:52
44.	Jim Cantor	18:00:02:00
45.	Terry Seaman	18:00:08:35
46.	Kazuo Kojima	18:00:29:28
47.	Rich Bosela	18:00:50:45
48.	Pat Danly	18:02:23:36
49.	Dave Breuer	18:04:49:29
50.	Chris Converse	18:05:09:50

THE KALTAG "TEN"

51.	Sepp Herrman	21:05:59:26
52.	Lynda Plettner	21:21:04:06
53.	Jon Terhune	22:00:11:04
54.	Gunnar Johnson	22:00:57:48
55.	Urtha Lenthar	22:01:05:09
56.	Tom Daily	22:01:06:50
57.	Mark Williams	22:01:06:58
58.	Catherine Mormile	21:01:18:28
59.	Don Mormile	21:01:35:16
*	Tom Cooley	22:01:43:43
60.	Brian O'Donoghue	22:05:55:55

Scratched:

David Aisenbrey
Nels Anderson
Roy Monk
Gary Moore
John Ace
Sonny Russell
Robin Jacobson
Steve Fossett
Alan Garth
Bill Peele
Barry Lee
Ken Chase
John Barron
Gary Whittemore

Disqualified:

Joe Carpenter

*Though Doc isn't listed in the official race standings, his arrival was dutifully logged in by Nome checker Leo Rasmussen.

IDITAROD'S FIRST AND LAST
Total elapsed time in days, hours, minutes, seconds

	RACE CHAMPIONS		RED LANTERNS	
1973	Dick Wilmarth	20:00:49:41	John Schultz	32:05:09:01
1974	Carl Huntington	20:15:02:07	Red Olson	29:06:36:19
1975	Emmitt Peters	14:14:43:45	Steve Fee	29:08:37:13
1976	Gerald Riley	18:22:58:17	Dennis Corrington	26:08:42:51
1977	Rick Swenson	16:16:27:13	Vasily Zamitkyn	22:09:06:06
1978	Dick Mackey	14:18:52:24	Andrew Foxie	22:03:29:54
1979	Rick Swenson	15:10:37:47	Gene Leonard	24:09:02:22
1980	Joe May	14:07:11:51	Barbara Moore	24:09:25:45
1981	Rick Swenson	12:08:45:02	Jim Strong	18:06:30:30
1982	Rick Swenson	16:04:40:10	Ralph Bradley	26:13:59:59
1983	Rick Mackey	12:14:10:44	Scott Cameron	21:04:36:41
1984	Dean Osmar	12:15:07:33	Bill Mackey	19:09:43:33
1985	Libby Riddles	18:00:20:17	Monique Bene	22:03:45:45
1986	Susan Butcher	11:15:06:00	Mike Peterson	20:13:42:21
1987	Susan Butcher	11:02:05:13	Rhodi Karella	19:09:01:01
1988	Susan Butcher	11:11:41:40	Lesley Monk	19:13:22:55
1989	Joe Runyan	11:05:24:34	Bob Hoyte	17:11:19:19
1990	Susan Butcher	11:01:53:23	Steve Haver	21:10:26:26
1991	Rick Swenson	12:16:34:39	Brian O'Donoghue	22:05:55:55
1992	Martin Buser	10:19:17:15	Vern Cherneski	18:13:05:02
1993	Jeff King	10:15:38:15	Lloyd Gilbertson	18:04:19:19
1994	Martin Buser	10:13:02:39	Mark Chapoton	16:16:17:35
1995	Doug Swingley	09:02:42:00	Ben Jacobsen	17:06:02:05

VINTAGE DEPARTURES

PECKED TO DEATH BY DUCKS
by Tim Cahill

In his latest grand tour of the earth's remote, exotic, and dismal places, Tim Cahill sleeps with a grizzly bear, witnesses demonic possession in Bali, assesses the cuteness quotient of giant clams in the South Pacific, and survives a run-in with something called the Throne of Doom in Guatemala. The resulting travel pieces are at once vivid, nerve-wracking, and outrageously funny.

"Tim Cahill [has] the what-the-hell adventuresomeness of a T. E. Lawrence and the humor of a P. J. O'Rourke."   —*Condé Nast Traveler*

Travel/Adventure/0-679-74929-2

FALLING OFF THE MAP
SOME LONELY PLACES OF THE WORLD
by Pico Iyer

Pico Iyer voyages from the nostalgic elegance of Argentina to the raffish nonchalance of Australia, documents the cruising rites of Icelandic teenagers, gets interrogated by tipsy Cuban police, and attends a screening of Bhutan's first feature film. Throughout, he remains both uncannily observant and hilarious.

"[Iyer is the] rightful heir to Jan Morris [and] Paul Theroux.... He writes the kind of lyrical, flowing prose that could make Des Moines sound beguiling."
—*Los Angeles Times Book Review*

Travel/Adventure/0-679-74612-9

RIDING THE WHITE HORSE HOME
A WESTERN FAMILY ALBUM
by Teresa Jordan

The daughter and granddaughter of Wyoming ranchers tells the stories of her forebears—men who saw broken bones as professional credentials and women who coped with physical hardship and killing loneliness. She acquaints us with the lore and science of ranching, and does so with a breathtaking immediacy that recalls the best writing of Wallace Stegner and Gretel Ehrlich.

"A haunting and elegant memoir."   —Terry Tempest Williams, author of *Refuge*

Memoir/Travel/0-679-75135-1

BALKAN GHOSTS
A JOURNEY THROUGH HISTORY
by Robert D. Kaplan

As Kaplan travels from the breakaway states of Yugoslavia to Romania, Bulgaria, and Greece, he reconstructs the Balkans' history as a time warp in which ancient passions and hatreds are continually resurrected.

"Powerfully argued...the most insightful and timely work on the Balkans to date."
—*Boston Globe*

History/Current Affairs/Travel/0-679-74981-0

A YEAR IN PROVENCE
by Peter Mayle

An "engaging, funny and richly appreciative" (*The New York Times Book Review*) account of an English couple's first year living in Provence, settling in amid the enchanting gardens and equally festive bistros of their new home.

"Stylish, witty, delightfully readable."   —*The Sunday Times* (London)

Travel/0-679-73114-8

MAIDEN VOYAGES
THE WRITINGS OF WOMEN TRAVELERS
Edited and with an Introduction by Mary Morris

In this delightful and generous anthology, women such as Beryl Markham, Willa Cather, Annie Dillard, and Joan Didion share their experiences traveling throughout the world. From the Rocky Mountains to a Marrakech palace, in voices wry, lyrical, and sometimes wistful, these women show as much of themselves as they do of the strange and wonderful places they visit.

A Vintage Original/Travel/Women's Studies/0-679-74030-9

IRON & SILK
by Mark Salzman

The critically acclaimed and bestselling adventures of a young American martial arts master in China.

"Dazzling...exhilarating...a joy to read from beginning to end."   —*People*

Travel/Adventure/0-394-75511-1

RIGHT ON THE EDGE OF CRAZY
ON TOUR WITH THE U.S. DOWNHILL SKI TEAM
by Mike Wilson

Mike Wilson follows the underfunded, underreported athletes of the U.S. downhill ski team through a World Cup season that culminates at the 1992 Winter Olympics in France. Juxtaposing scenes of raw courage and gonzo excess, the result is authentic enough to leave the reader windburned.

"The best [book] ever written about ski-racing."   —*Denver Post*

Sports/Travel/0-679-74987-X

VINTAGE DEPARTURES

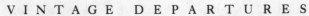